Gregory Smith (above left) was homeless for much of his adult life. He now has a PhD in Sociology and teaches in the School of Arts and Social Sciences at Southern Cross University.

Craig Henderson (above right) has worked as a writer and editor at Australian newspapers and magazines since 1987. Today the father of three lives on the New South Wales South Coast with his wife, Lizzie.

OUT OF THE FOREST

Gregory P. Smith

with Craig Henderson

PENGUIN BOOKS

PENGUIN BOOKS

UK | USA | Canada | Ireland | Australia
India | New Zealand | South Africa | China

Penguin Books is part of the Penguin Random House group of companies
whose addresses can be found at global.penguinrandomhouse.com.

Penguin
Random House
Australia

First published by William Heinemann, 2018
This edition published by Penguin Books, 2020

Cover photograph by John W. Banagan, courtesy of Getty Images
Cover design by Alex Ross © Penguin Random House Australia Pty Ltd
Internal design by Midland Typesetters, Australia
Typeset in Sabon by Midland Typesetters, Australia

Printed and bound in Australia by Griffin Press, part of Ovato, an accredited
ISO AS/NZS 14001 Environmental Management Systems printer

 A catalogue record for this
book is available from the
NATIONAL
LIBRARY National Library of Australia
OF AUSTRALIA

ISBN 978 1 76089 916 5

penguin.com.au

For Katie, my sisters, all the homeless and forgotten,
and anyone who thinks they're not good enough.

CONTENTS

PROLOGUE

I woke up on my back with a large snake on my chest. Surely it was going to sink its fangs into my throat and leave me to die in the ferns and the dirt.

I'd slept in enough roadside ditches to know I shared Australia with an all-star cast of nasties, not least taipans and eastern brown snakes. They're pretty much a slithering death sentence, especially if you have the misfortune of waking alone in a forest with one on top of you.

I can't say that my life flashed before my eyes that night as I lay there frozen, but even if it had I probably would have looked away such was the waste it had been. One thing was certain, though: I wasn't yet ready to die. I stilled every cell while the snake continued to explore my body and after minutes that felt like years its cold, scaly weight slipped off my left flank.

Cautiously I sucked in some air, rose to my feet, took a burning stick from the campfire and waved it around like a homeless Indiana Jones. There, on the forest floor near the edge of my camp, I saw it: a huge diamond python. One hundred per cent non-venomous. Just passing through.

The snake didn't stand a chance as I lunged and gripped tight behind its jaws. Dinner! I hadn't eaten in days. My terror was replaced by excitement as its body whipped and curled in the night air. I found my pocket knife, hacked the wide, flat head off the twisting creature and slung its body in the branches of a bush to deal with later.

I loaded up the fire with plenty of wood for the rest of the night and in the flickering amber I gave solemn thanks. I'd only been living in the rainforest for a few months but I'd developed a reverence for the natural world and deep regard for the spirituality of all things. I told the snake I was sorry that I'd had to kill it and how grateful I was that its flesh would sustain me. I vowed to never forget it.

I woke again just before sunrise eager to return to the business of the snake. The rewards for keeping my cool during the horrors of the night were even more apparent in the grey dawn. Suddenly I had at least a few days of food and I'd obtained an item of potential value – the scaly skin. I'd also been given something mystical and immensely powerful. Namely, snake blood.

After carefully separating the reptile into its component parts of skin, blood, meat and bone, I spent the rest of the day harvesting fern leaves for the coming night's bed and gathering wood for the fire. Later on, when the sun slipped behind the mountains to the west, I threaded strips of snake onto sharpened skewers I'd made from gum-tree twigs, and dangled them in the flames. As I chewed on the meat and gazed exhausted into the dancing flames, I had no idea I had just opened the door to a nightmare more frightening than any giant serpent. And it felt as if it might never end.

1

TAMWORTH

When I was a little boy I had a recurring nightmare about a huge ball. The damned thing would chase me through whatever dreamscape I happened to be trapped in and no matter how fast I ran, I could never get far enough ahead to feel safe. I was always on the brink of being crushed.

As is so often the way, my dreams simply reflected my waking anxiety. According to my mother I was two years old when my father picked me up by one foot and flung me head-first into the lounge-room wall. My left eardrum ruptured and I temporarily lost hearing in my right side, too. At least that's how Mum told the story – I was too young to remember.

Whether it happened or not, the salient thing about that nugget of Smith family history is that an act of brutality against a toddler fitted so easily into our overall story of abuse and dysfunction. Maybe it was an exaggeration, perhaps it was a bitter wife's tale, or maybe it happened exactly the way Mum described, but *something* bad happened to my head. Today I wear a hearing aid in my left ear as proof.

Violence was so common in our house that for a while I thought every father must beat his wife and children. The world terrified me. At bedtime I'd gather my sheets around me and take refuge behind fabric walls. It was my fortress; a flannelette barricade that nobody could breach. Hollywood Westerns must have been big at the time because I armed myself with an imaginary rifle that had a wooden shoulder stock and I'd shoot anyone or anything that came too close. I'd circle the wagons in my mind, take aim from behind my pillow and – *boom*!

When I wasn't getting flogged by Dad in one of his drunken rampages or defending my bed from imaginary raiders, I had to do nocturnal battle with that big rolling ball. My childhood, whether I was awake, asleep or somewhere in between, was like a never-ending bad dream.

Life began for me on the twentieth day of the fifth month in the common era of 1955. People do a double take when I say it like that, but it's my way of stating for the record that I'm not a Christian. I have no need, however, to qualify the place of my birth – the City of Tamworth, nestled in the Peel Valley in the vast New England region of New South Wales.

I may not be religious but I am a Tamworth boy through and through. Dad was born there, as was his father, and his father's father before that. In fact, we were once something of a pioneering family. Dad's great-grandfather, William Joseph Smith, had been a man for his time. The son of an English Wesleyan minister who'd arrived in the Colony on a ship full of convicts, William was the first of my paternal forebears born on Australian soil. Not content with life on the coast, he ventured inland from Sydney and fell in love with the riverside township of Tamworth in the 1870s. William was a tanner by trade and a progressive thinker who'd become intrigued by the new-fangled idea of electric street lights. Back then, Australia was illuminated after sunset either by moonlight or, in some urban areas, gas-powered lamps.

William won a seat on the local council and lobbied fellow aldermen that Tamworth deserved better. He faced down the naysayers for years and on 9 November 1888, half the town crowded around their newly constructed power plant to watch the mayor's wife turn on the lights. With the twist of a golden key Tamworth entered the history books as the first city in Australia – indeed in the entire southern hemisphere – to flood its streets after dark with the reassuring glow of electric light. William was the toast of the town.

In less than 100 years, however, the bright future that William Joseph Smith had promised would dim considerably. By the time I was delivered at Tamworth Base Hospital, the Smiths were no longer synonymous with the historic leap forward that had put the name 'Tamworth' up in lights.

Dad toiled at menial jobs and blew money at the pub while Mum worked on her hands and knees, cleaning the hospital where she'd given birth to me. My grandfather, Aubrey Peel Smith, was still quite a wealthy man, but he was also quite obnoxious – at least I thought he was. He owned a swag of properties, including homes and a general store in Darling Street, Tamworth, that was plastered in huge letters 'Aub Smith for Everything', and a banana plantation in the hills west of the New South Wales coastal town of Coffs Harbour.

Although Aubrey had placed a perfectly good, spacious brick home on one of Tamworth's nicest streets in my father's name, we were forbidden from living in it. The house was let out to a World War I veteran and the regulations of the day stipulated that the ex-soldier couldn't be evicted under any circumstances. To rub salt into the wound, the old Digger's war service meant his rent was frozen at a ridiculously small amount. It didn't even cover the council rates, which Dad had to cough up for.

By the time I was four I had been joined by four cute little sisters – Glenda, twins Lynette and Louise, and Wendy – and we were all sardined into a narrow, two-bedroom house that Aubrey owned in North Tamworth. I slept on the veranda and the four girls were sandwiched, top to toe, in a double bed.

The pressure of these claustrophobic conditions would help ignite my parents' arguments, not that any extra spark was needed when it came to their marital tinderbox. 'Just look at you, you worthless drunk!' Mum would holler. 'You can't even provide a decent house for your own family! You're pathetic!'

Dad would respond by getting more drunk and bashing Mum black and blue. Even as a small boy I felt compelled to jump up and try to protect her, or the girls if they were in danger, only to get belted, kicked and screamed at too.

Conspicuous by his absence during this mayhem was Aubrey. He couldn't stand Mum because word had somehow got around that she was part-Aboriginal. That was news to me. Mum had grown up 150 kilometres away in the tiny farming town of Guyra, where her mother had worked as a barmaid in the local pub. I don't imagine that back then publicans were tripping over themselves to hire Aboriginal women to pull beers for the boys. Besides, Mum, with her blue eyes and fair skin, looked about as Aboriginal as Elizabeth Taylor and she never, ever claimed to be part of any ancient mob.

None of this seems to have mattered to Aubrey. His mind was made up. This was the 'glorious' 1950s, a time of post-war prosperity when Aboriginal people were forbidden from voting and the Australian government catalogued their existence under the Flora and Fauna Act. People were herded off the land and had their children taken off them – all while enjoying the same rights under the law as kangaroos, bats, worms and snakes.

In the eyes of men like my grandfather, marrying my mother could only bring shame upon an established white family such as ours and it created a toxic relationship between the two men. Dad knew no other way of dealing with his problems than drinking and lashing out at the people closest to him. Alcohol was his primary weakness; it would make him lose control and morph into a monster. Things only got worse when his mother, Lilia, died in 1961. I was only five, but even I could see the crippling effect it had on Dad. He'd worshipped his mum who had been a foil to Aubrey's influence, and he depended on her for support and guidance. With Lilia gone, he lost the will to even try to become a better man.

Dad would finish work at the local starch factory at 4pm and head straight to his beloved boozer, the Tamworth Ex-Services Club, to get smashed with his cronies. He'd come home about 7pm, guzzle some of his home-brewed beer and get even messier. Mum would needle him and the arguments would kick off. 'Have a look at yourself,' she'd typically begin. 'You're a disgraceful excuse for a man. You're a joke.' At that point the punching and yelling would start, the girls would scream, I'd try to stop Dad and end up getting hurt too. Then it would be off to bed to try to outrun the evil ball.

Life at school was only marginally better. The very first thing I learned at East Tamworth Infants School was that I was different. My school uniform was a second-hand affair, and when I turned up on my first day in a pair of faded oversized shorts, Mum might as well have pinned a note to my forehead that said, 'I'm a dag! Tease me!'

Things deteriorated when news spread about my quirky middle name. You see, when William Joseph Smith (that bright spark who had lit up Australia) had sired a son, he'd named him William Peel Smith. It was a nod to the region's Peel River and Peel Valley, which in turn was named in honour of the former British Prime Minister Sir Robert Peel.

Old William Joseph could never have guessed that ninety years later, this sentimental adjustment to the family genealogy would result in his great-great-grandson, Gregory Peel Smith, being mercilessly mocked. I was buried under an avalanche of nicknames. I hated being called Banana Peel, Orange Peel and Potato Peel, but my forebears apparently encountered no such hassle. They dutifully passed their middle name down the line, right up until the kids in my class at Tamworth Infants School got a hold of it.

I'd retaliate the only way I knew how – by mimicking the violence I'd learned at home by observing my father. The moment someone said something 'wrong', he'd just explode, so that's what I did. This only led to extra ridicule and nicknames, which made me want to lash out even more. Soon I was stuck in a wretched cycle of bullying and violent reprisal. I became a withdrawn and stigmatised student who found it impossible to engage in classroom activities. People thought I was an idiot.

I knew something they didn't, though: I had a fire inside me that burned bright. I had a galloping passion for life, a sense of wonder and intense interest in the world and all of its mysteries and possibilities. Despite everything, I still imagined that one day I would be a roaring success of a man – possibly even the richest person in the country. I'd heard stories about the American business mogul Howard Hughes and how he'd take his lunch to work in a brown paper bag. I figured I'd probably do that too. Sometimes, when the mood of the house wasn't so bad, I'd fall asleep visualising my name on top of buildings – giant neon-lit announcements to the world that I'd made it.

2

MUM

Dad had a lot of serious problems. One of them was my mother.

I can only imagine that once upon a time Bruce and Beryl had been madly in love, with Panavision dreams for their future, but after the girls and I came along there was hardly a whiff of friendship in the air, let alone romance. Mum was a beautiful, charismatic woman who could turn on the charm in any situation. Like a lot of people in those days, it was important to her that she presented well to the outside world. At home, however, Mum was almost pathologically fixated on exploring the depths of Dad's flaws and she systematically pushed his buttons until he lost the plot. I can't say she *wanted* to be a battered wife – which she undoubtedly was – only that she seemed to revel in the chaos and disruption that resulted from belittling and provoking Dad. If he was the dangerous, unpredictable lion in the Smith Family Circus, Mum was the ringmaster.

She could be violent, too – particularly towards the girls. Like Dad, Mum policed a set of wildly arbitrary and shifting rules and enforced discipline in the same crazily inconsistent manner. Mysteries like, 'Who drank the last bit of cordial?' or, 'Who ate a biscuit without permission?' would be dealt with by way of inquisition. Mum would line up her four daughters and interrogate them at the top of her lungs. If the answers were inadequate or inconclusive she'd reach for her black studded belt, or, if she couldn't find that, the cord from the electric jug. My sisters would be bent over the bathtub while Mum whipped their bare backsides and legs as if she were driving slaves.

Mum disguised the results of her mischief with the jug cord by clothing the girls in long dresses or skirts that were several sizes too big. She papered over her own black eyes and swollen lips with make-up. It was harder to hide my injuries. I was in Dad's firing line more often thanks to my self-appointed role as protector of Mum and the girls, and often had cuts, grazes and bruises to the face. Although I was kept home from school when the evidence was too obvious, Mum would generally explain away my torn skin and swollen eyes as the just deserts of a clumsy boy. 'Oh, he's so accident prone,' she'd say with a theatrical roll of the eyes, if someone remarked on my latest shiner. Or, 'He's just too adventurous for his own good!'

Sometimes she even used Dad as a weapon by getting him to shift the focus of his anger on to us. We soon developed a sixth sense for when things were about to explode. Any time we suspected one of us might be drifting into

Dad's crosshairs, we would attempt to hide the target inside a closet, with coats and jackets piled on top. For a brood of little kids, we expended a hell of a lot of emotional energy just trying to understand what was going on each day.

Sometimes the warning signs were crystal clear. If ever we got home from school and Mum had rearranged the furniture, we knew we were in for a bad night. For some reason she seemed to think a spot of redecorating would distract Dad from whatever feud they were having. It never worked, and that's why I never move my furniture around today.

There were other troubles in paradise, too. Not least the fact that Mum was having an affair with a man known as Duker. He became a regular visitor when Dad was at work or on the drink at the Ex-Servo's. Duker would often be there with Mum when we returned from school and he'd press a shilling into each of our palms so we'd disappear to the shop to buy lollies. A small price for privacy.

On top of being a womaniser, Duker was a drunk. Just what Mum needed in her life. He always toted a brown paper bag containing a brown bottle full of brown 'medicine' that he'd swig at regular intervals. Apparently Mum's other drunkard, Dad, had extramarital affairs as well, but I never knew him to bring a strange woman into the house.

The Duker situation was toxic and it caused our already terrible home environment to corrode even further. The screaming, shouting, crashing and bashing increased. When things couldn't possibly get any more twisted, Mum and Dad welcomed another baby. A girl named Roma. Over the following years it became clear this adorable little newcomer was quarantined from Dad's outbursts. We would find out much later that she was strictly off limits because if word got out that Dad had laid a hand on her, Duker – her real father – would have throttled him.

Unlike the men in her life, Mum was never a big drinker. Instead, I suspect she was a speed freak. Everywhere Mum went she carried a little red and yellow bottle supposedly of Ford Pills – the herbal laxative of a generation. She was forever digging it out of her purse and popping little tablets into her mouth, four, five, six times a day. Instead of laxatives, I have a hunch the bottle contained one of the over-the-counter amphetamines, or so-called 'appetite suppressants', that were readily available in those days. Mum only ever ate like a bird and at mealtimes she'd often sit at an empty place mat and say, 'I sacrifice my meals for you kids.' In truth, I think she was simply cranked up on gear.

Growing up like this made it impossible for me to suspend disbelief in the way other kids did. In the early years, Mum made an effort to play happy families and inject a little magic at Christmas time, but I debunked it fairly quickly. I'd heard talk at school about a fat bearded guy who'd come down your chimney with a sack of toys, but the fantasy made no sense to me. I just couldn't buy it.

One Christmas Eve in the early 1960s I stayed awake to confirm my instincts. I wasn't the least bit surprised to see Mum carrying an armful of presents into the house. My world was black and white; there was no grey, no middle ground. You were either getting punched in the head or you weren't. You were either in trouble or you weren't. There was a jolly man in a red suit who lived at the North Pole or there wasn't. I knew the truth, and I made sure my sisters did too. 'There's no Santa,' I told them. 'He's not real.'

But we all knew monsters were real. Soon we'd be meeting some more.

3

NO MERCY

Mum was her usual intense, impatient self as she bundled me and the four older girls into the car for a Sunday drive. One of her best friends – a lady we called Aunty Muriel – lived in Armidale, a university town about 100 kilometres north up the New England Highway, and we were off to visit her.

It was mid-afternoon when we rolled into Armidale and headed up a long driveway to our aunt's place. The girls and I fell silent as a huge, imposing shape loomed through the windscreen of Mum's FB Holden station wagon. 'Geez,' I thought, 'Aunty Muriel sure lives in a big house.'

The gothic-looking structure was topped with three large Christian crosses, although it looked more like a medieval castle than a church. High up, right in the middle of the building's facade, was an arched niche that housed the marble statue of a gormless-looking bearded guy in a pointy hat. He was holding a staff in his left hand and he must have been twenty feet tall. I'd find out later that his name was St Patrick, the patron saint of something or other. Up until that point, religion had played zero part in my life. Apparently our family belonged to the Church of England, whatever that meant, but I never once went to Sunday school, Mass, Communion or any other remotely religious rituals. 'Jesus Christ' and 'God almighty' were just words people spat when they were angry or frustrated.

'What are we doing here?' I wondered as we tumbled out of the car.

It was as if Mum had read my mind. 'Come along, we have to go inside and see some people.'

As soon as we walked through the arches we were met by a group of women dressed in black robes – the Sisters of Mercy. With barely a word spoken they peeled me away from my little sisters and pulled me to the left while the girls were whisked right. Sensing a serious problem I started to scream. I imagine the girls did too but by then we were separated. It was a forced estrangement that would endure for decades to come.

Welcome to St Patrick's Orphanage, Armidale. My home for the next sixteen months.

One of the first orders of business for the Sisters of Mercy was to stand me in a hallway and give me a hiding. To be fair it was more of a mild, introductory series of slaps as opposed to the full-blooded beltings I'd grow used to down the track, but the message was the same: 'Stop crying! Don't be silly! Be quiet! Behave or else!'

Later, as the shadows lengthened through the high-set windows, I was marched into a large dining room on the ground floor. It was teeming with young children; boys on one side, girls on the other. I scanned all the female faces and eventually spotted my sisters huddled together at a table like little castaways clinging to a rock. They were all weeping, which only made me cry more.

Some kind of food was put in front of me but I was too grief-stricken to eat. This made the nuns angrier.

'Stop being silly! You're only making things worse. Be a good boy and eat up!'

I just couldn't, so the Sisters of Mercy dragged me out into a hallway and made me stand still until everyone else had finished their meal. After dinner we were taken to a large playroom with a wooden stage at one end. There were boxes full of toys; cars, wooden blocks, musical instruments. I absently fumbled with some castanets and was told to introduce myself to the other boys. I just burst into tears again.

None of the other boys appeared to be older than twelve. Later, I found out that the policy at St Patrick's was for girls to stay on into their teenage years while boys were sent somewhere else.

I missed bath time that night and was instead led up a large flight of stairs to the boys' dormitory on the first floor. The main dorm contained about twenty beds, but there were ten more on the adjacent covered veranda. My bed was on the veranda, second from the end and right next to a sweet Aboriginal boy named Gussy Nicholls.

Like me, Gussy was ten, and although his eyes were similarly bloodshot with tears, he could see I was struggling and asked me if I was OK. I stifled a sob and shook my head. That night Gussy and I listened to each other cry ourselves to sleep.

The next day I woke to the nightmare of nuns clapping and shouting. It was 6am.

'Out of bed! Out of bed! Get up and out of bed right now!'

Gussy was already on his feet and hurriedly making his bed. He shot me an urgent look. 'You'd better get up quick!' he whispered. 'We have to make our beds and be ready for Mass at seven o'clock.'

I followed Gussy's lead, and when I'd finished straightening my bedsheets I stood at the foot of my bunk like the other boys. That's when I first laid eyes on Sister Winifred. She was a squat, middle-aged woman with a permanently downturned mouth. Her first job every day was to check all the boys' beds were correctly made, and then to publicly humiliate those who'd had the misfortune of wetting theirs in the night.

Sister Winifred took to the debasement of little boys with a cruel relish. She made them strip their wet bedclothes in front of everyone and forced them to carry their sodden sheets to the laundry near the bathroom. All the while she shamed and abused the poor, wretched bed-wetters and refused to allow them to have a shower or even wash themselves at the sink. 'Filthy, dirty, lazy boys,' she seethed. 'You deserve to stink like that until bath time.'

Not only did she delight in punishing orphans for any number of vague misdemeanours or accidents, Sister Winifred would sometimes lash out pre-emptively. Every now and then she'd stand at the door near the top of the stairs and give each boy a solid slap across the back of the legs as they walked past; penance, she said, for the naughty things we were going to do that day.

I received one of her prophetic whacks on my very first morning in St Patrick's. It stung, for sure, but it hurt on a much deeper level. At least at home I could see Dad's anger rising and read the warning signs. But this was an institutional violence, an act of cruelty that was meant to punish me for nothing in the name of some supposedly loving god.

Every morning after the bed-wetters had been denigrated to the satisfaction of Sister Winifred, we were marched down the staircase and into the chapel on the ground floor. Boys on one side, girls on the other. The 7am Mass was an epic ordeal; a gruelling crash course in the finer points of wickedness, weakness, evil, filthiness and human frailty. It's a lot to learn about yourself at the age of ten.

After morning Mass – and only after Mass – could we file into the dining room to eat. And thus my first opportunity to dissent presented itself. I refused their food, partly because they served up bowls of lukewarm grey porridge with weevils churning in it, but mostly because I knew they couldn't force-feed me. This gave me some control over my life, which I found enormously empowering. It was my way of throwing a two-fingered salute, even if it did cost me a few slaps from the Sisters Most Merciful.

The religious immersion and brainwashing continued with afternoon prayers, and on Fridays there was benediction. Having gone from no religion to being forced to sit still while a priest shouted from the pulpit about Adam and Eve, Samson and Delilah, David and Goliath, Sodom and Gomorrah and sin, sin, sin, sin, sin – *my* sins – was a massive shock.

Although just a kid myself, I became genuinely disgusted at how children were being treated. There was one young lass who would occasionally be gripped by a seizure during morning Mass. It was a horrible sight to behold: the poor little thing's eyes would roll about in her head as she jolted in the hard wooden pews. I suspected that it stemmed from her being denied an early breakfast and I told the nuns so. This only earned me another hiding.

It didn't take long for me to get a reputation as a 'challenging boy' at St Patrick's. The way I saw it, the institution was the problem. I thought their methods were plainly cruel and unjust, and the first stirrings of socialist principles took a hold in me.

As is the case in wider society, food told a story of inequity at St Patrick's. Although I skipped their bug-spiked breakfast, I either ate dinner or I starved. In the evenings we were served up variations of meat and vegetables. I suspect they started boiling the vegetables about 2pm because by the time they hit our plates the carrots and greens were so overcooked they were almost translucent and had about as much crunch as a cowpat. The meat was no better. It was always tepid, pale flesh lined with congealed fat and infused with an off-putting aroma that made me think of internal organs. I don't believe any child ever looked forward to dinner in that orphanage; there were certainly no little Oliver Twists tugging at the Sisters' robes and asking for more.

But over on the nuns' table? They were on an altogether different gastronomic adventure. While we were forcing down mush, the Sisters of Mercy were tucking into steaks, lamb chops, mashed potatoes and fresh vegies.

I was outraged. 'Why should they be eating better than we are?' I screamed inside my head. Once, I even complained out loud.

Slap!

I doubted, too, that the nuns were forced to drink castor oil. Every Saturday morning we had to swallow a dose of the vile elixir, apparently because it was vital to our bowel function. We'd walk into the dining room, where a little cup had been set at each child's place. Sister Mary Joseph would hold one boiled lolly aloft. 'Whoever finishes their castor oil first gets the reward!' she'd trill. One boiled lolly among dozens of distressed children. Gee, thanks, Mary-Jo.

I never won the lolly because I never drank their stupid castor oil. I was learning to game the system and I'd realised that Saturday night was when we were given a change of clothes. So, while the other kids gagged as they tipped castor oil down their throats, I poured mine into the pocket of my pants. Sure, it was a bit messy, but only until that evening.

After a while I noticed that there was a distinct class system among the children in the orphanage, too. The child of a middle-class family that had fallen temporarily on hard times would be treated well. It was entirely different for an Indigenous kid put in there because his mum and dad were impoverished or because he'd been stolen by the government, as was the case with my mate Gussy Nicholls. Their experiences were like chalk and cheese.

I really liked Gussy a lot. We didn't judge each other, we didn't pick on each other, we didn't call each other names. He was just a nice kid and we looked out for one another. He told me great stories about his heritage. I learned that his family had lived in Australia for thousands and thousands of years, since the beginning and the Great Dreaming – much longer than the nuns had been around. Gussy's stories were the only things that brought colour into my own bleak world. The Sisters of Mercy, however, wouldn't hear of such heresy. Gussy's ancient roots meant nothing in the orphanage; he was a child of Christ who was born into sin. He was wicked and filthy and broken and he would have to make amends.

Like Gussy, my sisters and I clung to a pretty low rung of the social ladder at St Patrick's. We were from a poor family with an abusive, alcoholic father and a mother who apparently didn't want us around. Maybe Duker had run out of shillings. Our predicament made it easier for the nuns to give me a hiding. It wasn't as if a concerned parent would be regularly checking on our wellbeing.

Although there were one or two nicer nuns, in general the Sisters of Mercy were a heartless assortment of human beings. Their key philosophy was that 'The spirit of a child must be broken so that the spirit of the Lord may enter'. When that's your jumping off point in caring for children it's never going to end well.

Sister Winifred was a gifted breaker of spirits. Early one morning we were getting ready to go downstairs for Mass when she began swinging at the boys as we filed past her. *Whack! Slap! Crack!* As I approached, I could see there was no way I was going to escape being belted, but I ducked reflexively and slipped and fell down the staircase just as Sister Winifred took a swipe at me. It was a long way to the bottom and I cracked my head on the steps several times on the journey. When I got to my feet, blood was pouring out of my mouth and a large chunk of my front tooth plopped into my palm as I cupped it to my face. I could see in Sister Winifred's eyes that she was worried about what the implications might be for her: it had happened so fast it appeared she had pushed me down the stairs.

I was taken to a dentist in Armidale to have my busted mouth patched up. A few weeks later I was back in the dentist's chair to have the tooth capped. The procedure had to be repeated two or three times because the filling kept falling off. It must have cost the church a bomb.

Years later I'd discover that the entire episode – from being 'thrown' face first down a staircase by a nun, to emergency dentistry and multiple botched attempts at orthodontics – didn't appear on my records at St Patrick's. As far as they were concerned, it never happened.

4

RUN!

Bath time at St Patrick's was the worst. Every afternoon before dinner, several dozen boys would be herded upstairs and made to queue for a tub. It was a depraved ritual that every single boy dreaded. It wasn't that we didn't want to be clean and hygienic, we just didn't want to be groped while naked by teenage girls.

Strangely, for a pious religious order that took an over-weening approach to gender separation, the Sisters of Mercy thought it was perfectly fine to parade nude, fright-ened little boys in front of pubescent females.

A conga line of traumatised lads would snake out of the first floor washroom and down the hall like lambs to the slaughter. When you were fourth in line from the bath, you had to strip and stand there, freezing and vulnerable with your hands over your crotch until it was your turn. Once they got you in the bathtub, the sniggering fourteen- and fifteen-year-old orphans would go to work. It was a highly efficient sexual-abuse factory.

Some of the girls delighted in making cruel remarks about the boys' genitalia, while others put extra vigour into washing our supposedly private parts. It was a perverted circus that yielded lifelong shame for me and a lot of other young fellows. At the time I didn't have the capacity to consider what effect the sordid ceremony might have had on the girls involved, or what abuses may have been visited upon them at St Patrick's. All I know is that it warped my future interactions with the opposite sex and left me terribly hung up when it came to any kind of intimacy.

And that was just the official abuse.

I was singled out by a blonde-haired girl called Bev who was fifteen and pretty much had free reign in St Patrick's because she worked in the laundry. As an eleven-year-old boy I never really took much notice of her, until the day I decided to take a leak behind one of the sheds out in the orphanage grounds.

Later that afternoon Bev cornered me near the boiler room across from the chapel. 'I saw what you did!' she hissed. 'You did a piss behind the shed!' Then she issued the first of her demands: 'If you don't kiss me, I'm going to tell the nuns.'

I was terrified of the nuns, and although Bev was scaring me with her talk of pissing and kissing I thought it couldn't be worse than what would happen to me if the Sisters knew I'd taken a leak behind the shed. Urinating was a filthy, disgusting, heinous sin. Just ask the bed-wetters. 'You have to come with me and do whatever I say,' Bev commanded.

I reluctantly followed her to the recreation hall where the toys were stored. It was always quiet in there between 4pm and 6pm on weekdays and there was rarely anyone in there at the weekend either. This meant Bev could abuse me seven days a week if she pleased.

Things might not have been so bad if she'd just black-mailed me into kissing her once to atone for my toileting misdemeanour, but the terms of her ransom grew more and more deviant. She systematically sexually abused me for months.

Once she'd finished it would almost be time to go upstairs for a bath.

In some ways, entering St Patrick's was like being admitted to prison. The common denominator was that you were homogenised, dehumanised and bent to fit into the system. The first thing they took from you was your clothes. I can't remember what I was wearing on the drive to 'Aunty Muriel's', but I spent the following two years in pants and tops several sizes too large and in various shades of faded red. Perhaps the crimson was meant to make it easier for the Sisters of Mercy to see us. Maybe it symbolised the blood of Christ. I don't really know, but I've hardly ever pulled on a stitch of red clothing since.

One morning, I awoke to find a blue and grey school uniform laid out on the end of my bunk. Sister Winifred was hovering menacingly on the veranda and she paid special attention to me to make sure I put the uniform on. I'd be going off to school with the other boys and I would have to behave or else, she said.

Each day we were loaded onto a bus and driven a short way to the boys' school in the grounds of St Mary's Cathedral in Armidale. It was another imposing Catholic colossus made of dark bricks and darker personalities. I didn't stand a chance there. For one thing, my only friend, Gussy Nicholls, wasn't allowed to attend school for some reason.

The other students at St Mary's poured scorn on the orphans who were bussed in each day, and, just as at Tamworth Primary School, I was pigeonholed as a simpleton who was too disruptive to bother trying to educate. The Brothers didn't want me there so I found myself walking around the cathedral grounds all day doing nothing, hanging out down near the incinerators, or playing with a broken pen and getting ink all over my hands.

If the Sisters were merciful I don't know what that made the Brothers at St Mary's. There was one particularly cruel man who'd stalk the grounds with a steel whistle clenched in his fist. You might be playing with a ball or running around when he'd sneak up behind and crack you hard on the top of the skull with the whistle. The pain was unbelievable. The first time it happened to me I dropped to my knees and saw stars. I hadn't been doing anything particularly evil, just playing. It was a completely unprovoked, vicious attack.

I hated the Brothers with a passion. They were all sadistic but some seemed to truly delight in hurting children. I was attacked so savagely once that I was left with a profusely bleeding head. What could I do about it, though? There was no one to turn to, nowhere to run. I staggered to the toilets and pressed handfuls of toilet paper against my torn scalp until the bleeding slowed. Then it was back 'home' on the bus for a plate of slop at the orphanage and some sexual humiliation before bed. Did Mum or Dad have any idea what was happening to me? If they did they obviously didn't care. And if they didn't know then they didn't care enough to find out. I hated them with a passion, too.

The only person I could confide in was Gussy. He understood and sympathised. He was being sexually abused too, not that he ever spoke about it. I knew he was because he asked me about it one night after lights out. 'Hey, is anybody touching you?' he whispered. 'I mean in a bad, sorta dirty way?' I told him about Bev's program of molestation and the beatings I copped at the hands of the Brothers. 'You're lucky you don't go to school,' I said. Gussy didn't say anything, he just let out a soft sigh. A few months later I shuffled in from school one afternoon to find Gussy gone. To this day I don't know what happened to him.

If an orphanage is a place for children on the fringes of society, then I was an outsider among outsiders. Just as in Tamworth, I was ostracised, rejected, mocked and put down – and I reacted accordingly. I was volatile and depressed. I was devoid of ambition, and although my life was just beginning, my dreams of becoming a titan of business had already faded. I felt I had no future. There would be no buildings with my name on them.

I hated what was happening to me and rejected it in my heart. I refused to simply bow to the injustice, and for my defiance I was marked out as a troublemaker. The nuns had their methods for breaking a strong spirit: when they'd had enough of my recalcitrance they would lock me in a pitch-black storeroom underneath the main staircase. I'd be in there for up to eight hours at a time. When they were really fed up, they'd shut me away in a tiny room for days on end. It was literally solitary confinement for kids.

In the blackness under the stairs, however, I learned to dissociate. I carefully dug a little cave in the recesses of my mind where no one could reach me. The cave had a force field at the entrance and inside I gathered the things around me that I liked and trusted: animals, pets, horses, cats and dogs. I spent a lot of time in the cave as a child and it helped me to cope, but I knew deep down that retreating into my mind was only a temporary respite from the miserable reality of life. I figured I'd be better off just jumping the fence and running for the hills.

In the beginning my escapes were purely opportunistic. Often I'd bolt when the nuns took us on outings or walks around Armidale. I'd see an opening and when no one was looking, *whoosh*, I'd be off like a shot. The problem with that approach was that with no forethought, planning or idea where I was, I'd be rounded up pretty quickly.

Sometimes I was so desperate I'd run away without any shoes on. One night I made it past the outskirts of town by following a bitumen road. It was freezing cold and my bare feet started to bleed. It was getting to the point where I couldn't go on when I came across a single adult-sized rubber thong. Hallelujah! I pressed on, alternating the thong between each foot for ten minutes at a time. I limped along all night in that fashion, shivering and on the brink of hypothermia. 'When the sun comes up I'll be OK. When the sun comes up I'll be OK,' I kept telling myself. When the sun cames up the nuns found me and took me back to St Patrick's for an almighty beating.

It got to the point where I was escaping once a week, only to be picked up by the police, the nuns or a 'concerned member of the public'. After a while I was considered such a flight risk that I was excluded from organised outings and locked in solitary instead.

Usually I'd follow a road or railway track when I attempted to escape, but one time I tried cutting across country to increase my chances. I scrambled through the orphanage fence and darted into a nearby paddock. Although I had remembered to wear shoes and take a jumper, I hadn't given any thought to food or water. The main objective was simply to get away.

That night I slept under a tree that had been popular with cows. I could smell them on the grass, which made me apprehensive as I was still only eleven and large animals scared me. The next morning I set off through the dry fields and when I came to a bank of overhead power lines I decided to follow them, thinking they'd lead me out of Armidale to some other town.

It must have been nearly autumn, because while I had shivered through the night I began to sweat in the heat as the morning wore on. I picked my way through barbed-wire fences and stumbled on the rocky terrain. I could see there had been cattle or sheep in some of the paddocks but my luck held and I never ran into any.

About midday I came upon a lonely puddle of water in a depression in the dirt. By then I was hungry and extremely thirsty. The puddle was as brown as a cup of coffee and about as big as one, but it was water so I didn't spend a lot of time debating whether or not to drink it. I dropped onto all fours like a kelpie and slurped it off the earth. The next decision, however, was a bit harder. I had no idea where I was, how far I'd walked or even what direction I was heading in. With the taste of soil in my mouth I had to weigh up whether I should go back, where I knew what was waiting for me, or keep going on a potentially water-less trek. In the end, fear of the known outweighed any apprehension I had of the unknown – by far. I kept going.

As night fell I huddled next to an old tree stump and slept in fits and starts. By mid-morning the next day I came across a main road that led to the town of Ebor, eighty kilo-metres to the east of Armidale. I decided I was far enough away from the orphanage to risk following the bitumen. I'd only been walking for a short while when an old-timer pulled over beside me and asked me where I was going and if I'd like a lift. I had no answer to the first question but said I'd love a ride as far as he was going.

He dropped me off about twelve kilometres outside Ebor, where I had visions of scrounging some food and guzzling water from a public bubbler. Ten minutes into my walk, I heard the slowing of a motor and the rubbery scrunch of braking tyres on loose gravel behind me. I hadn't even seen the cops coming but they'd been briefed about me – my name, where I'd come from, what I'd be wearing. I dare say they knew what a filthy, trouble-making little sinner I was, too.

After two days on the run I was suddenly in the rear of their patrol car and on my way back to the orphanage.

The coppers were frightening men and they gave me a hard time all the way to Armidale. The passenger-side cop would turn in his seat intermittently, lean over and crack me across the head or shove me hard in the chest.

'You're an ungrateful little arsehole. Do you know that?' he growled. 'You have no idea how lucky you are to have the nuns taking care of you.'

But the cops weren't there later that day to see the nuns beating me and locking me under the stairs. Lucky them.

5

TROUBLE

I was twelve years old when Mum finally collected me from the orphanage. She acted as if nothing had happened; like we were on the return trip from 'Aunty Muriel's'. But I would never look at her the same way again. I had completed a crash course in the power relationship between adults and children, and while I didn't grasp the theories or mechanics behind it all, I knew that every grown-up had the power to embarrass, humiliate and hurt me.

At thirteen I was enrolled at Oxley High School alongside several dozen other kids, none of whom wanted anything to do with me. I was one of the unfortunate kids who was earmarked to break out in acres of acne. The eruption on my skin was severe, and before long I was allocated a new nickname: Pus Head.

At home after school I spent my afternoons studying the rooms in our house for the nearest exit point, be it a door or a window that I'd strategically prised open. I'd mentally review the previous day's violence, agonising over where best to stash a weapon so I could fend off Dad when he staggered through the door. My sisters may have been responsible for cleaning the house but I always knew exactly where the broom handle was.

I lived in a constant state of fear and anxiety. The mental capacity I used just to make it through each day's barrage left me with very little wit for anything else, certainly not for school studies. Simply existing became emotionally crippling. There wasn't even any relief when Dad finally collapsed in a heap, only dread about the inevitable repeat performance the following day. Algebra, homework and spelling tests barely registered in my mind.

As usual I was in constant conflict at high school, and as the teasing and bullying gathered momentum I grew ever more hostile. I was volatile at the best of times but as the suffering at home intensified, my fuse was often shortened by exhaustion. Unable to sleep, I'd sneak out of the house at night and wander the streets of Tamworth in the small hours when the world was silent. To slip out unnoticed I had to slide across the kitchen floor on my backside to keep the floorboards from creaking. I'd then stroll through the dark streets trying to plan elaborate ways of escaping home and Tamworth for good. My dream destination was usually the same: Queensland. The Sunshine State offered a new beginning. It was a clean slate across a real border with different people and subtropical warmth thrown in. I realised that if I was going to run away – properly run away forever – I'd need money for food and transport.

I decided that stealing milk money would help me amass a bank to fund my escape. In the 1960s a battalion of milkmen in little trucks fanned out across the country before dawn each day to deliver glass bottles of fresh milk to Australia's homes. In exchange, householders left a payment in cash (usually a few silver and copper coins) in pre-agreed hidey holes near their letterboxes or on their front steps. I started raiding these during my nocturnal wanderings. I'd discovered an uninhabited house not far from where we lived and started to use the place as a hide-out on days when I couldn't face the playground nasties. It was a funny old joint – a throwback to the 1920s – and felt a bit like stepping onto the set of a Hollywood Western. There was a room with frilly gowns, long gloves, fancy shoes, gaudy jewellery, and all manner of artefacts and knick-knacks. I was particularly taken with the rings with big, colourful stones set in them: 'diamonds', 'rubies' and 'sapphires'. I was more fascinated with the stones than anything else.

While my classmates at Oxley High were doodling on their pencil cases and wondering why Pus Head was absent again, I'd dress up in the gowns, thread the rings onto my fingers and swan around in the quiet solitude of the empty house. It was safe, I could be someone else for a while and no one knew I was there.

A few weeks later, however, someone *did* see me exit the house when I should have been at school. It was a relative of the old lady who used to live there. She knew who I was and went straight to the police. A subsequent search of the house revealed three rings had been 'stolen', so I was arrested and taken to Tamworth Police Station for questioning. I readily admitted to being in the property and told the cops I had indeed taken the rings, but that I hadn't removed them from the house at all – I'd stashed them underneath it. I also confessed to taking the milk money when asked about cash that had disappeared from front yards in my neighbourhood – $8.78 to be precise. I was charged with break, enter and steal for my escapades at the abandoned house, despite the rings still being there all along and easily recovered, and with thirteen counts of stealing relating to my moonlit removal of milk moolah. The magistrate ordered that I be 'committed to an insti-tution', but suspended the sentence provided I entered a ten-dollar good-behaviour bond for two years. On the charges of stealing, I was released on probation. The court had taken into account Mum's teary statement to police that, 'He has never given me any trouble before this.'

I would soon provide her with a whole lot more.

There had been weeks of conflict in the house: yelling, screaming, beating, crying, name-calling. It was not a nice place to be and it was wearing me down. We'd given up calling the police years before; nothing ever eventuated and inviting the authorities into our defective world was as good as ushering in more violence once they'd driven off.

After a particularly bad weekend, on a cold Monday afternoon in August 1969, we braced ourselves for Dad's return from the Ex-Servos. Mum had primed us by scream-ing at the girls 'Clean this! Tidy that! MOVE!' almost non-stop. I looked at my little sisters, all tear-streaked and sobbing. It reminded me of our first night in the orphan-age, alone and grief-stricken in the dining room.

As usual I'd been watching out for Dad because I knew what was going to happen as soon as he got home – the exact same thing as the day before, and the day before that, and the day before that. As he staggered up the big hill to our house I suddenly felt the tether slip straight through my fingers. 'No!' I told myself. 'Not today.' I bolted out into the freezing afternoon air and got as far away as I could.

It was just on dusk when I saw a horse looking rather lonely in a paddock a few miles out of town. I leaned against the fence and he sauntered over for a bit of a nuzzle. There was no one home, at least not that I could see, and the poor old nag was virtually begging me to liberate him. A horseback escape was suddenly on the cards. I reckoned I'd be able to make it a fair distance on a horse; further and faster than on foot. Spying a saddle and bridle lying on the back veranda of the adjoining house, I crept over, gathered them up and worked out how to fit them. Then I opened the gate, pulled myself into the saddle and we clip-clopped out of town.

Apparently somebody *had* been at home at the house, however, and they had called the police. After a mile or two I heard the whine of approaching sirens. Soon lights flashed behind me and turned the gloom on either side of the road a flickering blue. I put the horse into a full gallop and got low over his head. We were off.

He might have been an affectionate and compliant old horse, but what he made up for in personality, he lacked in stamina. After seven miles he tired and started panting heavily. Not wanting to harm him, I let him slow to a trot. I dismounted while the horse was still moving and sprinted into open land with the cops hot on my heels.

It was dark by then so I didn't see the barbed-wire fence across the paddock until I ran into it at full tilt. I was badly lacerated – and I was under arrest.

The cops untangled my bloodied frame from the fence, threw me in the back of their car and drove me straight to Tamworth Base Hospital. My legs had been sliced open quite severely, and one gash in particular was leaking a decent amount of blood. The doctor wasn't at all sympathetic, though; he didn't bother to suture the wound and bandaged it instead. After 'treatment' I was taken to the lock-up for some more 'attention'.

That night I learned that you don't run from the cops without a bit of payback. They'd been professional enough while I was in the hospital, but once they had me back on their own patch at Tamworth Police Station they were eager to administer some of their own special medicine.

You hardly see telephone books anymore, but back then they were ubiquitous, especially in police stations. Cops used them to bash you in a manner that hurt you and not them. I may have only been fourteen years old but I was about to get acquainted with the White Pages of justice.

Where a police baton will leave a welt or a mark, and knuckles can bruise or break the skin, a phone book slammed hard across the back or the chest delivers a lot of pain but, conveniently, leaves no evidence of assault. There was no point in my complaining to anyone about it. As if anyone was going to believe a little kid. Besides, who was I going to tell, a policeman?

It had been seven months since my last conviction, which meant my spur-of-the-moment horse rustling had violated the terms of my good-behaviour bond. Serious trouble. I was charged with two counts of stealing (one for the horse and one for the saddle) and bailed to appear at Tamworth Children's Court. In the meantime, an officer from the Department of Child Welfare Services paid a visit to our humble home and a social worker met separately with Mum.

I was interviewed by a psychologist who prepared a Clinical Psychological Report for the court stating that I functioned 'at the lower level of the dull range in keeping with [my] educational record'. She continued:

Gregory is a quiet, conforming and polite boy. He is a very inhibited person emotionally: he spoke of distressing events in the home with an immobile face and showed no ability to invest emotion in anybody. He shows signs of insecurity; his tension emerges in his disturbed sleep, frequent nightmares, talking in his sleep and severe nail-biting.

I must take issue with the 'lower level of the dull range' remark. Plus the fact that, as a trained psychologist, she might have concluded that rather than being 'insecure' and 'inhibited' I was severely traumatised and depressed. It might have gone some way to explaining the immobile face. But other than that, her assessment was reasonably competent.

In each case, however, these court-appointed assessors said that locking me up in juvenile detention – as per the conditions of my bond – would be a bad idea. So would any notion of sending me home to face more of the same from Dad. Despite his promise to the social worker to repent, it was pretty clear that it was beyond his faculty to ever change. Instead, the court, in its infinite wisdom, decided the best thing to do was uproot me from the community and send me to live in a distant city with a pair of complete strangers.

6

COLD WINTERS

Apparently the Winters were my great-aunt and great-uncle, though I'd never heard of them before, let alone met them, and I had no idea how we were related. The court might as well have sent me to live in Timbuktu with two middle-aged people selected at random from the back of a bus. But there I was in an unfamiliar house in Sydney where I was supposed to stay until my sixteenth birthday.

Tommy and Eileen Winters lived in a neat brick house at Greenacre, a tough suburb in the harbour city's south-west. While I was given a room, clothed and fed, the Winters made it abundantly clear that I was in their world by order of the court and that the arrangement was a burden on them. There was no warmth.

Aside from the fact I wasn't getting bashed every after-noon, life with the Winters wasn't a lot better than back in Tamworth. It didn't take long for me to realise that

Tommy was a drunk, a womaniser and a gambler – a trifecta of destabilising vices that charged the household with tension.

At first the Winters enrolled me in a local private school that was brimming with priests and Brothers. I hated the place; it was a bit too 'orphanagey' for me and I told them so. Eventually I was allowed to transfer to Punchbowl Boys High School. Were I any other boy with a stable home life I might have really liked it there – maybe even flourished. We were allowed to conduct science experiments, which I found fascinating, and the other kids were pretty good to be around for a change, too. I don't recall being addressed as Pus Head and I managed to pay attention to what we were being taught most of the time.

I was also amazed at the blurred lines between the hierarchy. The students played pranks on a couple of the teachers and I was shocked to discover these adult educators didn't mind. It confused me at first. When the boys in my science class plotted to secrete some famously pongy hydrogen sulphide in a dissolvable capsule inside the teacher's drawer, I was terrified that we'd all end up getting flayed with a cane. If you pulled a stunt like that on a Brother at St Mary's you'd just about get your head caved in.

But the Punchbowl jokesters had no such fears. 'Don't worry, it's OK,' one of them reassured me. 'He'll get the funny side of it.' Halfway through the lesson the teacher suddenly reeled away from his desk in hilarious spasms of revulsion as sharp wisps of rotten-egg gas wafted out of his drawer. The boys burst out laughing and, sure enough, so did the teacher. I was blown away.

The relatively decent time I was having at school only brought the misery of life at the Winters' into stark relief. I dreaded going back there of an afternoon. There was nothing familiar about where I was or what I was doing. I'd sit around the dining table with virtual strangers who'd ask me how my day had been and I'd wonder if I was in a waking nightmare.

Practical jokes or not, I had failed to make a single friend at school or even remotely be 'part of'. I've forgotten what the lesson was but our teacher was halfway through giving it when the instinct to run kicked in. I picked up my schoolbag, strode out of the classroom, across the playground and out the gate of Punchbowl Boys High. After a few blocks my bag grew too heavy so I hurled it over a fence and kept walking. Had I been in Tamworth I'd have no doubt plotted a course for Queensland. But in Sydney I was a fish out of water. I had no idea where to go so I just walked as far as I could in the opposite direction of the Winters' house.

It was getting on towards evening when the police finally caught up with me. They asked me why I'd run away so I told them. 'I'm in foster care and I hate it and just want to get away.' I waited for the customary beating from the coppers but it never came. Maybe it was because they were from the city. Country cops wouldn't have mucked around, yet these guys were really nice to me. Strangely, it made me teary.

I was still weeping when they dropped me back at the Winters' house. I told them I'd lost my schoolbag and Tommy said not to worry, someone had found it and returned it. The Winters were a bit kinder to me for a day or two. Pretty soon, though, they were back in the swing of telling me that I was in *their* house as a favour to *my* parents and not to forget it, right?

The tension built up and I started to break. Home alone after school one day, I went around the house and bashed the walls with a plumber's plunger, leaving big, black, circular marks all over the place. I spent another afternoon spraying flaming jets of poison around the house while 'playing' with a cigarette lighter and a can of Mortein.

I didn't last at the Winters until my fifteenth birthday, let alone my sixteenth. After four months, they'd had enough. I was back in Tamworth in time for the new school year and to resume my life as Pus Head.

I always thought the Oxley High School emblem, a ship's anchor, was a bid odd. After all, Tamworth is roughly 250 kilometres from the coast. I knew John Oxley was a British naval officer turned pioneering explorer of Australia, but I didn't imagine he'd discovered my landlocked home town by frigate. At any rate, I attended the school by bike.

Although I was in second form (Year 8) my level of education, which had been derailed by my years in the orphanage and stunted by domestic violence, hovered around the standard of a child in the lower fifth class. I had always been considered a 'difficult' student and in many ways I undoubtedly was. Bullying, ostracism, mental scarring and beatings will do that to a kid. A lot of the time, however, I was simply misunderstood by the people who were being paid to understand and nurture me.

I had my own grasp of the world, my own intellect, and I often wondered, when I was two or three steps ahead in my own mind, why my classmates had to have things spelled out to them. I definitely knew nonsense when I heard it. During one social studies class at Tamworth Public School a few years earlier we'd been learning about Australian history when our teacher, a lady who was a newcomer to town, explained that a fellow by the name of Captain Cook had discovered Australia.

'No he didn't,' I piped up firmly.

'I beg your pardon?' the teacher snapped.

'Captain Cook didn't discover it!'

'Greg, Australia was discovered by Captain James Cook in 1770 during an expedition aboard the HMS *Endeavour*.'

'Nup. The Aborigines discovered Australia.'

'That's enough!'

'The Aborigines discovered Australia thousands and thousands of years ago – before anyone else did.'

By then all eyes were on me. There were a few sniggers, giggles and mocking 'retard' looks from the other boys and girls, but they didn't realise I was just trying to help them. Back in the orphanage Gussy Nicholls had told me all about the real history of Australia. I had no reason to doubt what he said. I trusted Gussy's word, whereas this teacher, she was new. What did she know? I believed the other students deserved to be told the truth.

'Greg, stand up now and wait outside for me.'

After the class, Mrs New Lady scolded me and marched me to the principal's office, where I mounted a strong defence of what I'd said and refused to apologise or back down. I was told that 'teacher knows best' and given six cuts of the cane to make sure I understood the rule. It's what you get for being a 'problem child'. But I knew I was right about the Aborigines. So did they.

In a way that one episode encapsulated why school was such a challenge for me. It demonstrated the inflexibility of the system, my willingness to be outspoken and challenge what I thought to be wrong, my disdain for authority, the default to exclusion and corporal punishment, the bullying and ostracism from peers, and the utter failure to even attempt to understand my problems or my perspective. If they'd just tried to do that, even a little bit, I was sure I'd do well at school.

I remained an outcast at Oxley High School, but the overt bullying had generally stopped, mainly because I put an end to it with my fists. One day a small group of boys thought they'd test the limits by calling out 'Pus Head! Pus Head! Pus Head!' over and over again. I copped it for three or four minutes until, without any warning, I flailed into them like a crashing helicopter. I knocked one kid straight down and mercilessly laid into the other two. The onslaught was so intense they ran away, genuinely frightened. For that I had to front Mr Rankin, the deputy head, who duly administered six cuts of the cane. As usual I didn't flinch, and I asked him, 'Is that the best you can do?'

On another occasion I was minding my own business in French class (I took French as an elective because I thought it was romantic) when I was called outside by Rankin. He told me I was going to be punished for sparking a brawl in the playground earlier that day. Although I pleaded innocent I was made to sit outside his office for the afternoon. Eventually he called me inside and delivered six of the best. I gave him another F and told him, 'I thought you'd be able to do better than that with the practice you get.'

The next day Rankin sought me out to apologise. It had come to his attention that it had not been me who was involved in the brawl after all. Furthermore, he said I had a credit for six cuts of the cane. As far as I'm aware I still have that credit to this day.

My troubles at school weren't limited to boys and principals. Religious hang-ups and Catholic-engineered molestation had caused a yawning chasm to open up between me and the opposite sex. One afternoon I was shuffling along a corridor when I heard music coming from one of the classrooms. I slowed down to have a look and saw that inside there were six girls dancing on the tables to some pop song or other that was chirping out of a cassette recorder. When they saw me, one of the girls turned around and spoke up for all of them. 'Piss off, dick. You're a grub.'

Out of the blue the schoolyard angst suddenly stopped just before the end of the first term. As soon as I turned the legal leaving age of fourteen and nine months, Dad pulled me out of high school. As far as he was concerned, my education was over. He explained that I wasn't cut out academically and persisting would be a waste of time. Instead, I was instructed to get a job to help pay the bills at home. I would not get my leaving certificate and I would not wear the Oxley senior uniform with the anchor on the tie. Instead I was given a pair of baggy overalls, a broom and a cleaner's job at an engineering firm in Tamworth.

The men there were even worse than school kids – they treated me like garbage and one bloke in particular delighted in bullying me every chance he got.

I reacted the only way I knew how. I ran.

7

CAGED

The older I got, the further I'd make it away from home. As a boy of five or six I'd run a few blocks or maybe a kilometre before I was found by Mum or Dad, or picked up by a neighbour and once by the police. By the time I was eleven I was high-tailing it dozens of kilometres from the orphanage. As a teenager I was sometimes able to put hundreds of kilometres between me and my troubles, only to find new ones waiting for me.

On one occasion I hitchhiked more than 200 kilometres north to Glen Innes. I came unstuck trying to fend off hunger. I'd entered a shop looking for something – anything – to eat. I spied a tray of fruit by one wall and as I reached out to take a piece a voice boomed, 'Are you going to pay for that?' The shopkeeper made a lunge for me but I dropped the fruit and bolted out the door. He rang the police, who didn't take long to find me. I was treated to the obligatory kicks and slaps about the head and driven back to Tamworth and my living hell.

Thumbing rides proved to be the most effective means of flight by far. It was a hell of a lot better than walking with half a thong, running through paddocks or riding a geriatric horse down the middle of the road. By the time I was fifteen, however, I had learned to drive a car myself. Well, sort of. No one had ever taught me, I'd simply watched Mum and Dad use the pedals and gear stick and tried to mimic what they did.

Trouble at home had been escalating. I'd grown a bit bigger and although I wasn't as tall or as strong as Dad, I was large enough to fight back more convincingly and sometimes cause damage to him, too. Often this simply meant that he'd attack me with added vigour lest I get one over on him. It was after one such vicious clash that I ran away and vowed to make it to Queensland and stay there for good, no matter what.

I stole a couple of cars but they kept breaking down (or I kept breaking them, thanks to my DIY driving techniques). I finally made it to Armidale, where I stole four dollars, ten packets of cigarettes and two packets of biscuits from a shop. The biscuits were for sustenance, the four dollars was for buying more food along the way and, since I wasn't a smoker, the cigarettes were to be traded or sold for food at a later date.

After years of failed attempts, this teenage crime spree had finally delivered me across the border and into the promised land – Queensland. To my dismay I found it to be just as callous a place as New South Wales. In the town of Toowoomba, west of Brisbane, the cops caught up with me after I was observed showing suspicious interest in a parked car. They tackled me hard onto the ground and went to the extra effort of driving their knees into my back and pushing my face into the dirt as they handcuffed me. At the police station I was fingerprinted and asked to give a statement. I was terrified and didn't say a word so they locked me up overnight with several grown men.

In the cruellest of twists, the very border that I had long dreamed would set me free instead formed the basis for my imprisonment. With no local crime to hang on me, the police charged me with one count of taking stolen goods (namely the bickies and the smokes) into Queensland. It was a crime deemed so grave that I was driven to Westbrook Training Centre, an infamously brutal gaol for juveniles on the outskirts of Toowoomba, to await my day in court.

Being in Westbrook was a hardening experience. On arrival I was thrown into a large cage full of troubled children. It was separate from the main buildings and had no solid walls (just metal bars topped with a tin roof) so it was open to the elements. There were ten to fifteen other boys locked in the cage with me; youths of all different shapes and sizes but each wearing the same haunted expression while pretending not to be scared. The wardens brought food to us as you would scraps to a pig-pen, and at the end of the day we were marched inside to a dormitory to sleep and then herded back into the cage the following day.

With boys under such stress and despair it's no wonder fights broke out. I've forgotten how or why my first brawl in the cage started, but I remember the guards didn't intervene. They just let me and the other kid tear into each other until we could fight no more. The next confrontation was a barbarous encounter. Another boy and I beat each other with such desperation that we were well splattered with blood. Eventually the guards stepped in and stopped that one.

After a week behind bars I was driven to Toowoomba Children's Court where the charge of taking stolen goods into Queensland was thrown out through lack of evidence. Who knows why? Perhaps the cops ate the biscuits and smoked all the cigarettes. There was no relief, though, because New South Wales Police had applied for my extradition and a few days later I was back in the cells at Tamworth Police Station for a White Pages welcome. When they'd finished, the cops composed themselves and set about trying to pin a large proportion of the state's unsolved crimes on me, including just about every car theft within a 200-kilometre radius.

I may have committed crimes but I was honest; I always had been. Although I'd already confessed to everything I had done the coppers interviewed me for hours on end – twice. I was so freaked out that I screamed at them, which simply made them laugh at me and tell me what an idiot I was. In the end, the only surplus crime they could find that fitted the rough timeline of my movements en route to Queensland was the theft of a wallet in Glen Innes some time 'during October'.

'I didn't steal that wallet,' I protested truthfully.

'Yes you did, dickhead. You might as well own up to it.'

'I told you exactly what I did,' I shot back, 'BUT I'M NOT A LIAR!'

They seemed to think pushing a kid to the point of hysteria was a hilarious joke and they charged me with stealing the wallet as a punch line. I was convicted, but this time around the magistrate saw no need for long-lost relatives from Sydney to intervene – he ordered that I be committed to an institution. In other words, I was going to a gaol for children.

After a brief stint in Yasmar Boys' Home in Sydney, I was shipped by train 250 kilometres north to a place called St Heliers, a 700-acre prison farm outside the town of Muswellbrook in the New South Wales Hunter Valley. My travelling partner was a massive Corrections Department guard who kept an enormous fist clamped around the belt at the back of my pants. It seems everyone knew I was a runner.

'D'ya smoke, son?'

'Huh?' My forehead had been planted against the window as I watched the scenery roll by and pondered what horrors might lie ahead.

'D'ya want a smoke?' As the guard spoke, a lit cigarette teetered precariously on his lips. He proffered his packet to me.

'Yeah, yeah, sure,' I said and clumsily plucked one of his smokes from the box. The guard struck a match and lit my first ever cigarette for me. Like everybody else in history, I coughed so hard as the poisonous gases flooded my lungs that I nearly threw up. Mr Corrections just smiled.

At St Heliers, I quickly learned that smokers had status among the inmates and were even given a weekly ration. Big tobacco would have loved it. But the irony of being introduced to state-sponsored smoking while being punished by the state for stealing cigarettes was not lost on me.

While I'd grown used to being beaten by adults – from Dad through to teachers, the Sisters of Mercy, the Brothers of Brutality and various members of the New South Wales and Queensland Police – I was introduced to more considered types of penance in juvenile detention. I was forced to stand on an 'X' chalked on a concrete path with my upturned arms outstretched at right angles and a pillow balanced across my forearms. I had to stand still like that for an hour, minimum, in the December sun. The pain was excruciating, as was the humiliation.

Even the 'training' they administered at 'training schools' like St Heliers amounted to a self-perpetuating punishment. The inmates were divided up among various 'houses' and overseen by 'house parents' who ordered us to work. We had to scrub every centimetre of the enormous dining-room floor, and the toilets were cleaned in a similar fashion, except with an abrasive sandsoap. One day I hadn't finished cleaning the dining tables in time for them to be set for lunch. For that I was told to scrub the dining-room floor by myself and I was to be 'unprivileged' for the rest of the week.

Being unprivileged meant you faced a suite of punishments for a set period, usually seven days. These included cleaning out fetid grease traps, having to stand up while you ate your meals, being forbidden from speaking, scrubbing the concrete walkways while the other boys had recreation time, and various other demeaning and humiliating privations. I got so angry about it I laid into the dining-room wall with my fists, ripping skin off my knuckles and denting the plaster in the process. After five or six weeks of my insubordination and volatility I was transferred to another house called Hunter.

In complete contrast, Hunter was run by a kindly Italian couple. The female house parent took a liking to me because I'd taken a shine to her cats. I'd sometimes stray near the boundary line at Hunter to pat and confer with her large collection of felines. Early in the piece she made a point of coming over and talking to me as I knelt on the ground and scratched one of her moggies behind the ear.

'Do you like cats?' she asked me, smiling.

'Yeah, I like them more than people,' I admitted.

A few weeks later I was honoured when the Italians asked me to take care of the cats while they went on extended leave. That's when the real trouble started.

A man named Joe, who was in charge of another house, was given responsibility for Hunter while the Italians were away. I distrusted and disliked Joe right from the start – something that was obvious to him and everyone else – so Joe had to show me who was boss. First he cut off my tobacco. Then, he started to slap me across the head or sneak up behind me and deliver a vicious kick in the backside whenever he felt the need or sensed an opportunity.

On another occasion he choreographed my suffering from the sidelines. Sport was compulsory at St Heliers and on Sundays inmates competed against each other in various codes, including rugby league. Like a lot of boys I loved watching footy, but I had never played in an actual game until Joe selected me to be in the front row in a clash against the biggest, toughest inmates in the place. I was a skinny runt and my beefy opponents relished the opportunity to tear me to shreds. I was pummelled, belted, trodden on, crushed and left so concussed that I don't recall finishing the game (the last I ever played in, too). Joe was over the moon.

The worst of the abuse, however, had nothing to do with physical pain – at least, not for me. It was the Italians' brood of cats that suffered, and in the process, a deep emotional wound was inflicted upon me.

While the Italians were on holiday, perhaps comfortable in the knowledge I was taking good care of their pets, Joe ordered me to round up all the cats at Hunter and castrate the males. 'Stick 'em head first in here and use the knife to cut their nuts off,' Joe instructed as he handed me a large black rubber boot and a small pocket knife. I couldn't quite believe what he was saying. Aghast, I outright refused.

Crack! He belted me so hard in the side of my head that I saw stars and my good ear was left ringing. I held my ground and said there was no way I'd torture animals in such a way, but Joe was going to force me to do his bidding one way or another. Finally, he agreed to let me put the cats into a hessian sack instead of jamming them into an airless boot, but I still had to castrate them.

I cut a small slit in the sack and for the next hour I bundled cat after cat – more than a dozen of the petrified creatures – into the bloodied bag, wrestled them into place until their testicles protruded from the slit and did the deed. The purpose of the macabre exercise was to stop the cats from breeding. The purpose of forcing a boy to do it? I'll never know. I'd been very fond of those cats and I'd given an undertaking to care for them, not butcher their organs. Some days I still ask the cat gods for forgiveness.

My resentment towards Joe distilled into pure hatred. I truly would have murdered him if I'd had the opportunity. I knew then that I had it in me to be a killer.

Two months later I was free to resume my place in society, whatever that was.

My father didn't set out to be the person he turned into. I never would have produced him. It has had happen to a person who had to be to me to be adults. But I can'd like a new the certains teachers places away. where we may at some

8

DAD

My father didn't set out to be the person he turned into. Nobody in their right mind would. On my birth certificate his occupation is listed as a salesman, and I have a photograph of him holding me as a baby alongside his father, Aubrey. They both looked very sharp and professional in collar and tie. Something must have gone awry very quickly.

The first job I remember Dad having was at the wheel of a petrol tanker, carting fuel to the Shell service stations in the little satellite towns that orbited Tamworth: Kootingal, Moonbi, Bendemeer and Wallabadah. One of the very few pleasant childhood memories I have is riding high in the passenger seat of the old lorry on days I joined Dad on his rounds. It almost felt normal – like two pals out on the road sharing an adventure. Neither the feeling nor the job lasted.

Dad's primary occupation was as a labourer at a Tamworth starch factory. He left home early every morning in a pair of white overalls that made him easy to spot as he walked up the hill towards home at the end of the day – never a welcome sight. Dad wasn't a hands-on type of parent and, like a lot of men of that era, he didn't appear the least bit interested in raising kids. Aubrey had been the same so I don't think Dad had a clue how to do it or even what to say to us.

I once managed to get a job with Wordsworth's news-agency, doing a paper round and going to all the pubs in town to sell copies of *The Sun*, *The Daily Mirror* and *Best Bets*. I slogged away at it for about a year and saved every penny with the aim of buying myself a pushbike. It was a second-hand affair that had a broken cotter pin, so it made an annoying 'clump' sound every time the pedals rotated, but I'd worked hard for it and was chuffed that I'd bought it off my own bat. The afternoon I rode it home Dad was in the yard taking the head off a chicken.

'Look, Dad, I bought a bike!' I said proudly.

'So what?' he grumbled, hardly even bothering to look up from the blood and feathers.

I can't remember him ever teaching me anything much other than how to lose control. Dad's idea of a swimming lesson, for instance, was to throw me into the local dam and watch to make sure I didn't drown as I flailed about trying to figure out dog paddle for myself. It had literally been sink or swim. There were no fun games, no father-and-son camping trips or memorable afternoons where he'd teach me how to fish.

On an emotional level, the main things I learned from

Dad were fear and hate – mostly of and for him. I got more out of my relationship with Mum's brother, Uncle Robbie, who lived in Oberon west of Sydney. In the brief periods I spent with Robbie he took the time to show me how to make snares for rabbits and some bushcraft tricks that would one day come in extremely handy.

For a man whose life was a mess, Dad was quite the stickler for domestic order. Luckily for him, he had five daughters to push around. The girls were constantly press-ganged into cleaning the house and Dad would assess the results during fastidious forensic inspections. My sisters were ordered to clean underneath the bath, in the gaps between bricks and even inside the keyholes of doors. Any trace of dirt or grime was enough to send Dad off his rocker.

He was like a crazed maitre d' when it came to clean dishes, too. If he detected the slightest smear or a skerrick of 'muck' on a plate or fork once the girls had finished washing up, he insisted they empty the entire cupboard of crockery and cutlery, then wash every single piece until it passed muster. These strict standards didn't apply to Dad, though. He was particularly volatile when he was slaughtered on sherry and home-brew, and there were times he'd hurl plates of food onto the ceiling or out the door. That kind of mess was OK, apparently. And so was the mess he made of his children.

If alcoholism is weakness, it was true of my father. He would drink himself into such a state of malfunction that, as I grew older, I sometimes got the upper hand. He'd be too far gone to fend me off as I belted into him with a stick or whatever happened to be in reach. Unlike Dad,

DAD

I didn't need alcohol to lose control – those circuits had already been fried. I would scream while I attacked him, 'You're like scum crawling up the toilet. I hate you. I hate your guts! You're a pathetic drunk.' In times like those I became a confluence of my parents – Mum's mouth and Dad's fists.

I also developed guerrilla tactics to exact a toll for the terrible things he'd done to us and would no doubt do again. Dad loved sherry and he downed at least one half-gallon bottle every day. But he was also fond of his home-brew. Sometimes, after he'd bottled a new batch of beer and waited for it to ferment, I'd sneak around and open them all up, add half a teaspoon of salt and reseal the lids. This killed the carbonation process and left him with flat, salty beer. I'd also 'accidentally' spill salt all over his meal before he got home or set his transistor radio on full volume and slightly off channel so it would scream white noise in his ear when he switched it on. I could be a right little bastard.

I learned to be pre-emptive, too. It got to the point where as soon as I'd hear raised voices I'd be straight into whatever room it was coming from to start laying into Dad before he even lifted a finger. The day I tried to kill him was just another strategic strike.

Dad used to keep a bottle of sherry planted in the back garden so he could go for a wander and enjoy a quiet swig in the great outdoors. On one particular afternoon he was walking through the backyard towards his stash when I ran up from behind and took him down with a flying shoulder charge. As he lay on the grass I jumped on top of him and wrapped my hands around his throat. I hadn't planned on killing him, but since it seemed to be happening I was

63

willing to go through with it. I had no choice. Something in my mind had snapped.

Fortunately for both of us, a neighbour was able to drag me off him. I sometimes wonder what would have happened had no one intervened. I suspect I might have gone to gaol for murder. It didn't really matter, though, that I'd failed to choke Dad to death. I was back in a cell soon enough anyway.

9

NO SAINT

I lit upon the idea for committing burglaries while watching the British mystery-thriller TV show *The Saint*. The series followed the adventures of Simon Templar (played by a suave, pre-Bond Roger Moore) who was a Robin Hood–style burglar who stole from criminals but kept the proceeds for himself. I decided to adopt his ways to bankroll my disappearance from Tamworth – a never-ending obsession for me.

While Roger Moore had access to a great wardrobe department and costume designers to fit him out for small-screen heists, I had to make do with pieces of daggy black clothing gathered from around the house. And unlike The Saint, I was easily caught. Mr Mitchell, whose house I broke into in our neighbourhood, was a fairly big fellow and he had no trouble throwing me onto the floor and sitting on me while his wife rang the cops.

Around that time I'd also been breaking into cars and stockpiling the pilfered loot in a shed in the backyard. I was questioned about these break-ins, too, and – never one to lie – I confessed. A catalogue of the stolen items reveals pure opportunism and my overall stupidity. In addition to small amounts of cash, the stolen gear included: bottles of wine (I didn't drink), a stethoscope (I had no patients), a cassette holder and cassettes (I hated music), a set of darts (I didn't play darts), a whistle (as if I wanted to call attention to myself!), binoculars (see what I mean?) and some house numbers (yes, house numbers). I imagined it all had some value that I could convert into cash at a later date – maybe even enough to buy my own car and drive off somewhere far away to start my life anew. This stuff was also returned to the rightful owners. And I was returned to detention.

I was made a Ward of the State on 12 March 1973 and sent away for a year.

The Minda Juvenile Detention Centre in Sydney was truly horrible. Although inmates slept in dormitories instead of cells, everything else left me in no doubt I was in prison. The brick perimeter walls were so high you couldn't see out, while all the walls inside were so low that guards could watch your every move. Even the toilets had waist-high partitions and no doors; same with the showers. There was no dignity, but in any case I'd already lost mine in the bathtub at the orphanage. Those groping teenage girls had scrubbed it right out of me.

Minda did have a few cells, though – solid concrete boxes that were used to separate and punish inmates – and it wasn't long before I was locked inside one for forty-eight hours. The trouble started, as it often did, when another boy began to niggle me. He was a big guy (a lot bigger than me) and I suppose he felt he could tease me with impunity and just bash me if I tried to do anything about it. There's an old saying, however: 'It's not the size of the dog in the fight, it's the size of the fight in the dog.' Or, in my case, it's the size of the rage in the damaged skinny kid.

I attacked him fast and hard. It must have shocked onlookers to see this scrawny little critter erupt. I was only slight but I learned to be mean. Very mean. My facial features would change and my eyes would pop out of my head. I know it frightened people, especially the unlucky ones on the receiving end. In an instant I had the big guy on the ground and by the throat. I could feel his Adam's apple and windpipe twist and crack under the crush of my fingers. Just as I had him in dire straits I was dragged off and thrown into solitary, possibly as much for the safety of others as it was for punishment. I was sent to see a psychologist who concluded I was severely depressed and traumatised. She referred me to a senior State psychiatrist, Dr Freeman.

I was feeling particularly hungry on the day I stood in an office at Minda, across a desk from the very well dressed Dr Freeman. I was asked questions along the lines of, 'How do you feel about what you've done?' and, 'Do you see it affecting other people?' I couldn't have been less interested in what was going on and didn't say a word. I just kept wondering when it was going to be over and what I might be having for lunch. Looking back, I'm not sure Dr Freeman was paying much attention either, given the conclusions he reached:

Gregory is a personality disordered adolescent, socio-pathic type, who at present appears to be unable to conform to the norms of society. I do not consider him depressed and their [sic] certainly is no indication for psychiatric treatment. His transfer to a Training School should be expeditiously carried out.

So there you had it. I wasn't depressed or traumatised – I was a sociopath! I would never change and I was beyond the reach of psychiatric intervention. When I was told this, I had no reason to question it. After all, the man was an actual doctor – and a snappy dresser, too. In some ways I considered the diagnosis a badge of honour and I was even proud of it. At least now I had a label and a place in the world. 'Hey, I'm a sociopath!' Tragically I believed Dr Freeman's nonsense for a very, very long time.

No sooner had I arrived at Yawarra (a 'training school for boys' thirty-five kilometres west of the New South Wales port city of Newcastle) on 4 May 1973, than the screws made a point of telling the other inmates I was in for burglary. On top of being a card-carrying sociopath, I was also regarded as a sneaky, conniving little bastard who couldn't be trusted. Apparently burglars were among the lowest of the low. The torment and baiting was relentless.

Yawarra was different from the other detention centres I'd been in, in that a lot of the boys knew each other. They came from similar areas and had established histories and relationships, or at the very least knew someone who knew someone else. There were networks, alliances and connections. And then there was me, the reviled prison outcast.

Inmates were under strict surveillance and forbidden from speaking to anyone without permission. The only time boys could talk and mingle without fear of punishment was during designated 'smoko' breaks. I was excluded from smoko because I was deemed to be trouble with a propensity to become violent. The trouble, however, only started because the inmates needled me.

'Hey, Spiderman,' someone would sneer, 'you're a famous cat burglar – you should be able to get out of this place really easy, eh? Why don't you just climb up the walls, you sneaky little fuckwit?' I'd explode and attack until the screws dragged me away to a cell.

One particular inmate fancied himself as a real fighter. He was supposedly a state champion boxer and he carried himself as though he was ready to shape up at a moment's notice, deliver a flurry of crisp punches and claim the belt as the crowd went wild. One day he started in on me. 'Oh, you're a bit of a fighter, are ya, Smithy?' he said, possibly oblivious to the fact I hated being called Smithy. 'So, you're a burglar *and* a tough guy, are ya, Smithy? Well, I'll tell ya what, Smi–'

My forehead slammed into the bridge of his nose with such force he dropped to the concrete floor like a sack of spuds, but I wasn't anywhere near finished. If this guy really was a champion boxer I had to neutralise him once and for all. I leapt on top of him and pounded his already damaged face with my fists. He wasn't moving and he was losing blood at quite a rate so I stopped punching, gripped him hard by the throat and tore at the muscles and tendons in his neck. I felt several pairs of strong arms grab hold of me but even the screws had trouble putting an end to my sickening demolition job. I refused to let go of his throat. Finally, I was put in a vice-like headlock and hauled away.

Since admission Smith has responded to training excellently, my subsequent progress report noted. *No adverse mentions have been recorded and the lad has lost very few points.*

There was no mention of my assault on the boxer, no mention of the fact I was locked in solitary confinement for a week as punishment, and not a peep about any of my numerous other fights, infractions and the many weeks I spent unprivileged. Since I was a Ward of the State – and thus the responsibility of the government – these incidents may have reflected worse on the powers that be than on me. If there was violence and chaos behind bars it seems their policy was to not mention it.

I very much regret the damage I did to the poor boxer. I hurt him very badly. At the time, though, I felt as if I had no choice. He threatened me in front of other inmates, his shoulders wide and standing tall on his reputation. Unfortunately for him, reputation meant nothing to me. I'd been fighting my father – a grown man – since I was five years old and I didn't care how big people were, I just concentrated on making the threat and the fear go away. I didn't even mind being locked in the concrete box for seven days. At least I was safe in there and could retreat into the cave in my head, behind the force field where I made the rules: 'Animals only.'

When they let me out to rejoin the general population, Golden Gloves never came near me. And I mean he never came *anywhere* near me for more than a year. Few people did, and nobody in Yawarra ever called me Smithy again.

Smith has continued to respond to training in an exemplary manner, the Yawarra superintendent wrote on 10 January 1974. *Gregory is a very well behaved boy and it is envisaged that a recommendation for discharge will be made after a further brief period of training.*

My 'training' in the boys' homes taught me the finer points of how to: peel potatoes, scrub floors, polish floors, launder clothes, iron clothes, fold clothes, scrub pots, wash dishes, clean toilets, castrate cats, sweep paths, empty bins, roll cigarettes, make beds, not talk, stand up, sit down, languish in cells and march left-right, left-right.

It is difficult to see how Greg's response to training could have been improved, the superintendent stated on 19 February 1974. *It is therefore recommended that steps be taken to implement his discharge.*

Three months later and just a few days after my nineteenth birthday, the screws at Yawarra handed me a baggy set of second-hand clothes, $2.25 in change and some advice: 'Don't come back.'

When I returned to Tamworth I was an adult in the eyes of society and the law. If I wanted to I could legally vote in elections, drink in pubs, marry in holy matrimony and serve time in adult prisons. But with all these wonderful possibilities at my feet, I was hopelessly unprepared to face the world. Institutions, not to mention my parents, had failed to teach me any of the things that are crucial for a young man to get along. I didn't know how to hold a conversation, how to introduce myself properly and I could only just read and write. I hadn't the foggiest idea how to talk to girls, how to interview for a job, and I had no clue whatsoever how to control my searing anger at the world and everything in it.

I figured it was time I picked up a gun.

10

PUNCH DRUNK

Throughout my youth I'd heard dispatches about the war raging in the jungles of Vietnam. Maybe in the Australian Army I could be 'part of'. Even if it had occurred to me that the traumatised Diggers limping home from South-East Asia were being spat on and abused in the street, I doubt it would have put me off a military career – it was just the kind of treatment I was used to anyway.

Australian troops were all but withdrawn from Vietnam when I caught the Glen Innes mail train down to Sydney to sign up in 1974. The army had sent me the train ticket, which I thought was very decent of them. But for someone who was heading off to battle I was totally unprepared. All I had were the clothes on my back, and even then not nearly enough. I almost froze as the leaky old red rattler lurched through the high hills of New England and across the western plains of New South

Wales. I had to hug the foot warmers all the way to stave off hypothermia.

During the eight-hour journey I tried to imagine what life in the military would be like and I concluded it would probably be a good fit for me. Juvenile justice had taught me how to scrub floors and march, while hierarchical discipline had ruled my life since Mum dumped me at the orphanage. I was in no doubt whatsoever about my ability to kill people.

At the army recruitment office near Central Station I was put through my paces. I seemed to do well in the medical and physical fitness tests. So far so good – I could almost feel the uniform on my skin and the jungle boots on my feet. It was the psychological component that brought me unstuck. Just one question actually:

'Tell us, Gregory, why do you want to join the infantry?'

Too easy. I didn't have to think twice about my answer. 'So people will shoot at me.'

And that was that. I bombed out of the Australian Army's psychological aptitude test on the spot. I would not be going to fight in Indochina or anywhere else. I was deemed too much of a loose cannon to serve in a war that had been full of them.

I caught the next freezing train back to Tamworth with my tail between my legs and a foot warmer up my jumper.

By the time I'd been released from juvenile detention I was getting through twenty cigarettes a day, so it only made sense that my first job as a free man was at a tobacco farm. I found the position while scouring the employment pages of Tamworth's *Northern Daily Leader*. The ad said workers were needed to 'sucker' tobacco plants and offered a rate of $1.20 a row.

Despite not having a driver's licence, I borrowed Mum's old Austin Wolseley and drove a short way out of town to Moore Creek to see the farmer who'd placed the ad. He put me to work that same day suckering his tobacco plants under the mid-summer sun. The job required me to remove, by hand, the little buds (suckers) from the stems of each tobacco plant in order to make the bush grow in a more upright manner. There were dozens and dozens of tobacco bushes per row and it took me at least two hours to sucker each row. It was hard, repetitive manual labour that paid me less than one cent for every minute I toiled.

After two days slaving away I was contacted by a bloke named Chico Cameron. I'd seen him drive past the farm with a carload of workers the day before. Chico had noticed me working out in the field by myself and, being a bit of a socialist like me, he felt my rights as a worker were being impinged. 'You're being ripped off, mate,' Chico informed me. 'You're better off coming to work with me.' Chico and his crew picked and suckered tobacco at other local farms and were paid a pretty reasonable $1.20 an hour. Double the money? I didn't have to think twice.

About 5.30 the next morning Chico pulled up outside Mum's place in Tamworth. (After years of increased separations, time apart and estrangement she and Dad had finally divorced.) I was still asleep, but when he leaned on the horn I launched straight out of bed and piled into the back of his battered old FC Holden station wagon with the other blokes.

I felt awkward around other people, partly through a lack of social awareness and partly through self-loathing, yet I somehow managed to get along. I could no longer look at myself in the mirror and had let my beard and hair grow long and wild. It was Chico who first nicknamed me 'Beardy'. It was hardly creative but preferable to the alternatives, so I answered to it only slightly begrudgingly.

We worked at all the tobacco farms around Moore Creek to the north of Tamworth and Kootingal to the east. We'd generally start about 6am and work until 2pm. Although picking and bundling tobacco is hard yakka, I had been blessed with long, strong fingers that were perfectly suited to the work. I was, it has to be said, a gun tobacco picker.

I don't know if the New England tobacco farmers had shares in Joe Maguire's pub in Tamworth, but it would have made for a wise investment. Every day we pickers would repair to the boozer after work to have our daily pay cheques cashed in order to hand the money straight back across the bar. By the age of twenty-one I had developed an affection for the numbing properties of alcohol and was fast becoming a drunk. A very nasty one.

Having grown up in a house where alcohol poisoned the well of everyone's happiness, I had never been in a hurry to start boozing myself. The first time I ever bought a beer I did so with some milk money I'd pinched to finance another failed escape from home. I'd made it as far as Tenterfield – 300 kilometres to the north of Tamworth and just twenty kilometres shy of the fabled Queensland border – and had snuck into a local pub to escape the cold.

It was lovely and warm inside, with a fireplace glowing in one corner. I was sitting at the bar by myself when the barmaid ambled over. 'What'll ya have, love?'

I had no idea what the correct answer was so I just pointed at a crusty old bloke who had his fist wrapped around a schooner glass. 'I'll just have one of those, thanks.'

I didn't really know what I was drinking but it had bubbles in it and tasted like something you'd use to clean floors. After I'd forced it down, a woozy warmth flushed through my synapses. Realising I'd be sleeping outside, I ordered three more. That night I slept in a park and didn't move until morning.

Even though it had proved its worth, alcohol remained off my radar for most of my teenage years. You don't get to drink in the boys' homes so I never had the opportunity, even if the desire had have been there. By the time I was twenty-two, however, I not only had the desire but an aching compulsion to get drunk. The growing addiction helped fulfil another need that constantly gnawed away at me – the strong desire to be hurt. From my earliest days I had been in conflict. My whole life had been about physical punishment, and when I became a young adult the punching and kicking suddenly stopped. Far from it being a relief, I felt that if I wasn't being belted in some way then there was something wrong.

I started to find the answer in booze. Not only did it temporarily numb the anguish and torment I carried with me everywhere and every day, it was helpful in loosening my big mouth so that people might punch me in it.

Getting into a fight can be harder than you think, but after a while I settled on a bit of a system. I'd normally start off on beer, just to see what kind of mood was lurking below the surface and to relax enough to strike up a conversation. When I moved on to drinking bourbon I'd get a bit snarkier and be on the lookout for opportunities to take offence. When I switched to rum, violence of some kind was almost always assured.

People could push my buttons without even realising it. It could be as innocent as someone telling me, 'I've got a wife and two kids at home.' I could lose the plot over something as benign as that. Politics was another hair trigger. I had all kinds of socialist views and didn't mind 'educating' people about them. Now and then, however, the people I wanted so badly to smash me in the face would sit and laugh at me instead. No matter what I did I couldn't get a rise out of them. Nights like that were disappointing; a waste of grog and time.

Sometimes I made 100 per cent sure the night would end in fisticuffs. The first time, coincidently, was in Tenterfield – the same town I'd had my first beer in as a boy. I walked into a pub there one night itching for strife. I wanted to hit and be hit. I ordered bourbon, took off my coat in anticipation and started with the mouth. It didn't take long for someone to say the wrong thing and he happened to be twice my size. Perfect.

I launched at the big fellow with a flying shoulder to the neck and he crashed to the floor with a thud and shatter of beer glasses. Then he got back up.

Over the next little while Mr Big went about belting the daylights out of me, not realising that by doing so he was pummelling me into my comfort zone. When he'd finished, he and the barman picked me up, dragged me through the pub and threw me into the street with a bruised and bloodied face, and a shredded shirt.

In some ways the night had been a roaring success – I'd knocked the bloke down and got repaid with a hiding. Just terrific! I had, however, made two critical errors: I'd left my coat inside and hadn't had enough to drink to ward off the cold. I had to sleep rough that night and it was bloody freezing.

I would repeat that performance in pubs all along the eastern seaboard. There was only one hotel I refused to fight in – the Central Hotel in Tamworth. That was my safe place. After all, I had to set aside one pub in Australia where I could just go to relax. Everywhere else was a battle zone.

11

DANNY

I couldn't find a single reason to smack the guy in the mouth.

I'd chucked in my job in Tamworth and hitchhiked more than 1500 kilometres to the town of Bowen on the coast of North Queensland, where I was minding my own business at the bar of a local pub. A man who was a few years older than me struck up a conversation. Under normal circumstances that kind of fraternising could easily have ended with a shoulder to the throat or a headbutt to the face. I tried hard to give myself permission to attack the affable stranger but I just couldn't do it – he was just a really nice guy. More than that, he was quite possibly the first person, besides Gussy Nicholls, who I ever liked right off the bat.

His name was Danny Doyle and he was out recruiting workers on behalf of his boss. The tomato-picking season was just getting underway in Bowen and they had some work to offer. 'Do you want a job, mate?' Danny asked.

'Yeah, I might. Doing what?'

'Shed work. We've got some pickers coming in and we need someone to help in the shed unloading the tomatoes and that sort of thing.'

'Righto. How much does it pay?' I asked, getting straight down to business.

'A dollar fifty an hour.'

'Yeah. I'd be into that. But I've got nowhere to stay.'

Danny didn't hesitate. 'Stay at our place with me and my dad. There's a bed on the veranda. That's your bed.'

'Oh yeah?' I replied, hiding a grin. 'Cool. I'm in.'

I couldn't have been happier. I had a job, a place to stay, a lift to and from work every day and a nice bloke to knock around with. Danny was a hoot. We took off from the pub in his little red 4WD with the windscreen dropped down flat and a warm wind in our faces. The next day we drove out to the tomato farm to start clearing up and to get ready for the first pick to arrive. During a break I wandered outside to check out a battered grey Ferguson tractor that looked way older than me. Danny sauntered up beside me. 'You ever driven one of these, Beardy?'

'Nah,' I said.

'Well, allow me to teach you.'

Learning to operate the tractor saw me promoted on my very first day. Danny's boss, the old bloke who owned the farm, came by the shed and Danny introduced me to him. His name was Clary Lewis.

'So, you can drive the tractor?' Clary asked me.

'Yep. I've got it going pretty good,' I said confidently.

'Oh, well then, you can do the carting.'

'The what-ing?' I asked.

'We'll show you.'

The carting was a great job by the standards I was used to. I'd hitch a trailer to the tractor then drive out into the fields to pick up the buckets of produce the pickers left behind as they moved along the rows of plants. I had to keep a tally of how many buckets I loaded, then cart them back to the shed where I'd unload and head back out for more. Some might consider it a pretty dull occupation, but to me it represented a massive breakthrough into meaningful and enjoyable work. I wasn't cleaning grease traps, mopping up filth, plucking plants or breaking my back under a heavy load. For the first time ever I loved my job.

The downtime was fantastic, too. As soon as we'd knock off, Danny and I would go out looking for adventure. We went fishing, crabbing, shooting and even tried to catch sharks in the creek behind the meatworks. Danny was great company and had the knack of making me laugh – a rare gift. We were out on a shooting trip in his little 4WD one day when I heard Danny say, 'Quack, quack!' I was standing up looking around for wild pigs and quickly turned to face the front, when a low-hanging branch knocked me clear out of the car.

'What's with the quacking?' I demanded to know as I dusted myself off and checked for injuries.

'Mate, I told you to duck!' Danny said, cackling as if it was the funniest thing anyone had ever said. His laughter gave me the giggles, too.

Danny wasn't the only bloke on the farm who liked to have a lend. A bloke called Tom, who was the waterman responsible for irrigation, was also a bit of a joker. I gave him a lift in the tractor one afternoon and dropped him at the edge of an embankment that led down to a big well so he could start a water pump. When he got to the edge he looked into the hole, then turned around and said, 'Er, Beardy, it's probably about time you learned how to do this. You just climb down there and start the pump. Pretty simple.'

'OK. Sure.' I headed down into the hole but when I got to the bottom I was horrified to find a massive snake staring back at me. I flew back up the bank like an Exocet missile, as Tom rolled around laughing. When his sides had stopped hurting he went back down and caught the snake. It was a coastal taipan, one of the most aggressive and deadly snakes in Australia. Tom showed me how to tell the difference between that and a python. It was all about the scales and the shape of the head, he said.

I learned a lot that season, and not just about snakes, practical jokes and tomato farming. I discovered that Danny was a genuinely lovely man who at that time was the closest thing to a friend I'd ever had. He never once asked me anything uncomfortable like, 'Where are you from?' or 'Why are you different?'

Clary Davis was also a wonderful, big-hearted human being who treated me extremely well. Towards the end of the season, Clary told Danny and me that we could have the last two picks of a section of the crop. It was quite a bonus. We harvested the tomatoes, weighed them, crated them up and sent them down to the Sydney markets where they went for eight dollars a box. We did that twice and when our cheques came in a couple of weeks later I was bowled over by how much we'd earned.

The bonus came at just the right time. I'd been sending money to Mum back in Tamworth because, while I wasn't particularly fond of my mother, I didn't like to think of her and the girls living in poverty. I stuck cash into an envelope and mailed it to her every week, sometimes with a short note. It also meant my family knew where I was. I dutifully peeled off a chunk of my end-of-season bonus and put it in the post, too.

A bit later on Clary thanked me for my efforts. 'You should come back next year,' he said. 'If you'd like to come back a bit earlier you can help me plant.'

I didn't even have to think about it. In fact, I intended to wait right there in Bowen. Danny and I had plans.

The first time I ever got stoned was on a Saturday afternoon in Tamworth. I was nineteen years old and I'd been innocently drinking beer in the Central Hotel. As I chewed through another schooner I got talking with a local girl; just my usual awkward chitchat. Before long her boyfriend slipped into the bar and said, 'Who wants a smoke?'

The girl grabbed her bag and was on her feet in a jiffy. I didn't really click, so the guy turned to me and said, 'You smoke, don't ya?'

'*Yeahhh*?' I replied, wondering if he meant cigarettes.

'Well, come on then.'

Bemused as to why we didn't just have a ciggie in the pub like everyone else, I followed them outside into a little laneway. There the boyfriend sparked up a joint. I'd never laid eyes on one before and the first thing that struck me was how much it stank. The second was how much I loved it.

A few minutes after my maiden tokes of marijuana I started laughing my head off. I giggled like a little kid and completely embraced the strange, spacey, silly feeling of being stoned. I was instantly in love with it. We went back inside and kept drinking and I ended up extremely messy – what's generally known as pissed and stoned.

The second time I got high I was in Bowen with Danny. He'd invited me to spend the off-season at his place and we had all kinds of adventures that year: croc wrangling, mountain climbing, pig hunting and drinking. Now and then Danny would go off shooting pigs and bush turkey by himself, which I thought highly irresponsible. One day he came back from one of those solo expeditions excited. 'Beardy, d'ya know anything about dope?'

'I know a dope if I see one,' I replied, pointing at him.

'Nahhh! Dope! You know – marijuana. Do you know much about it?'

'Oh yeah, I suppose.' (Translation: 'Not really.')

'Do you know when plants look like they're ready to be harvested?'

'Oh yeah.' (Translation: 'Nup.')

And with that I was in the little red 4WD at sunset, riding shotgun with Danny into the darkening forest about fifteen kilometres from town. He explained that he'd found a massive dope plantation while out hunting, and now I was on hand as his expert advisor for an impending dope heist.

Danny stopped the car about a kilometre from the crop, and we slowly and carefully crept the remaining distance through the bush like thieves in the night (which we were). Eventually we broke through thick grass and into a cleared pocket of forest. There must have been 200 plants visible in the moonlight, each of them about six feet tall and as fat and round as big Christmas trees. The sweet, sappy aroma that hung in the air was beautiful. Yo ho ho.

'Do you reckon they look ready, Beardy?' Danny whispered.

'Oh yeah, I suppose,' I replied.

We sat down to hatch a plan and concluded it would be best if we took half a dozen plants each and left the rest. We did the deed and drove back to Danny's place where we hung them up under the house. We were so thrilled that we checked the plants three times a day to manicure them and see if they were drying out. About three weeks later they were ready to take down so we could separate the buds from the leaf. We ended up with a ridiculous amount of pot. I couldn't help wondering what 200 plants worth looked like.

We sold a fair whack of it but we smoked a lot, too. The first time I got stoned with Danny I was as sober as a judge. We had shared a big, fat joint and gone out for a night-time drive. It was different from the giggly high I'd had the first time back in Tamworth. My mind was racing but time seemed to slow down. Every mile we drove felt like ten, each turn of my head was a highly resonant experience that seemed to account for several long minutes, and whenever Danny spoke it sounded like he was in another dimension. I absolutely loved it – even more than the first time.

From then on a lot of our adventures were undertaken while stoned. Sometimes it had consequences. We started going after feral boar using bows and arrows with full-on hunting tips attached. One day I was climbing up a hill when I felt a sharp pain in the back of my leg. Danny had shot at something, missed and got me instead. Fortunately, the tip only penetrated halfway in, but the bleeding was profuse and the gash was bad enough for a trip to Bowen Hospital.

I found that marijuana helped me to relax and take it a bit easier in between my ears. Like alcohol, I used it as a buffer between me and the horrors of my childhood, the deafening echoes of which were impossible to silence.

When the next season rolled around I was excited to head back to work at Clary's. I helped him plant the new crop, and in return he pretty much set about teaching me the basics of being a farmer. He taught me how to plough a field using the tractor, how to drill with it, how to dig fields in a straight line. One afternoon I was working in the shed when Clary walked in with a face like stone and told me he'd just got off the phone with my mother in Tamworth. One of my sisters had attempted suicide. 'You're needed at home, mate,' he said solemnly.

I had no idea what to think or how to react, but Clary had it all figured out. 'Don't worry, Beardy, I'll have someone fly you to Brisbane and then we'll get you the rest of the way somehow.' I was bundled into Clary's light plane and taken to Brisbane where, out of the kindness of his heart, he'd chartered another plane at his own expense to fly me directly to Tamworth Airport.

My sister was in a pretty bad way so I stayed in town until she was out of danger. Then I caught the train back up to Bowen. When I arrived, though, something had changed. At the time I couldn't put my finger on it, but it was almost as though Clary's immense act of kindness had destroyed whatever balance I felt in Bowen. Maybe it was a sense of owing him something, a kind of obligation. Perhaps I was wary of them getting to know who I really was. Maybe I was unable to process what had happened to my sister. Whatever it was, I just couldn't handle it. Pretty soon afterwards I left Bowen and slipped off their radar for good.

When I look back today I realise that I was so damaged I couldn't grasp the opportunities that came my way. Here were some beautiful people who were prepared to befriend me and train me in the art of farming, but the barren soil of my life had left me stunted in every way.

Clary Davis would be long gone now. I've often thought about trying to get in touch with Danny but it's never happened. I hope he forgave me for running away.

12

JULIE

After a while I resigned myself to the rather bleak reality that I'd probably live out my days working in backbreaking, grimy or tedious jobs. The cleaning gig at Fielders Flour Mill in Tamworth was all three in one. The mill was a local landmark where men like me toiled at horrible, filthy tasks in order to help Fielders give the nation its daily bread. I needed to take two showers after a shift just to scrub the flour dust out of my pores. The soft, fine powder clung to every millimetre of exposed skin and every hair. It would even get caked inside my nostrils. It also made my throat extremely dry, so naturally I needed to drink a lot of beer to clear it away.

That's how I first met Julie – blowing the pipes clear with schooners of Reschs Pilsener one Saturday afternoon at the Post Office Hotel in Peel Street. She was in a corner having a couple of beers with her sister and some friends when I walked in. I slapped a coin on the pool table and ordered a beer. Julie said something to me or I said something to her and by the end of the night we were deep in conversation, which was unusual for me. I even found myself flirting with her. It must've been the beer.

Julie was like a little doll. She was about five feet tall with fine, delicate bones, rich red hair and a pair of dazzlingly green eyes. She may have come across as petite and demure in her pretty dress, but she could hold her own in an argument. She was beautiful and I was taken by her. We went our separate ways when the pub closed but not before Julie invited me to take her on a picnic the next day to the banks of Lake Keepit, a massive valley west of town that had been flooded to make a dam.

'Yes, ma'am.'

I picked her up at the Post Office pub just before lunchtime in my VF Valiant, a lairy looking mobile in canary yellow with big pink monkey stickers on the rear fenders. We stocked up with a couple of sandwiches and a carton of beer, slammed the heavy doors shut and lit out of town. That afternoon we lounged in the sun, chatted and downed the beers when, without warning, Julie up and kissed me. Even though I was out with a girl on my own and we were getting drunk together I was completely taken aback. I didn't know the first thing about women and how I was supposed to behave around them. Abuse had left me extremely anxious about sexual activity. Suddenly I felt intimidated by Julie, but I managed to push my fear down enough to continue canoodling until late in the evening.

Over the next few weeks Julie and I started to become an item. I don't quite know what she saw in me. Maybe she thought I was a brooding rebel. After all, I'd taken to wearing thick leather cuffs on my wrists à la Spartacus. Most evenings after work I'd have my two showers, put on some clean duds and meet her at the pub, where we'd drink and play pool.

Alarmingly, she insisted on meeting my parents who both lived right in town. The thought of this filled me with dread. I'd become comfortable, even a little bit secure, in the developing relationship and I worried that if Julie met my horror show of a family she'd run away screaming. But Mum and Dad met her separately and managed to behave. Julie said they were nice. So, beautiful *and* kind. I reckoned my girlfriend was something else.

I already knew I was punching way above my weight with Julie – my workmates at the flour mill had made sure of that with a barrage of teasing remarks that spoke of their envy. While we were dating I started to climb the ladder at work. I'd graduated from cleaner to packer and, finally, to top man, responsible for all the packers as well as ensuring the smooth flow of flour on the packing floor of the mill.

The extra responsibility came with extra bucks. I'd often work seven days a week for months at a time and I was really pulling in the cash. The best part of being a top man was that I worked independently of others. On most shifts I wouldn't speak to or see another human being. Just fine by me.

There I was with a gorgeous, caring girlfriend and a well-paying job. Was this what life was all about? Was

I suddenly living the dream? I had no idea, I was just going along for the ride and when Julie suggested we move in together, I jumped in with both feet.

She chose and organised a furnished one-bedroom place in South Tamworth that had a deep bathtub, wooden floors and a small backyard – all for twenty-three dollars a week.

The first time we went shopping together Julie accidentally put a mop head in the fridge while packing away, giving us a cutesy couple nesting story that we could both laugh about. Occasionally in the afternoon, after she'd finished work at an industrial laundry and I'd come home from the mill, we'd go out in the backyard and I'd teach her some of my fighting tactics. We used to laugh about that, too. Most of our entertainment centred around alcohol, though, and blowing money at pubs. Still, I managed to save enough to trade in the yellow monkey mobile for a nice Ford Falcon XW, diamond white in colour. Living the dream.

Then I got sacked. An Italian bloke had started working at the mill and he was being given a hard time. Some of my redneck colleagues started calling him 'dago', 'fucken wog' and 'spaghetti dickhead'. I found out a couple of the store packers had been slicing the tops of flour bags with a knife, so when the Italian fella went to hoist them onto pallets he'd end up covered head to toe in sixty-seven kilos of flour. That was the last straw for me. 'He's got the same rights as you,' I bellowed. 'Treat him with respect or else!'

'Or else what?'

I knocked the first packer down in a trice and had turned my attention to redneck number two when I slipped in some oil on the concrete and found myself on the floor.

Punches and kicks rained down on me and I tucked myself into a ball to ride it out.

Later on, I was summoned to the supervisor's office and grilled about what had happened to my head.

'I fell down some stairs,' I said.

Word about the workplace fight, however, had got around and I was fired on the spot. Not for brawling, but for lying about it. The knucklehead racists kept their jobs and, no doubt, kept up their bigotry too.

Rather than blow up about it, Julie supported me and said I'd done the right thing in standing up against bullying. In a stroke of luck, my brother-in-law at the time said he could get me a job as a cleaner at a spring manufacturing business in the inner-city Sydney suburb of Alexandria. Julie and I decided we'd try our luck in the big smoke.

Julie found us a small second-storey flat in Wiley Park – a gritty working-class suburb in south-western Sydney. As fortune would have it, the flat was just a short walk from the Wiley Park Hotel. I'd become a supporter of the Canterbury-Bankstown Bulldogs during my short stint at Punchbowl Boys High, but I grew fanatical while drinking at the Wiley Park – the unofficial spiritual home of the team. A few weeks after we moved our meagre bits and pieces down from Tamworth, Julie scored a job working at Woolworths opposite Sydney Town Hall. One day after work she asked me to marry her.

'Yes, ma'am.'

I dutifully, if not romantically, scurried off in search of an engagement ring. We didn't have any close friends to throw us an engagement party, but we'd become drinking buddies with the couple who lived directly opposite our unit. One constant in my life was my inability to make friends. I'd never had any, outside of Gussy and the relationship with Danny that I'd walked away from, and I didn't know how to begin. Instead I relied on alcohol to form shallow acquaintances that revolved around getting plastered. I have no idea what their names were but we asked our pisspot neighbours to be the best man and bridesmaid at our upcoming nuptials. They jumped at the chance; they loved a drink.

The wedding was held on a Saturday at the Tamworth City Bowling Club. Julie had just turned twenty and I was twenty-four. There were around twenty guests in total – mainly family and a handful of 'friends' (like the virtual strangers who served as the wedding party). I know there was a cake and that my Ford XW served as the bridal car, but beyond that the rest of the wedding was a blur. It was a frightening day for me. I was self-conscious, unsure, and a large part of me wished I could be anywhere else. I wasn't much more than a prop at my own wedding; a clueless kid playing a part that he thought was expected of him.

For our honeymoon, Julie and I drove the seven hours back to Sydney so we could both front up for work on the Monday morning. I had to get up at 4.30am each day to catch a train into work so I could clean up after the skilled guys who made springs for car suspension. Julie didn't have to start until 9am so we didn't see each other in the mornings and she didn't get home until about 7pm. I, on the other hand, would knock off at 2pm. Rather than go home and make myself useful, I'd head straight to the Wiley Park Hotel and get busy downing schooner upon schooner of Tooheys New.

By the time Julie got home from work I'd already be there, drunk and abusive. The only thing missing from the picture was the bottles of home-brew and the violence. Other than that I was mimicking my father. It became apparent that I had no other understanding of what a relationship was all about. I had no reference point. Instead, I'd wait around half-paralytic and expect Julie to feed me. 'You're my wife! You cook my dinner!' Truly Cro-Magnon stuff.

After a while I started eating dinner at the pub instead. I was sitting there one afternoon nursing a schooner when I suddenly had the familiar impulse to run – to just bolt and never look back. I resisted and went home as I always did to flake out in a chair. When Julie walked in the door I was straight into her, pushing her buttons. It might have been about something she'd said, what she was wearing or what she was doing, but I actively and deliberately tried to get a rise out of her. It was exactly what Mum used to do to Dad.

Even on weekends I refused to let up. We'd share the housework in the morning and then I'd sit in my chair with headphones on listening to Tchaikovsky's 1812 (still my favourite piece of music) while I inhaled ten beers. By late afternoon I'd be back in belligerent mode. I was never physically abusive to Julie, but if you lived next door, like the wedding party did, you'd have been worried by all the screaming and banging that came from our flat. After a couple of months of newly-wedded bliss, Julie started to arrive home later and later, obviously in the hope that I'd have passed out. Of course, I started accusing her of having an affair. That was the last straw for Julie. She realised she'd made a big mistake.

A day or so later, after just eight weeks of matrimony, I arrived home from the pub, slid my key in the lock and got a surprise when it wouldn't turn. I tried again: nothing. Julie had gone and had the locks changed. I was ropeable and started trying to bash the door down when someone – possibly my best man – thought it might finally be time to call the police.

'What seems to be the problem, sir?' the constable asked as he stepped into the stairwell.

'No problem at all thanks, pal. I live here. This is my place.' I was being a prick.

The constable glanced at the door. 'Then why don't you try using your key instead of your feet?'

'Because she changed the fucken locks on me, that's why.'

'Well, that means you don't live here anymore.'

'Yes, I do!'

'No, sir, you do not.'

At such an impasse the general rule is that the person with the gun is right. I had no choice but to walk away and leave all of my belongings behind. By then we'd traded in my Ford for a nice new Chrysler Centura, but Julie had the keys. Not long after I lost my wife, my home and my Tchaikovsky records, I lost my job, too.

I hit the drink hard after the cop evicted me from my marriage. I'm not 100 per cent clear on the details but the bender ended with a bang to my head. It could have been a fight or it might have been a fall. Whatever it was, it was bad enough that I wound up in Canterbury Hospital with a concussion. What I do remember is starting to sober up and getting nasty towards the medicos.

'Fuck off, all of you! Leave me alone. I just want to kill myself. Just let me die!'

The realisation that I'd not only trashed my life again in record time but made a mess of Julie's, too, had hit me hard. Maybe it was a cry for help but I can't say for sure whether those were genuine suicidal threats. Not that it mattered; pretty soon a doctor appeared with a clipboard and a serious expression that didn't bode well.

'Look, we simply can't let you leave, Mr Smith. You're threatening suicide and we're concerned for your wellbeing.'

He scribbled on his chart and told the orderlies to arrange my transfer to Callan Park, another hospital across town at Rozelle. When I arrived I was surprised to note that the hospital was made up of a series of beautiful 100-year-old sandstone buildings scattered among pleasant, meandering gardens. Callan Park (originally known as Callan Park Hospital for the Insane) is a fine example of public architecture that was typical of 19th Century Sydney – until you notice the twelve-foot-high stone walls that are designed to keep the patients in. That was when the penny dropped. 'I'm being committed!'

Callan Park was crammed full of mentally disturbed people who wandered the sterile-looking hallways doing all manner of strange, unsettling and disgusting things. With nothing better to do, I joined in. I actually built on my performance at Canterbury Hospital by thrashing about, screaming gibberish and making wild threats. It didn't take me long to realise that every time I went off my head, the nurses would give me a nice big injection of Valium to calm me down.

With the lie of the land sussed, I settled into a bit of a routine in the loony bin. I'd pretend to be on the verge of a psychotic tantrum, the staff would come running and I'd hold my arm out while they injected me with more Diazepam. Then I'd settle on a bench in the sun with a dopey smile on my face to watch the birds. It was like being on an all-expenses-paid Valium vacation, until the world came crashing back in. After a few days, Julie got in touch. Not because she was worried about me; no, she was anxious to wind up our marriage as quickly as possible. I started thinking about the future, too, and I got talking to another patient about how I might escape.

'Escape? You know if you really want to get out it's not that hard,' he said. 'All you have to do is show them that you look after yourself.'

'Oh yeah? How's that exactly?' I asked.

'Have a shave every morning for a start. Just take care of yourself, don't act crazy and they'll let you go.'

As much as I was enjoying the Valium, I also cherished my liberty. I hadn't shaved in a long time so I lost the beard the next day and kept the shaving up. The change was noted in my medical reports and within a few weeks a doctor walked in and said, 'OK, Gregory, you can discharge yourself now if you'd like.' It was late in the afternoon and the nurses were kind enough to give me one final shot of Valium before I left, after I'd assured them I was going to catch public transport. I certainly wasn't planning on driving. 'No, ma'am!'

Complete bullshit. The truth was that Julie had parked the Centura a little way down the road and left the keys under the front seat on the condition that I left Sydney at once and didn't come back. Fine by me. I climbed behind the wheel and headed where I always did when my life went to hell – straight back up to Tamworth.

A few hours later I was propped at a table in a little bowling club in the backblocks of Maitland guzzling schooners. I'd decamped Sydney using the Putty Road, a treacherous ribbon of tarmac that snakes north-west across the Great Dividing Range en route to the northern tablelands. Although still doped up on Valium I must have cut a reasonably coherent figure because the barmaid kept serving me. After all, how was she to know I'd just been let loose from an insane asylum? I ploughed through at least eight beers before I was asked to leave. The barmaid said it was because they were about to close up but it might have been because I was getting wobbly.

Back in the car I set a course for Tamworth, still four hours' drive away. In those days I only knew two speeds: dead stop or flat out, and with hardly another car on the road I decided it was a good time to put the Chrysler Centura – a six-cylinder beast with an excellent power-to-weight ratio – through its paces. The last thing I remember was being surprised to see a concrete pylon speeding straight towards me.

It was the stroke of midnight when I slammed into the Branxton Railway Bridge at 100 miles per hour. I learned that later from the cops who said the metallic explosion of Chrysler on concrete had sounded like a bomb going off.

It jolted the local sergeant awake and he looked at his bedside clock to make a note of the time.

I was in a horrible state; trapped in the crushed Centura, out cold and suffering massive chest trauma. The Police Rescue Squad had to use the jaws-of-life to cut me free. I came to in the intensive care unit at John Hunter Hospital in Newcastle with a tangle of tubes protruding from me. I was in recovery for months. As soon as I was well enough I finally slunk into Tamworth, where a $25,000 repair bill for the damage I'd caused to the Branxton Railway Bridge was waiting for me.

The year 1980 had already been an *annus horribilis*, but then Dad died. He'd developed complications from cirrhosis of the liver, the result of thirty years spent poisoning himself and us along with him. Grandad Aubrey had given him a little flat in Tamworth to die in, and in the end Dad couldn't even get out of his chair. He just sat in his lounge room surrounded by empty sherry bottles. If ever there was a man who drank himself to death it was my father, Bruce Aubrey Peel Smith.

Interestingly, Mum still loved him and had visited him every day to make sure he was fed and comfortable right up until the very end. I only saw Dad once before he died, but his mind was misfiring so much by that time that I doubt he even recognised me. My memories of life as his son, however, were crystal clear. I felt obligated to attend his funeral, just so I could make sure they buried him. Then I spat on his grave.

Dad's physical departure from my world made no difference whatsoever to the appalling state of it. I found myself at a crossroads. Rather than try to pull myself together, I let myself fall apart. I crawled away from Tamworth and into the gutters of an uncertain future.

13

HOMELESS

My homeless life played out right up and down the east coast of Australia; from the harsh sidewalks of Darlinghurst, Kings Cross and Surry Hills in Sydney to Red Hill and Woolloongabba in the back lanes of inner-Brisbane. I drifted all over New South Wales, into the little hamlets, the big regional towns and the empty spaces between them. I slept out in the open in North Queensland, too. Cairns, Townsville, Rockhampton, Mackay. It was always warmer up there.

Wherever I lay down to sleep, safety was the number one concern. I got attacked a few times over the years and even wound up in hospital. There are people in this world who get off on bashing homeless people. They want to hurt you. I've come to with my face smashed in, my head wet with blood, and burning, busted lips. I'd be miserable for days after a bashing, with grazes, bruises and lumps all over my body. I trusted no one and everywhere I went I'd look at random people and wonder, 'Was it you? Did you do this to me?'

When you're homeless you learn pretty quickly that if you have any money, you hide it. If you've got any drugs or booze – anything of value – you stash it somewhere else before going to sleep. Sadly it's not unheard of for the homeless to rob the homeless, no matter how small the takings. I've had shoes ripped off my feet while sleeping and it's not easy to come by another pair.

Other times it's just the system that's against you. One of the worst developments for homeless people happened when local councils hit on the idea of watering public parks at night. You could be sound asleep when suddenly a hidden sprinkler nozzle two metres from your head would go 'click' and start spraying jets of water into your face.

It's far better to find shelter if you can. I've slept on stinking, urine-spattered tiles in public toilets, inside grime-coated industrial rubbish bins, at railway platforms, in boiler rooms, on the verandas of unsuspecting Australians, under country churches, in a big plastic bag on the side of a road, in a cardboard box, in cars, in police lock-ups . . .

Out in the open is worse. Aside from sprinklers and the threat of a random beating, the elements can go against you. It only takes one cold snap to figure out that warmth is essential to a half-decent rest. Then there's the rain, the dew and the creepy crawlies to worry about – the ants, spiders, ticks, wasps, mozzies and snakes.

Homeless life is a hard, hard slog. You're always hungry, you're always tired, and society always thinks the worst of you – especially cops and security guards. They'd think nothing of cracking me in the sternum with a baton or kicking me in the ribs only to tell me to piss off, to where I do not know – it wasn't as if I had a nice cosy room around the corner. Years can disappear in what seems like hours when you're homeless. Time means nothing when you have no foothold in society. The usual calendar markers like Christmas, birthdays, holidays, footy grand finals, long weekends, the Melbourne Cup – none of these things exist anymore. Instead, the sun comes up and then the sun goes down. Days are just days that are either hot, cold, windy, warm, wet or dry. Night-time is the same, just with darkness and apprehension thrown in.

Despite being ground down by society's heel I always tried to uphold a personal code of conduct and preserve some measure of dignity. I never touched or hurt another homeless person and I never begged. That's not a judgement on people who do beg – it's just that I'd rather steal or scavenge in bins than plead for anyone to help me.

Soup kitchens were OK. The Matthew Talbot Hostel at Woolloomooloo in Sydney was the best as there was a certain amount of autonomy there. People didn't ask questions and you were just allowed to blend in. Other places rubbed me the wrong way, like a certain soup kitchen at Red Hill in Brisbane where they wanted too much information. 'Who are you?' they'd ask. 'Where do you come from? What's going on?' I didn't like that, even though I knew they were only trying to help. It's demeaning enough to avail yourself of a helping hand – you don't want to be quizzed about why you need it.

Still, I far preferred Brisbane and Sydney to Melbourne. I hitchhiked to the southern capital once because it was somewhere I'd never been and I thought I might have a chance of finding some work. Big mistake. There was nothing familiar about Melbourne. I wanted to know where the soup kitchen was. I wanted to know where I could find somewhere safe to sleep. I wanted to stay out of trouble. I couldn't find anything. And where were all the pubs? Even the boozers were different down there – Melbournians went in for wine bars instead. I only lasted a few weeks in town before I blacklisted Victoria for good.

Pubs were important in my rudderless life on the road. I picked up some good jobs over the years just sitting in public bars and keeping my ears pricked, particularly in the regional towns. I'd be having a couple of beers and someone would say, 'Joe Blow down the road is hiring and wants pickers.' I was always actively trying to work, not just to make money but to also participate in society. I was still trying to be 'part of'.

Although I usually stuck to the coastal towns, I decided once to try my luck in the outback. I'd been sleeping rough around Townsville in North Queensland for a couple of weeks, and noticed road signs to a town called Charters Towers a few hundred kilometres inland from the coast. It sounded slightly exotic (were there even towers there?) so I started hitching. As the afternoon stretched on, an old bushy bloke gave me a lift but dropped me in the middle of nowhere when it was time for him to turn off down some barely perceptible dirt track. The sun was going down and I suddenly found myself all alone beneath a very big sky. I curled up in a ditch by the side of the road.

Although it had been a hot day, it wouldn't have been more than an hour after dark before I started to shiver uncontrollably. I didn't know it then but I was at an elevation about 300 metres higher than balmy Townsville. The temperature plummeted and I had serious concerns about whether I'd make it through the night. Old mate the bushy had dropped me on a long, straight, flat stretch of road, and as I stepped out into the middle of it I could see no sign of houses or vehicles. But I did feel warmth rising up from below. The bitumen had acted like a massive heat sponge, soaking up the North Queensland sun and storing it into the night. I lay down on the road and the shivering subsided. I slept on the tarmac on and off all night, confident I'd hear any approaching trucks before I ended up as roadkill.

Late the following day I straggled into Charters Towers and wasn't really surprised to discover it was just another unremarkable corner of the map. I looked around for a safe place to bed down and settled on a bench on the platform of the train station.

I don't know how long I'd been asleep when I was woken by three guys. 'Oi, fella. What're ya doin'?'

And so it started. Initially they weren't too bad and shared their grog with me. As we got more and more pissed, though, I realised one guy had a set against me. I was getting woozy and I clearly hadn't read the situation at all. I went to take another swig on their bottle when *crack*! Mr Attitude king hit me hard in the jaw. I don't remember much after that but when I came to I was bloodied, bruised and fairly beaten up. A priest was bent over me asking if I was OK. A silly question – my ribs were probably fractured and I'd lost a fair bit of blood out of the gashes on my head.

The priest helped me to my feet and took me to his home behind a nearby church. I stayed there for a couple of days while he fed me, gave me a bed and looked after me. I repaid him with intense distrust. I'd lost all faith in priests and nuns at the age of ten. As soon as I was able to walk without too much pain, I got the hell out of there and hitched back to Townsville. It had been a lot to endure but at least I could faithfully report there are no towers in Charters Towers.

14

FISH OUT OF WATER

I may have been a drifter but I was as motivated as the next person to bring in a pay packet. One reason my employment was fragmented and itinerant was due to a lifelong compulsion to be anywhere other than where I was. I'd hitchhike from point A purely to get to point B, not really caring where point B was. Next stop was point C, D, E, F, G and so on through the alphabet. If there happened to be a job somewhere in the mix I'd stop and grab it – for a while at least anyway. That's how I ended up with the wind in my hair fishing for coral trout on the Great Barrier Reef.

I arrived in the coastal Queensland town of Rock-hampton sometime in the early 1980s. I had money to buy enough beer to get good and drunk, and maybe get in a fight too. After finding a suitably seedy early opener I settled in to get hammered.

About 10am I looked up from my schooner when four

or five rowdy blokes barrelled through the door. They were all big, tough bastards but there was something disarming about them. They seemed happy, and were roaring and laughing at each other, giving off good energy. I hunkered down with my beer and kept one ear on what they were saying. After downing a few more drinks I made a tentative foray into the outskirts of their conversation.

'So, what do youse blokes do?'

This was one of my survival tactics in a pub: go on the offensive and ask questions before anyone asked one of me. Other times I'd hide behind my beard and not engage at all. Then there were the occasions I'd run off at the mouth and explore the opportunity for a punch-up. On this day I opted for Plan A: a civil inquiry. The guys turned out to be professional fishermen who spent their days angling for coral trout on the southern outcrops of the Great Barrier Reef. And, it just so happened, they were looking for a 'decky'.

'Are ya interested, mate?'

'Yeah, for sure. I can do that. What's a decky?' I responded.

This brought laughter from the boofy boys – another sign that the day was unlikely to end in a bar fight.

'Nah, seriously, do you want a bit of work as a deckhand? It's like a cleaning job.'

'Yeah, bloody oath.'

'We're going out tomorrow morning. If you really wanna work, be outside here at 5am. We'll pick you up and take you down to the boat.'

And that was that. I'd passed the job interview. I stayed at the pub for hours and drank myself to a standstill before lurching into the park across the road to sleep. At 5am the next day I was the early bird sitting bushy-tailed on the pub steps. Just as they'd promised, the fishermen arrived in a ute, pulled me aboard and we set off for the nearby port of Yeppoon.

An hour later as the sun came up I was standing on the deck of a forty-foot fishing boat, steaming out to the Coral Sea for a three-week voyage. Ah, Queensland! Homeless one day, a sailor the next. The skipper was a focused, no-nonsense bloke who spent most of his time on the radio and shuffling through charts in the wheelhouse. The rest of the crew totalled eight, including me.

'Righto, Beardy, as the deckhand your job is pretty straightforward: just make sure the deck is clean and clear.'

'No worries.'

'We'll be gutting and filleting the catch and you'll need to scrub down the deck and keep it from fouling up with guts and whatnot.'

'Yep. Sweet.'

This was a good start. I was an expert at cleaning floors. The trawler towed a string of four dories, which were smaller boats that had a tub-like section in the middle for the fishermen to put the catch in. Once on the fishing ground, we'd stop near a section of reef and the guys would pile into the dories, spread out and start fishing the sea floor using handlines.

With the others out fishing there wasn't much for me to do on deck, so after a few days I was invited to join them in the dories. There was nothing scientific about fishing for coral trout. You'd bait up the hook and just drop it over the side. As soon as you got one on the line you had to haul it up as quickly as possible before the reef sharks charged in and took it.

It turned out I was pretty good at fishing and I was loving it. I may have been the decky but I got paid by the kilogram, the same as everyone else. Once you got back onboard and weighed up your catch, that was your cut. Then the blokes would get about the filleting and I'd do my job clearing up all the blood and guts and scales.

Although they were nice to me, the fishermen never asked any questions, and I never offered any information. Fortunately there was no booze onboard, which was a major factor that prevented things from getting ugly. If we'd been drinking out there, somebody would have eventually asked me a really stupid question like, 'Who are ya?' or 'Where are ya from?' or 'What's yer story?' and I would have lost it. As soon as people started to pry I almost always lost it.

That was part of my secret inner-self. These blokes – any people I met – never knew how much danger they were potentially in with me around. To the crew I was a reasonably benign creature. I was Beardy the quiet deckhand. They had no idea that I was a sociopath and that the wrong look or the wrong question could result in an almighty eruption of violence.

It never came to that on the Coral Sea. When we got back to port the skipper handed me my pay cheque and I nearly fell over. It was just over $1000. The wage I was used to at the time was maybe $180 to $200 a week. On the boat I had all my food paid for, plus board, and I still walked away with a grand. I was thrilled. Maybe I was destined to find my place as a fisherman.

*

I became ambitious after that and decided that if I was going to be a professional angler I'd better get some qualifications. I stuck around in Rockhampton and signed up with a Maori prawn trawler captain named Wiremu. He was offering a deckhand course, which basically entailed me going to sea with him while he showed me the ropes – a bit of old-school on-the-job training to help me get my deckie's certificate.

Prawning with Wiremu was a totally different kettle of fish. For starters it was just the two of us on board. And rather than it being a dry boat, he'd polish off a bottle of Bundaberg Rum for breakfast every day. That worried me. Wiremu was a big, big boy and as I watched him steadily inhale the Bundy I saw a familiar look come across his face – namely the 'I've just drunk a bottle of rum' look.

Although I was wary, Wiremu turned out to be a really pleasant, gentle man. He wasn't a belligerent drunk like I was, and he liked to sing. Importantly, he never once asked me any difficult questions and he never shared his rum. Good things, both, and as a result the trawler ran like a well-oiled machine.

I couldn't believe the size of the prawns we were pulling out of the brine. Some were as long and as thick as bananas. 'Hey, Wiremu, how come we never see these on our tables?' I asked.

'They're the biggies we put aside for the top shelf,' he explained. 'They're going to Japan.'

Although we'd only go to sea for three to four days at a time, we'd sail far enough offshore to be at the mercy of the weather. One night we got caught off guard by a pretty big storm. We'd been so preoccupied scooping up net after net full of big, juicy bananas that we ignored the rising wind and the hastening seas. Before we knew it we were battening down the hatches for a very bumpy ride back to port. When Wiremu went to pull in the retractable stabilisers that arced away from the hull, one of them became jammed. He turned to me with a big smile.

'One of us is going to have to go out and untangle that.'

'Oh yeah? Which one of us?'

'Well, I'll tie a piece of rope around you.'

He thought it was hilarious but I was terrified. Two minutes later I had a rope cinched around my waist as I shimmied out on a pole that dangled over the boiling, black ocean. The boat was bucking like a bronco and sheets of rain lashed me as I struggled to free the steel chain that had jammed the stabiliser in place. I got dunked a couple of times and for a moment I thought I might be going the way of the *Titanic*.

Despite Mother Nature's best efforts, however, I held on and got the job done. Wiremu reckoned it was because he'd trained me so well. Back on the safety of the deck I was excited and pumped with adrenaline. 'Did I really just do that? I did OK!' It was one of the rare moments in my life where I could say I was extremely proud of myself.

With our freezer full we chugged back to Yeppoon and took the banana prawns to market. It was only a two-way split with Wiremu so my cut was thousands of dollars after expenses. In the space of a month or two I'd gone from drinking my last dollars in a pub to being on the verge of a promising career in commercial fishing. But there was a problem: Wiremu liked me. And I figured if I stayed and worked for him he'd probably end up asking me questions about myself. I started drinking my earnings and grew increasingly agitated. What if he found out what I was really like? He wouldn't like me if he knew the truth. The thought mortified me. It was time to leave.

A few days later I was on the outskirts of Rockhampton, thumb in the wind as the cars and semitrailers rushed by. A long-haul trucker picked me up and I headed off to point H.

15

A BEANBAG AND A BIBLE

I had a deathly attraction to Tamworth. Every time I'd
return there it would end up a complete disaster. I couldn't
help it, though. Tamworth was my home town, it was where
I was born and even though I had no meaningful connections there (not even with my family), I always ended up
crawling back there like a beaten dog.

And so it was in the winter of 1984. I was sleeping on
people's couches, drinking and taking drugs – pursuits
that required money. I needed a job to fund my 'lifestyle' but no one wanted to hire me. One afternoon I was
wandering through Tamworth Arcade on Peel Street
when I noticed how filthy the place had become. 'You'd
think they'd clean the joint!' I thought. Then I stopped
dead. It was a light-bulb moment. I walked straight to the
arcade management office and opened negotiations using
my usual charm.

'Yeah, so I'm gonna clean the arcade for you. How much do you wanna pay me for it?'

'We'll give you fifteen dollars an hour.'

It was that easy. They hadn't had a cleaning contractor for a while. It showed and they knew it. Furthermore, I didn't have to outlay one cent to get started. I gave them a list of the equipment and products I needed, which were duly purchased, placed in a storeroom and I was handed the key. I got stuck into it straight away, working at night after the customers and retailers had long gone home. Christ it was boring. As I mopped, polished and scrubbed until all hours with nothing but cockroaches for company, I started to think there had to be an easier way.

Since management was paying me fifteen dollars an hour I didn't see why I couldn't put someone else on to do the job for five dollars an hour so I could go and do something else. I found a bloke who was willing to subcontract and I pocketed ten dollars an hour for his troubles. He was happy to have the gig but, not long afterwards, he was offered a job out of town and moved on. 'Listen, I've got this place where the rent is all paid up in advance,' he told me. 'You can move in and take it over if you want.'

It was a furnished townhouse at one end of a block of three on Chelmsford Street, not too far from the arcade. I moved there in a trice. From destitution just a few weeks earlier I suddenly had cash coming in and a roof over my head. I felt obliged to share my good fortune so I instituted an open-door policy. Homeless people and drifters started wafting in and out and there was always booze and drugs around. I even kept a bowl of pot on the table.

Around this time I had another bright business idea.

I'd found a replacement to take over the five-dollar arcade contract, which freed me up to have a few beers at the Imperial Hotel. I was sitting there one afternoon when I noticed how disgusting the carpets had become after years of beer and ash raining down on them. The floor was so sticky that when you went to the bar it felt as if you were walking across Velcro. 'Oh yeah!' I thought. 'Carpet cleaning!'

The acquaintance I'd been drinking with fancied himself as a bit of a salesman. 'How good are you really?' I asked as I returned to our table with two schooners.

'Pretty good, as a matter of fact.'

'Give us a demo then. Go and talk to the publican over there and tell him we're gonna shampoo his carpets.'

'Whadaya mean?'

'You convince him that we'll shampoo his carpets, then we'll go down to Woolworths or wherever, rent one of those carpet cleaners and we'll come back and do the job.'

It turned out the salesman was very good indeed. He quoted the publican $450 to shampoo the Imperial's fetid floors. Jackpot! Earning $450 for a single night's work in 1984 was like winning Lotto. Of course, I wasn't going to get dirty, so I employed another guy to help Willy Loman. The business, which I called My Mates Cleaning Service, went from strength to strength. Between the arcade and the shampooing of Tamworth's commercial carpets, the money was fairly rolling in. I even had enough cash to buy a little pantech truck to cart our gear around.

The open-door policy at Chelmsford Street, however, wasn't such a raging success. I got home from cleaning someone's floors one day to find a mountain of dirty dishes piled up on the bench and assorted crap strewn throughout the place. People were lying on the couches and sprawled on the floor mulling up, drinking and generally not giving a stuff. If there's one way to upset a cleaner, that's it.

I walked over to the kitchen and, with a big smile on my face, stretched one arm across the benchtop and walked it to the other end, mowing all the crockery and glasses onto the floor in the process with a mighty crash. That got their attention.

'Nahhh,' I said as they looked at me in alarm. 'If you're gonna use this place, respect it. Keep it clean. Yep? OK?'

They tidied up and kept the little townhouse neat for a few weeks, but then the mess and indifference returned. I did the same thing as the first time: dishes, cups, cutlery and glasses crashed to the floor in a heap. 'If this happens again,' I told them evenly, 'then I'm gonna blow the place up.'

Sure enough, I got home one night the following week and the place had reverted to a pigsty. 'Righto, everybody,' I announced, 'you've got about two minutes to get your things and get out of here 'cos I'm gonna blow it up.' Ever since childhood my word had been important to me. I was not a perfect human being but I was an honest one. If asked whether I had stolen your milk money and I had, I would admit it. If I told you I didn't steal your wallet in Glen Innes, you could believe that too. And if I said I was going to blow up the house, then I would have to follow through. If nothing else I am a man of my word.

Still, no one bothered to drag themselves off the sofas in a hurry, so I walked calmly but purposefully back out to the truck to retrieve a spare can of petrol. Back inside

I started sloshing it all over the walls. The couch potatoes began to look a bit worried and then it dawned on them that this was really happening. 'Oh, Christ!' There was a stampede for the front door.

With the place to myself for once, I dropped the empty fuel can, then grabbed my favourite orange vinyl beanbag and a copy of the Bible I'd seen lying around. I knew where I was going in the afterlife, but I figured that if I had the Good Book with me when I arrived, I might just be redirected upstairs. I plonked myself down in the middle of the room, fished my Zippo lighter out of my pocket, sparked it alight and lobbed it at the nearest petrol-sodden wall.

Whoomph!

I hadn't anticipated burning myself to death so I was a bit surprised by the ferocity of the fire. At least I was keeping my word, though, and it'd be over soon enough so I could finally be done with it all. I closed my eyes and waited. I heard the smashing of glass and splintering sounds. The flames were everywhere.

'It'll be over soon . . .'

Strong arms gripped me and yanked me off the beanbag. I heard urgent shouting and a woman's panicked voice as I was dragged outside and onto the grass. The fire brigade had driven the 800 metres from their station in record time.

No sooner had Tamworth's bravest saved me from the burning building than the cops had me in cold steel handcuffs. The next thing I recall was waking up in a locked and guarded room at Tamworth Base Hospital. Amazingly, I wasn't burned and had no serious injuries.

But I knew I was in a lot of trouble and that my business was gone, for what it was worth.

Amid these grave and sobering circumstances, chocolates and flirty notes started arriving for me. They were from the woman whose voice I'd heard when I was being dragged out of the house. I don't remember formally meeting Nicola but she was apparently one of the Chelmsford Street lounge lizards who I'd strongly suggested should run for their lives. And now she was sending me flowers and cute little cards.

'If you need anybody to talk to when you get out I'll be here,' she wrote. 'I'm available.' And, 'If you need somewhere to stay, we can get a caravan and live together.' I couldn't quite believe she was courting the man who'd just torched the place she'd been in. But Nicola's mind was made up. I had won her heart through arson. Who knew there could be such a thing?

'I can't wait till you get out.'

But I wasn't sure I'd be going anywhere any time soon, other than prison. I was facing very serious charges – arson, maliciously setting fire to a dwelling, and recklessly endangering human life. When I'd started my little beanbag barbecue it hadn't occurred to me that people might be innocently going about their lives in the adjoining townhouses – the ones that were connected by the same roof. The result could have been catastrophic and tragic. Yes, it looked like I'd being going away for a long, long time.

I was contemplating what I might have to do in order to survive in gaol when a psychiatrist named Dr Tan walked into the room. Over a few days he interviewed me at length, asked me to do some tests and made various assessments and evaluations in his charts. When he finished he looked straight at me and asked, 'Would you like to get off this?'

I breathed a sigh of relief. For once I had a lot to say. 'I really don't want to do twenty-five years in gaol, doctor. I understand there are consequences for what I did and I need to take responsibility for my actions, and I –'

Dr Tan cut me off. 'You're not responsible for your actions. I think there are things happening inside you that you actually don't have a lot of control over. If you work with me for a period of time and do what I ask, I think we can convince a judge that you were not fully responsible for what happened.'

He had me at 'Would you like to get off this?' Of course I'd do anything he asked. And so the process of working with Dr Tan commenced. Step one was to prescribe me the anti-depressant Tryptanol and the anti-psychotic drug Largactil. Step two was to get me out on bail under the care of the good doctor.

When those drugs kicked in, however, I honestly wondered if I might have been better off just getting a full frontal lobotomy instead. They were brain hammers that left me completely zombified. I didn't need to drink, didn't need any drugs. I was totally smashed. I moved like a cartoon character in slow motion and talked very s . . . l . . . o . . . w . . . l . . . y. When the time came for me to leave hospital Nicola was waiting outside.

How she'd escaped my attention back at Chelmsford Street is beyond me. She was a stunning blonde and brimming with kindness and tender concern. We jumped into a taxi and headed for Tamworth's Thunderbird Caravan Park. Nicola had organised everything, and, just like that, we moved into a van and began a life together. She cooked me a beautiful meal. She soothed me and took care of me. And I allowed myself to think that she loved me, as abstract as my understanding of love was.

I didn't really have a clue who she was. Nicola, however, was happy to fill me in. She'd been born in England. Her father was a Cockney boxer but she'd come to Australia with her mother and settled in Tamworth. She liked drinking and taking drugs so we were a perfect match. We settled into domestic caravan life, and although I wasn't drinking because I was bombed out of my scone on Tryptanol and Largactil, it didn't stop Nicola. My kind of girl.

After a few months and a couple of court appearances, as my case clunked its way through the judicial gears, I decided it was time I had a couple of beers as well. It didn't take much to get me scrambled. Then Nicola came home with some pot. 'Oh, alright, let me have a cone, too.' I was gobbling the elephant tranquillisers and now alcohol and pot on top. I doubt very much that Dr Tan would have approved.

During my next hearing at Tamworth Local Court the magistrate told me my case had been adjourned to the District Court. I had no idea what that meant, or what the guy was on about to be honest. I couldn't get my head around any of it. I was just popping my pills and doing whatever Dr Tan said. Apparently, though, the District Court was a serious escalation. Gaol was getting closer.

In all my years of homelessness, going to gaol was one of my biggest fears. For that reason I tried hard to avoid doing anything too outrageously criminal. When they released me from Yarrawa and said 'Don't come back', I took the

122

advice to heart. From that day in 1974 I'd maintained a spotless record. But then the dirty dishes started piling up. It wasn't as though fire-bombing Chelmsford Street was a simple misstep or a misdemeanour; it was a heavy, heavy crime. And society was going to make me pay.

In the meantime, I wanted to support my new spouse. I slowly adjusted to the mind-scrambling medications and my movement improved, so I managed to get a job at the Millers Tyres factory. From 8am till 5pm I lifted truck tyres and I started to buff up. I had muscles popping out of muscles.

In mid-1985, with a lengthy prison sentence hanging over our heads, Nicola fell pregnant. I was pretty happy that I was going to be a dad. Nicola and I were great together – a fearsome double act with a rock-solid routine. I'd work all day tossing tyres then come home where Nicola would be happily cooking dinner. The cartoon *Inspector Gadget* was usually on TV so I'd smoke a couple of cones and sit down to watch it. Then we'd get pissed. It was a perfect little world. We'd be fine with a baby!

I don't recall doing much in terms of getting ready for parenthood. There were no antenatal classes and I had no thoughts about a cot, clothes, nappies, toys. I really didn't have a frame of reference to understand those things, having never encountered or experienced them. I figured they would just happen. It was the same way I thought watching *Inspector Gadget* with Nicola was exciting and the sign of a happy relationship. Living the dream.

Not that we didn't have our issues. We were asked to leave a number of caravan parks due to our raucousness when drinking and the constant reek of our dope in the air.

It didn't worry us too much, we just moved on to another site. But inevitably we started to fight. I could be as abusive as ever and Nicky was no shrinking violet either. After all, she had the blood of a Cockney boxer pumping through her veins.

Our last port of call was a caravan park on the banks of the Peel River. We'd make fires down near the water and sit around partying. One night I'd finished my first bottle of rum and was into my second when I blacked out and fell face first into the fire. Nicola kicked me off the coals and burning branches and rolled me down the bank into the freezing river. *Plunk*.

That did the trick and woke me right up. Nicky had only been trying to save me from char-grilling my head and I repaid her by flying into an ugly rage. I staggered sodden back up the riverbank and tried to grab her. 'You bitch! What did you do that for? Wait until I get a hold of you.' I careened around the park hollering a stream of bile at a defenceless pregnant lady. It was a shameful performance that only ended when I staggered and fell chest first into a steel star picket and broke a rib.

Looking back I really can't say why Nicola wanted to be with me in the first place, but I can take a guess. I think she was addicted to the adrenaline and the thrill of being with a loose cannon like me. She loved the idea of excitement, risk, adventure; of being Bonnie to my Clyde – even if Clyde was a sociopath.

Then we had Katie. I was right there when she was born, in the same room at Tamworth Base Hospital where I'd entered the world thirty-one years earlier. Katie arrived just before 2pm on 17 March 1986. Nothing could have prepared me for the feelings that welled up and exploded in a supernova of gratitude and wonder. I was amazed, relieved and overjoyed all at once. I didn't care if it was a boy or a girl, I was just happy. Katie was beautiful. *Is* beautiful. A few days later we brought her home to join us in the caravan. A week after that she was gone.

I got home after work to find Nicky had cleaned out all of her things. There was no sign of her. No note. Nothing. She'd been decent enough to leave all my stuff there, except for one thing – my ten-day-old baby girl. I hadn't seen it coming but I guess it's hard to make sense of the world when you're on Trypto-dope-Largactil-rum.

I had a fair idea where Nicky had gone. Her mother lived on the other side of town and when I knocked on the door it was Nicky's mum who answered. 'She doesn't want to talk to you.'

'Well, she needs to tell me what's going on,' I demanded.

'She doesn't want to talk to you.'

Soon after that, a message came through to me at the caravan park. Nicola wanted me to sign over full custody of our daughter to her. I wasn't about to do that because I reckoned if I did, Nicola would take Katie straight to England. I was adamant that I should be allowed to have a relationship with our daughter, and hired a family law solicitor to help me stop her leaving the country. I might as well have hired Nicola's. For reasons I could not understand, my solicitor said I'd be better off just signing the custody papers.

'Huh? Why?' I wanted to know.

She just kept it up. 'It's really in your best interests to sign the papers.'

'You need to convince me why it's in my best interests to sign custody over.'

She couldn't, or wouldn't. I thought they were all too hung up on the word 'custody' when what I wanted was to establish a *relationship* with my daughter and to have my rights to that relationship ensured before I signed anything. In the meantime I had been granted 'access' (another word I hated) to Katie for one measly hour a week at the local community centre. Under supervision, of course.

'That's not a relationship,' I told my counsel. 'You're sacked.'

I complained about her to the professional ethics standards board, who gave me another solicitor. I went around to her office to meet with her. 'I've had one person try to screw me around,' I began, turning on the Smith charm, 'and I'm not in the mood for another one.'

The new lawyer already had the brief on her desk. In fact, I'm sure she had more than the brief. 'Tamworth is a small town, you know, Mr Smith.'

It most certainly is, and it was made pretty clear to me that I was the only sociopath-arsonist-soon-to-be inmate on the loose. I never did manage to secure that relationship with Katie but I never signed the custody papers either. No one really cared, though. Nicola took her to England anyway.

I was alone, save for my Legal Aid solicitor and Dr Tan, as I waited for the District Court magistrate to arrive. We'd been told there was every likelihood that I'd be committed to stand trial and if that happened I could say goodbye to my freedom. I was sad more than nervous. After all those years of trying to find a place in the world where I could be 'part of', it was just so disappointing that it was going to be in a prison.

When the magistrate entered the courtroom, everyone bowed their heads, although I was the only one who felt like hanging mine low forever. 'After careful consideration,' he began, 'it is the decision of this court to grant the application.' It took a few moments for the words to sink in. In the eyes of the law it had been demonstrated and accepted that I could not be held responsible for firebombing the dwelling and putting human lives at risk. Most significantly, mine.

A few weeks later I crawled away from Tamworth – again – and back to the land of the lost. Nicola eventually returned to Australia with Katie but, many years later, I found out that the beautiful girl who had once been intent on saving me after a suicide attempt had taken her own life. Nicky wrote a three-word note. 'Fuck the world.'

I knew what she meant.

16

MEREDITH

Around 1987–88 I found myself back in Sydney staying at the Matthew Talbot Hostel. I'd been drifting around and doing the odd seasonal job in North Queensland, but decided to hitch 1800 kilometres south to the big smoke in the hope of picking up permanent work and pulling my life together. As usual, I kept striking out.

After a string of knockbacks it occurred to me that listing a homeless person's shelter as my residential address might have been hampering my prospects. With that in mind, I moved into a backpackers hostel in Stanley Street, Darlinghurst, and my luck changed when I answered an ad for a store packer's position at a business in the city.

At the interview I was informed that I didn't have enough qualifications. I was taken aback. I mean, what qualifications does one need for warehouse work? I refused to take no for an answer and argued the toss with the company's owner, telling him I was quite capable of learning a warehouse position, thank you very much, and if he was in the market for a hard, honest worker then he need look no further.

Perhaps the guy took pity on me, perhaps he was impressed by my ritzy inner-city address, or maybe he liked my front. Whatever it was he gave me a chance and suddenly my life was a fraction brighter. He had a son working for him at the time, and I made friends with him. He was a good guy. He was kind to me and loved hearing my harrowing tales about life on the edge of society while we shuffled stock around the warehouse.

After work we'd go our separate ways. I'd trudge to the local bottle-o, buy a flask of bourbon and down it on the walk back to the hostel. Once there I'd figure out how to get more alcohol on-board so I could get to sleep in a room with eight other chaotic people in it. Consequently I sometimes found it hard to hit my stride in the warehouse the next day. The boss's son had a great way of boosting productivity, though. He was using cocaine at the time and started bringing free tastes into work for me to sample. It wasn't long before these furtive chemical appetisers gave rise to a full-on hunger. Soon I was searching for powders elsewhere. I didn't have to look very far.

I'd first met Meredith in a sleazy Darlinghurst pub. She was an attractive girl in her late twenties, a tall-ish five foot ten and very goth-like, with long black hair, black clothes and beautiful pale skin. She was also a drug dealer and she'd sometimes drop through the backpackers hostel to do business.

That's where I noticed Meredith dealt in narcotics, as opposed to green.

One day she was sitting on the steps out the front of the building where I worked when I finished my shift. It was pretty obvious what was going to happen.

'Hey, umm, do you know where I can score?' I began.

'What are you looking for?'

'I don't care. Cocaine, marijuana. Heroin? Anything.'

Meredith looked me up and down. 'Alright. Meet me back here in half an hour.'

She joined the passing current of pedestrians and when she returned thirty minutes later she was smiling.

'How much do you want?'

At that point I could have asked her 'How much of what?' but I just pulled a fifty-dollar note out of my jeans pocket and handed it to her.

'This enough?'

She took it and palmed me a small plastic sachet containing a dirty cream-brown powder.

'You ever used this before?'

I shook my head.

'OK, why don't you come back to my place and I'll help you?'

'Yeah. Sure. What's your name again?'

'I'm Meredith.'

Meredith lived alone in a one-bedroom flat with a tiny kitchenette, a single bed, a small three-drawer dresser and a skinny wardrobe. The sink was strewn with utensils and the single-element electric cooker looked like it was an afterthought. While it was tidy enough, the joint stank of urine, sweat and mould. Meredith closed the door behind us and busied herself at the dresser with a spoon, a hypodermic syringe and the little bag of heroin. I sat on the floor.

'What's it like? I mean, how does it make you feel?' I asked.

If I'd had any second thoughts about injecting drugs, Meredith neutralised them with the perfect answer. 'It takes all of your pain away.'

Sold. And with that, the pretty goth from the pavement gently took my arm in hers, jabbed my vein with a second-hand needle and watched with a satisfied smile as the opiate went to work.

Whoosh! The heroin flowed through me like rays of warm summer sunshine. Blissfulness bloomed in every cell of my body. Then I vomited. And vomited. And vomited. But I was amazed by how much I was enjoying throwing up. In fact, throwing my guts up was the best feeling I'd ever had.

Puke or no puke all of my pain went away, just like the lady said it would. I melted onto the floor and we chatted for hours into the balmy, deeply stoned night. I told her I worked at the building where we'd met and that I had nowhere to live other than the overcrowded backpackers. Her response surprised me. 'It's not much but if you can get a blanket or a mattress or something you can sleep on the floor here.'

The next morning I went to work. When I knocked off I didn't worry about buying bourbon. Instead I walked straight back to Meredith's place. She greeted me and nodded towards the dresser and the 'present' she'd arranged for me – a loaded syringe.

Whoosh! I didn't vomit this time but my synapses were swamped by the same high tide of comfort. The conversation took up where we'd left it the night before. 'You really can stay here, you know. If you've got nowhere else, the floor is all yours.' I didn't need to be told a third time and over the next few days I organised some blankets from the local St Vincent de Paul outlet. I even bought a pillow.

Within a couple of weeks I'd transformed from being derelict into a gainfully employed man sharing the rent with a beautiful young woman in cosmopolitan Darlinghurst. I was also morphing into a heroin addict. So, swings and roundabouts. Given that it was built entirely on a foundation of smack, the relationship with Meredith was anything but intimate. We never had sex. We weren't even flirtatious. Ours was more of an understanding that boiled down to a shared trust: she'd never rip me off and I'd never rip her off.

I suspect all Meredith's money came from dealing drugs, but even if you're a link in the supply chain heroin is expensive. Although my income was regular we'd still sometimes end up low on funds. And when addicts get desperate, it's others who pay the price. Whenever we needed an injection of cash I'd simply steal some valuable item from work and bring it back to Meredith who had the connections to move stolen goods.

Supplementing our income by ripping off the guy who had given me a break in his business cemented our relationship. Meredith knew she could rely on me for monetary support and I knew she could help me build a barricade between me and my eternal misery, one deal of heroin at a time.

*

I don't know if it was because the drugs gave me confidence but I soon had a compulsion to follow up on something I'd been thinking about for a long, long time. The Sydney TAFE building at Ultimo was only a short walk from work and it wasn't too far from Belmore Park, the infamous oasis for Sydney's homeless opposite Central Station where I'd spent plenty of nights sleeping under a bush. The halls of learning at Sydney TAFE may as well have been a million miles from the world I inhabited, though. I was a junkie-alcoholic-thief who had no one – not even Meredith. In truth, she wasn't much more to me than a human heroin dispenser. I might have been stoned but I was fully aware that I was living a shit life.

I had never really let go of the notion that if I could only get a better education I'd be able to break the cycle and drag myself out of the gutter. Even though I was constantly written off as an idiot, I knew I was smart. I understood the world and the people in it in my own way, and I often found, sometimes to my surprise, that I was three or four steps ahead of the next person, just as I had been at school.

I must have seen an advertisement for Sydney TAFE or read a pamphlet somewhere, because one day after work I walked over to Ultimo and enrolled in night classes. It was the first time I'd been in a classroom since my fleeting appearance at Oxley High at the age of fourteen. I have no idea what the course was, but for a month or so I'd go to school in the evenings after work and study whatever it was we were studying.

After six or eight weeks we were told to write an essay on the topic of our own choosing. I don't know why but I produced a handwritten dissertation on the threat feral cats posed to Australian fauna. It must have been in the news at the time. My grammar and spelling were atrocious but a few days later my tutor called me aside. He was a switched-on guy and knew that I was a junkie. Addicts never fool anyone.

'I don't know if you'll finish this course, Gregory,' he said, 'but whatever you do, don't ever give up on the idea of studying.'

I hadn't seen it coming. Encouragement. A compliment. Some belief in me. It scared the hell out of me. I walked out of the building that night and never returned. I went out and got blind drunk. 'What would some college teacher know about me and my education?' My agitation escalated and a familiar default kicked in: be somewhere else – now!

Meredith wasn't in the flat when I got back there, so I grabbed my pack and hitchhiked out of Sydney with nothing but some spare clothes and a few hundred dollars in my pocket. Homeless once again.

17

INTO THE FOREST

I drank copious amounts of alcohol while I withdrew cold turkey from the heroin. I was lucky to get off smack. It had been a time of high purity in Sydney and by dosing myself with the twin depressants of alcohol and opiates I'd been tempting fate. I could have overdosed on any given day.

I don't know how long afterwards it was – maybe six months, maybe a year, maybe a week – that I found myself wandering at night along Redcliffe Beach in Brisbane feeling sick, alone and depressed. Up above the high tide mark I caught sight of some shapes in the sand and when I got closer I could make out a row of upturned canoes. I decided on the spot to run away to sea. I knew there were islands out to the east, on the opposite side of Moreton Bay, and figured if I could make it out to one I'd be able to live out my days as a castaway far from people and their endless crap.

I liberated one of the canoes, dragged it down to the water's edge and pushed it into the waves. It wasn't until I clambered aboard that I realised I didn't have any paddles, so I knelt down and tried to propel the thing using my hands. A stiff onshore breeze had whipped up a bit of wind-swell and as I stroked into the blackness I started taking on water. A wave crashed over the side, and another. Then it was all over – a third wave twisted the canoe sideways and I capsized in a pathetic spectacle about ten metres from shore. Defeated, I struggled back to dry land and fought back tears of frustration as I sank onto the sand, marooned on an island from which there was no escape. I'd just about had enough of the world.

When I rolled into Byron Bay in northern New South Wales six months later it wasn't an intended destination, just literally where I ended up. I'd stuck it out in Redcliffe doing a soul-destroying job cleaning faeces off the floors of a nursing home until I could take it no more. I grabbed my pack, bought a bike, and started pedalling south. A few days and 200 kilometres later, I came across an old piggery-cum-camping ground and stashed my bike there while I set off on foot to investigate the town that was famous for being the easternmost tip of Australia. When I returned the bike had been stolen. That night I slept on the sand at Byron Bay Beach, still homeless, still marooned and now bike-less.

The next day, as I sat destitute and depressed on the beach, I could see the mountains that marked the rough location of Mullumbimby. I remembered that someone had once told me I'd like Mullumbimby, so I started walking.

I'd always enjoyed travelling through the Northern Rivers region of New South Wales, where the steep, green farmland of lushly carpeted fields was skirted by neat crops of sugarcane and rambling rainforests. The climate was magic all year round and echoes of alternative culture still hung in the townships and country lanes.

When I arrived in Mullumbimby in the summer of 1989–90 I was chuffed not only to find it was a pretty little town, but the things I'd heard about it appeared to be true. There was music, crystals, incense, colourful clothes, dreadlocks and even the whiff of dope on the warm breeze. I scored half an ounce of pot which immediately came in useful in helping me get to sleep on a fairly decent park bench I found by a creek. Despite the loose vibe and the peace and love, to me Mullumbimby was just another park bench on another leg of another trek to nowhere. After a few days I'd had enough.

It was humid and overcast when I picked up my pack and walked south out of town towards darkening clouds. It was a typical northern New South Wales country road that twisted through hilly fields dotted with homesteads, cows, rusty sheds and the odd forlorn-looking horse. I trudged past a golf course and a farm where a bloke was completely oblivious to me as he cut his grass atop a ride-on mower. I remember thinking with a touch of envy how perfectly contented he looked.

After a few hours the road started snaking uphill. On my right a modest, thickly forested mountain range loomed larger and larger in my peripheral vision. The closer I got, the more dramatic the cliffs looked. 'What,' I wondered, 'is at the top of that?' I paused intermittently along the way to puff on some pot in my hash pipe and take a few lukewarm slugs from the nozzle of the 'silver pillow' wine bladder that was sloshing about inside my pack. Sustained only by booze, drugs and a handful of nuts, I trudged on until sunset, when I came to a comfortable place to sleep. I smoked some more pot, drank some wine and passed out.

In the morning I had a couple of pipes and a few swigs of wine to wake myself up, and hit the toe again. It was harder going as the road gained altitude up the side of the mountain. I had to dodge a couple of cars on the hairpin bends but I finally reached the top in the afternoon. A sign at a T-intersection said a left turn would take me back down to the Pacific Highway while the right promised to take me to a place called Crystal Castle. It was a no-brainer; castles beat highways hands down. I was disappointed, though, when a few kilometres down the road the Crystal Castle turned out to be a tourist attraction. I walked straight past it.

I followed the heavily tree-lined road along the mountaintop until I arrived at another intersection. This time the choice wasn't written on a sign, it was laid out by the fact that one option – going left – led up a dirt road compared to the bitumen on the right. 'Dirt road warrants a look,' I decided. I passed a couple of large orchards and some cottages and shacks hidden among the trees and vines. The further I went the narrower the road became and the taller, and strangely more present, the trees appeared to be. It was getting late.

As dusk fell, a battered, vine-wrapped weatherboard house came into view. I felt perfectly comfortable approaching the place because it was in disrepair and deserted, a little like me. It was dark, shabby and the roof on the veranda was falling down. I found the gate and stepped into the overgrown yard – straight into a cowpat. There was no front door so I invited myself in, had a couple of pipes and a drink and fell asleep on the timber floor.

When birdsong woke me early the next morning I was desperately hungry, so I plotted a raid on one of the orchards I'd passed the previous afternoon. I slipped over the fence and helped myself to a pawpaw and a couple of kiwifruit. After my pathetic diet of wine, nicotine, nuts and gritty pieces of dope ash in my mouth, the fruit tasted incredible. I felt so good and energised that I celebrated by smoking more pot and guzzling the last of the vino.

I stayed in the orchard for hours, just looking at the fruit trees and the insects that teemed all over them. I had no plans, so about midday I figured I'd keep exploring the mountaintop. I walked back past the abandoned house and after a while the road turned into a trail and, finally, a narrow track. I found myself being drawn deeper and deeper into a cathedral of trees.

The air inside the forest was still, sweet and moist, and towards the late afternoon dark clouds slid overhead and the light faded to grey. In between distant rumbles of thunder I could hear every bird in every tree. I could also hear rustling leaves and fast movement in the thick tangles of bush that lined the track. The darkening day and these mystery noises made me apprehensive. Fear of the unknown rose up and stomped on my mood.

I sat on the track and reflected on the hopelessness of my situation. I felt rejected, inadequate and full of guilt about my long list of sins and failures. Everything I did was sinful. The fact that I couldn't make connections with people was a sin. The fact I was homeless was a sin. Unemployed – sin. Alcoholic – sin. Addict – sin. Abused – sin. Divorced – sin. The guilt may have been a hangover from the Catholic orphanage but it had also been reinforced in society. 'Even out here,' I thought. I'd dragged myself to the top of that mountain only to have my place in the world confirmed. I was an outcast. Human refuse. I was immensely sad that my life had ended up that way. As if my spirits weren't low enough, the heavens opened up. As rain soaked me through I was completely vulnerable and without a shred of hope.

When I left Mullumbimby I'd been wearing jeans, a T-shirt, a pair of shin-high GP army boots and an Akubra hat. In my green army haversack I had a full-length Driza-Bone raincoat, a packet of Drum tobacco, matches, a candle, my trusty pocket knife, a three-foot-long piece of blue and yellow nylon rope, a water bottle, some nuts, a couple of packets of Tally-Ho cigarette papers, my little hash pipe, a briar pipe and about half an ounce of pot. The sum total of my possessions after thirty-five years on the planet.

These belongings may have been modest but each fulfilled an important role – not least the Driza-Bone. This quintessential Australian raincoat plus fancy hat had come to me a year or two earlier when I'd done a brief stint at a horse stud in Tamworth. John Parkes, a prominent figure in the racing industry at the time, had been looking for a gardener to help with the upkeep so I'd put my case forward. Somehow, as if by miracle, I wound up getting hired. As part of the induction, John took all of his new workers into town and kitted them out with a nice Akubra and a top-of-the-line, full-length Driza-Bone. He was a very decent guy.

Just a couple of weeks after John spent that money welcoming me into the fold I repaid him by leaving town. I didn't so much resign as stop turning up for work. It didn't trouble me one bit to leave John in the lurch and keep the expensive gear he'd given me. I just had to go, and the next thing anyone knew there was a homeless man wandering around Kings Cross dressed like The Man From Snowy River.

As raindrops the size of sultanas pelted through the forest canopy I was glad of John's generosity. I quickly dragged the Driza-Bone out of my pack, sat on my haunches and pulled it over my head. I had never been rained on so hard in my life. The water droplets felt more like bits of gravel and the storm showed no sign of relenting. I cowered in the slush and mud, miserable beyond words. Cramps gnawed at my muscles and pain shot up my spine.

Whenever I found myself in a particularly tough spot my mind would drift to my younger days when I'd been locked in concrete cells or under the stairs. That was where I'd first learned to separate mind from body. I could dissociate to the point where my physical self would absorb whatever punishment was being meted out while I protected my inner-self, to a degree.

I was just crawling into my mind-cave to escape the storm when I felt an itch inside my trouser leg. I reached down to scratch it and felt a sticky warmth on my fingers. I looked at my hand and it was covered in blood.

As I pulled up the cuff of my jeans I was horrified to see five or six leeches on my leg. Then the same on the other! In the gloaming I made out fifteen or so more sliding purposefully towards me across the sodden forest floor. The slimy raiders must have been able to sense my body heat, or whatever evil powers of detection leeches can call on to ruin a human being's day.

It was time for a big decision: either move forward or go back. Going back was out of the question and the status quo down there in the mud and the blood wasn't too appealing. But where could I go? I was already 'gone'. I rationalised that I could deal with the leeches and the wet, I just needed to find a better place inside the forest. I thought about looking for a hollowed-out tree or maybe digging a little cave – a real one. I was clutching at straws but deep down I was confident I'd be OK. I just needed some time to get organised.

Despite the pitch black and the rain it struck me that I was feeling strangely positive about the situation. Something was different in the forest, and I liked it. Then it dawned on me. 'There's no one else here!' Still, I was fearful to a degree and nervous about the creatures and the strange noises. 'Do I keep going or do I go back?' All that was behind me was guilt, pain, depression, misunderstanding, disappointment, anger and the fear of ending up in gaol. I was happier squatting in the rain, plucking parasites off my legs.

'I'm staying right here.'

18

CAMP

I hardly slept for more than a few minutes at a time and I was soaking wet and cold as first light turned the black silhouettes of the forest into different shades of grey. I hadn't smoked any dope all night for fear of risking my precious matches in the biblical downpour. I was also acutely aware that I'd run out of grog and I was a long way from a bottle shop – a scary no-man's-land for an alcoholic to find himself in.

But there was something really cool taking place, too. As the sun crept higher, the grey shapes turned into an array of glistening greens, and the warm rays that penetrated the canopy caressed my waterlogged skin. A beautiful blue sky materialised through the leaves high above and mist drifted up from the forest floor. It was as if someone had flipped a giant switch to 'magic'.

I found a large pool of sunlight by the side of the trail

where I dried myself off enough to organise a couple of hits on the hash pipe and reflect on what had been a challenging night. I named the spot Pompeii because it had felt as if the world was falling in on me. Adequately stoned, I marched about four kilometres back out of the forest to pinch more fruit from the orchard.

Along the way I noticed things I hadn't seen the previous day. For one thing the trees were colossal in size and beauty. All manner of palms were interspersed among the massive eucalypts. Fallen trunks were coated in velvety moss and strings of vine twisted skyward from the steamy ground. Even the dirt sparkled with a trillion grains of silica that lit up like tiny diamonds when the sunlight hit them at the right angle. I felt my face break into a smile; a strange and unexpected sensation that made me grin even harder.

As I approached the abandoned house I could see it was in fact mid-renovation. Oops. I quietly ducked past and retraced my steps along the dirt road to the bitumen, which I noted was called Mill Road in the locale of Goonengerry. I moved carefully and silently by the other homes and slid quietly through the orchard fence once again. I crept under a tree, plucked a ripe, bulbous pawpaw and sat down to the freshest food I'd ever tasted.

I slurped on the pawpaw and scanned the landscape for any potential threats, especially angry farmers. Instead I spied a chicken coop on a nearby hill crest. 'Yum! Eggs!' I edged closer to the henhouse, constantly pausing like a fox to review my surrounds. I could see two eggs in the chook pen, and as the ladies clucked among themselves a few feet away I dashed in, grabbed the booty and scurried back to the orchard. I cracked the eggs straight into my mouth as if I were baking a cake in it. Feeling extremely satisfied and buoyant, I stuffed more pawpaw and a couple of avocados into my pack and legged it back into the forest.

I strode past the scene of the previous night's leech storm at Pompeii and selected one of the random tracks that snaked off into the trees. After cautiously feeling out the trail for a while, I came to a large, roughly circular clearing about ten metres in diameter. Trails fanned off it in all directions; some very obvious and others difficult to see. The larger ones, I discovered, were walking trails while the narrow ones were old logging tracks that had all but been forgotten. Every path, it seemed, stemmed from this clearing. I named it Rome. Around lunchtime another thunderstorm dragged itself across the mountain-top, but this time it didn't worry me so much. There wasn't a leech in sight and although I was still on edge and fairly spooked by the constant movements in the undergrowth, I was also aware of a budding connection between the forest and me. By late afternoon I'd dived deeper and deeper into its embrace, following a track that wound down a long, curved hill until it came to a creek where cold, clear water rippled over mossy rocks. I drank my fill and topped up my water bottle before settling on a boulder to take it all in.

All of the sounds had a softness about them. There was no clanging, no revving engines, no loud or angry voices, just an orchestra of birds chirping, frogs croaking, water trickling, leaves whispering and, every now and then, a rustle in the bushes. The little gully looked as if it had been torn from the pages of a fairytale; the banks lined by Bangalow Palms, reeds, lilies and all manner of water plants I'd never seen before. I explored a little and found a couple of deep water holes. I was blown away to discover a large crayfish with a vivid blue shell living in one. There were miniature waterfalls, rivulets and dark rock formations coated in different mosses and fungi. The more I looked at it, the more beautiful all of it was.

The rain had stopped and over to the west, where the sun was starting to drift, I could hear the unmistakable sound of a waterfall – a big one. I carefully picked my way downstream in the direction of the cascade. After a short walk, the trees opened up to reveal the most breathtaking view I had ever seen. I stood at the top of a huge waterfall and gazed in silent wonder 180 degrees across a deep canyon. The immense valley opened wide to the south, narrowed through densely forested shoulders to the north and was hemmed in on either side by the mountain I was standing on and a range a kilometre or so to the west.

Across the other side four or five waterfalls streaked down the jagged cliff faces. Hypnotised by the majesty, I sat on a rock and stared. Something strange started to happen to me. I felt a relief and a calmness settle. It took a moment for me to put a finger on the feelings but after a while I was in no doubt: it was a kind of belonging. For the first time in my life I had arrived at a point on the map where the grass actually was greener. I was overjoyed that for once I had nowhere else to go. I was right where I wanted to be and I didn't want the feeling to pass.

If I'd had wine I would have toasted my arrival. Instead I gorged myself on pawpaw, marijuana and hand-rolled cigarettes. The shadows grew longer and, ever the homeless man, I knew I had to think about where I was going to sleep. Reluctantly I pulled myself away from the cliff-top vista and retreated back up the creek a way.

Sensing I was the only person in cooee I reckoned I could risk a fire. The bush around me, however, was soaking wet thanks to the steady bouts of rain. Undeterred and a little hopeful, I gathered up some damp twigs, leaves and a pile of wet branches. I cleared a spot on the ground and tried to light the kindling, but every failed attempt wasted another cherished match. I was already booze-less and if I was unable to take drugs or smoke cigarettes I would find myself in the direst of straits. Then again, I didn't want to be alone in the pitch black in the wilderness for another night either. I had to figure out something.

I remembered a story I'd heard about a bloke who'd saved himself by lighting a fire in the rain using a dry shrub he'd found inside a cave. I wasn't about to go looking for caves but it gave me an idea. The bark of one of the trees next to me was starting to peel back so I tugged it a little more and discovered that the woody, papery fibres underneath were completely dry. Bingo! I looked around for a more fibrous type of bark and after ten minutes or so I found a tree that fitted the bill.

Using my knife I stripped the wet surface bark away and pulled out clumps of the stringy inner material. It was bone dry and when I rolled it between my fingers it bunched up loosely like a cotton ball. I gathered a good handful of the stuff, put it on the ground with a few damp twigs on top and with the strike of a single match I had a fire.

It was a momentous achievement and I felt on top of the world. I was safe in a place where no one could kick me, I had a fire, I was warm, and I had an endless supply of water to drink. I stared into the flames for a long time feeling fairly comfortable outside and in. I dragged my Driza-Bone out and, using my pack for a pillow and the raincoat for a blanket, curled up next to the fire and went to sleep. Then, of course, it rained.

I was finding out the hard way why they call it rainforest. I scrambled to my feet and huddled on my haunches beneath the Driza-Bone for a second night. Although it didn't pour for as long as it had at Pompeii, I was camped right next to a creek and the level started to rise rapidly. Soon the creek was lapping at my spluttering, hissing campfire. Thankfully the deluge stopped after thirty minutes or so and I could soon see stars twinkling through the canopy. Once again the forest had left me cold and wet but I was oddly calm and at peace. With sleep off the agenda I sat in the darkness and watched the distant galaxies until they faded into the pale glow of the new day.

I chided myself for making camp on the bank of a creek. It probably hadn't been the smartest idea. I would need to find somewhere safer and drier, and I would have to sort myself out. A quick inventory revealed I had just over a quarter of an ounce of pot, half a packet of Drum tobacco, two packets of Tally-Ho papers (one of which had succumbed to the humidity leaving them all stuck together), about ten matches, seventy-five dollars in notes and a few loose coins. Hardly what you'd call a growing concern.

Something I did have an unexpected oversupply of was resolve. During the night I'd decided conclusively that the forest was now my home for the foreseeable future. But this meant I had to start planning and thinking ahead about survival.

I returned to the track and set off to explore my surrounds a bit more. I hiked for an hour in one way and an hour or so in another, weaving through the bush and scrambling over logs and rocks before returning to the creek and heading off in another direction. By lunchtime, after I'd covered a fair bit of terrain, it was clear I should make the creek central to my operations. Not only did it provide water for drinking, cooking and washing – it was just a beautiful place to live.

For lunch I forced down a greying, overripe avocado and almost gagged in the process. Food supply, I noted, was another factor I'd need to think hard about. As I scanned the bush on the south side of the creek I noticed the ground climbed about thirty degrees up a slope roughly twenty metres to the left of the waterfall. I headed over to check it out. The vegetation was different there. Rather than tall trees, vines and palms, the much rockier ground was crowded with smaller bushes and dense, thorny shrubs.

After ten minutes or so pushing through the undergrowth I stepped into a slight clearing. The ground comprised a large, slightly sloping bed of lava rock that tilted away by a foot or so on one side making it impervious to flooding. It was impossible to see the clearing from the creek or the walking track that led into the gully. The only way you'd be able to see it would be by helicopter. It was high up on the cliff-side flank of the waterfall and the view to the north-west up the sunlit canyon was magnificent.

Moving into my new place was easy. I simply retrieved my pack from where I'd stashed it down by the creek, clambered back up through the bushes to the clearing and sat down. Throughout my homeless years I always had the same name for the place I laid my head. Whether it was a public bench, a ditch or a depression in the long grass next to a river it was always 'camp' to me. This looked like an excellent one.

Although I was going to be nice and dry on the lava rock, I'd have to fashion some kind of mattress or bedding. I also figured that preserving the vegetation around me, so as not to create any kind of footprint, would be crucial to remaining undetected in the forest. I vowed to always collect firewood from further afield. Ferns and grasses, for use as bedding, would also have to be gathered at least half an hour's walk from camp.

Even though I'd removed myself a little way from the waterfall, I still considered the entire gully to be my domain. I came to think of the creek and the cliff top as my lounge room, because that's where I spent time just hanging out and relaxing. My camp up on the nearby shoulder of the waterfall was my kitchen and bedroom, because that's where the fire and the bed were. My bathroom was quite a hike away – across the other side of the creek and down another little gully. Far away from my water supply.

If I wanted to stay relatively comfortable I'd have to be diligent about chores. Firewood and bedding were the priorities so I generally got stuck into those tasks early, but never before smoking some dope to tweak my brain chemistry. I'd hike off into different corridors of the forest in search of dead-fall branches. I never pulled wood off trees lest someone read the signs. The bedding, however, was harvested fresh. Every day I'd go into secluded corners of forest to cut giant fern leaves and other soft foliage with my pocket knife. Once I had enough to make a comfy mattress I'd loop my little length of rope around the centre, hoist the bundle onto my shoulder and carry it all back to camp.

Sleeping in the forest grew a little easier as the weeks ticked by but it was generally a stop-start affair. I'd wake up several times through the night to feed the fire, and if it was raining it could be hard to get back to sleep. I'd almost always wake before sunrise when the birds started up. Judging by the wattage of the embers I could tell if the fire needed urgent attention or whether it could wait until later.

Most often I'd throw on a stick or two, and when dawn broke I'd zigzag through bushes and over some lava rocks down to the creek. I was always careful to never catch my reflection in the silvery pools. I'd stare straight ahead as I'd squat on the bank and scoop cold handfuls of water to wash the face that society didn't want to see and that I didn't really care to look at either. Whenever I did see myself it was enough to bring on days of guilt and painful introspection.

Depending on my mood after washing my face, I'd take a few moments to inspect the deeper recesses of the creek to make sure the crayfish was still there. Satisfied all was as it should be, I'd look to my left and behold the view that never disappointed. Some mornings I'd wander down to the creek to discover that humidity had worked some kind of alchemy overnight, filling the canyon from top to bottom with a thick, white cloud. I felt as if I could almost step out onto the misty floor and waltz right across to the other side.

Sometimes after big rains had swelled the creek, I'd strip naked at the top of the waterfall, lie on my back in the surging water and watch the birds do their thing in the canopy above. Or I'd sit by the edge of the cliff top and gaze for hours into the emptiness of the canyon. Now and then that lovely feeling would rise up again – the belonging. Soon enough, though, my past would lumber over and shoulder charge anything that even resembled happiness.

The scenery may have changed, and I may have felt more secure than I did in the cities and towns, but inside my head the needle was stuck largely in the same groove. 'You're in this forest because you're a sinner,' I'd regularly remind myself. 'You're not welcome in society. They don't have a place for you so you'd better stay right away from them.' Days could be spent re-reading a single chapter of my life, trying to make sense of it and how it had helped shape me into such a horrible person. I'd return to the orphanage or to the kitchen of my childhood where Dad was on the rampage. I'd think about all my crimes and sins and transgressions and wonder if I was somehow cursed. And, if so, why?

It was fortunate there was a laundry list of pressing tasks in the forest, otherwise I might have hated myself 24-7. For one thing, the same humidity that turned clouds into magical bridges in the sky could also ruin my food, and thus my entire day, pretty quickly. The damp of the rainforest wasn't so bad that it caused my fingertips to prune, but some days it wasn't far off. It was a relentless, penetrating mugginess that could turn a fresh pawpaw black within twenty-four hours or render a perfectly good box of Redheads useless.

I'd finally run out of tobacco, so on my first trip back to Mullumbimby – a two-day walk away – I stocked up on Drum, a couple of casks of wine, some cans of Sunshine powdered milk, flour, rice, boxes of matches, candles and salt. I also grabbed a few copies of the local newspaper, the *Byron Shire Echo*.

On my return to camp I painstakingly swaddled the matches in strips torn from the *Echo* and then wrapped the bundle in a piece of cloth. I had made the process of lighting a fire harder for myself by refusing to use cigarette lighters. I had decided that plastic was an abomination and a sign of consumerist greed. In the forest I only wanted to use natural materials.

Later on I'd use the *Echo* to store perishable food, marijuana, magic mushrooms and anything else I wanted to keep for more than a day or two. But no amount of newspaper could stop the rain. It was just part of life. If I was going to be drenched for two weeks straight, that was just that. I got used to it. It's amazing what you can get perfectly comfortable with after a while.

The rain turned dirt into mud, and lava rock into slippery stepping stones that presented a thousand ways for me to fall and hurt myself. Like everything else, injuries sustained in the forest were measured on a different metric than in the civilised world. Badly twisted ankles, deep lacerations, violent gastro illnesses? These didn't count as serious. Ticks burrowing into the middle of your back where you can't reach them? Hardly worth mentioning. A brigade of leeches sucking cupfuls of your blood? Nothing to see here.

While trifling discomforts abounded in a day in a life

in a rainforest, I was also aware there were some nasties living up on that mountain that could definitely cause me serious harm or even end my life. One of them, I'd find out, was me.

19

THE FOOD CHAIN

I know what it's like to be truly hungry; to say the words 'I'm starving' and not really mean 'I'm a bit peckish'. I've been so animal ravenous that I've rummaged around, gagging, in the reek and slop of public garbage bins, in search of something to force down my throat. In the forest I discovered a whole new level of starving.

Sometimes I would go three or four days without eating. It's not that there wasn't any food around, I just had to catch it first. At one point I was so weak from hunger that I literally crawled on all fours at the creek in search of a morsel. I looked for frogs and even tadpoles, and turned rocks over using my very last kilojoules of energy. Blessedly I came across a thumping big worm twisting in the silt on the bank. I hadn't eaten in four days so it never stood a chance. I dunked the worm into the creek and squeezed the dirt and guts out between thumb and forefinger. Once I'd jettisoned the goop I was left with a slimy outer tube of worm skin about thirty centimetres long. It took an almighty effort to convince myself to put it in my mouth, and I dry-retched at the thought, but billions of hungry cells egged me on so down it went.

I dined on other creepy crawlies, too – grasshoppers, bugs, a massive beetle (crunchy and bitter). In the early days there was only one species that I refused to eat, simply because I found it too beautiful to destroy. The crayfish was about thirty centimetres long and had a thick tail and robust claws that were no doubt crammed with tasty meat. It would have been so easy to reach in, lift it out and boil it up over the coals in a Sunshine milk tin. But if I did that, I knew I'd miss looking at it and be filled with a deep regret. I had enough of those already.

I could hear critters of the air and land around me all day, every day. I began to recognise the calls of the different native birds and the squeaking, grunting noise the bats made in their treetop bedrooms. I could see my feathered friends, too: Willie wagtails, currawongs, drongos, bush turkeys, noisy pittas and lyrebirds.

On the ground it was a different story. I'd hear things moving more often than I saw them. To begin with this was accompanied by a jolt of fear that I was about to be attacked. But after a month or so I grew more in synch with nature and could spot the 'monsters' that had been terrorising me. The most prolific land creatures in the forest were lizards, and the most common of those was the Egernia major, or land mullet. They are shy, highly strung little creatures, about thirty to forty centimetres long with dark, glossy scales – and they dash into the undergrowth or rocky crevices at the first sign of danger.

There were other reptiles, too – slightly scarier ones, like the big monitors. The ones I saw were about as long as my arm but I knew they grew quite a bit bigger. Monitors have an impressive set of claws and they also pack a bite that's laced with a slow-acting bacteria. I knew if I got chomped by one I'd be in a spot of bother so I tended to give monitors a wide berth. And of course there were all kinds of snakes. The first time I saw one I was sitting on the lava rock watching a little marsupial meander across the ground. Out of the corner of my eye I caught a movement in the tree above it. I was just about to say something when a large python dropped on the little critter, swirled around it and squeezed.

I was shocked and surprisingly upset. My first instinct was to save the mammal – the same kneejerk response I felt when I leapt up to defend my sisters from Dad. I got to my feet and started towards this outrageous mismatch when something stopped me dead. 'What right have I got to interfere with this?' It was a whole different concept from little girls being hurt; that was abuse whereas this was about survival. As uncomfortable as it was for me to watch the cute critter die, the snake had every right to have dinner. There was a flipside to that realisation, though, and I was getting hungry.

I heard the bats before I saw them. I was out walking when a familiar sound caused me to look up. The thing I'd noticed about bats was that they didn't seem to be afraid of me – the advantage of sleeping at the top of a tree, I guess.

I walked right up to the base of the trunk and figured if I could knock one out of the branches with a stone I'd eat like a king. I was, after all, quite the marksman. When I was a child I used to nick Dad's air rifle and discovered I was a very, very good shot. I used to pick off birds, hitting them in the head every single time. I don't feel good about it now, but back then I was pretty impressed with myself. As soon as a bird would come into range I'd lift the barrel and *bang*. I hardly even bothered to aim. It was just instinct.

Throwing a rock up at a tree was a different proposition altogether. My first effort missed by a mile and even after I corrected my aim I kept coming up short. The problem was the bats were a good six feet higher up the tree than my maximum range. My stones would crunch into the leaves and twigs beneath them and they'd just move a few feet away, resettle and go back to sleep. I had to figure out how to gain that extra six feet, so I decided I would be David and the bats would be furry little Goliaths. I tore a sleeve off my T-shirt and fashioned it into a sling, which turned my throwing arm into a bat bazooka. After ten to fifteen goes I scored a direct hit. I could hardly believe it. 'Food!'

The bat was only stunned but it careened out of the tree and thudded haphazardly onto the forest floor. It flapped and struggled on the ground for a second before I pounced. Hunger had focused my every fibre and there was no mucking around; I snapped its neck. The warm, limp body stank of urine, but I didn't care. I'd slept in public toilets that smelled ten times worse. To me it was the reek of survival. On the walk back to camp I swapped my hunter's cap for my chef's hat. 'How do you cook a bat? Do you skin it? Should I just throw it in the fire?'

In the end I dug a little hole in the coals. I rolled the bat up, folded its wings around it, placed it in and covered it with more coals and ash. I was surprisingly ceremonious about the process, although I had no idea where the sentiment sprang from, other than deep within me. I just knew I felt for this creature. 'I'm really sorry, I'm really sorry,' I kept saying. 'I had to do it. I need to eat.' All the while I kept testing it until I thought it was about ready. It didn't smell like urine anymore. It actually smelled nice, like meat cooked on a fire. The gut had shrivelled up into a ball and I could easily pick away at the flesh around it. Next I peeled the skin off and ate it. That was particularly tasty. It didn't taste like chicken – it tasted like bat – but it was hot, reasonably flavoursome and it helped keep me alive.

Barbecued bat became a staple for a while after that. It would have been nicer if I could have seasoned them with a few spices and a bit of pepper or chilli, but at least I had salt. And compared to some of the other items on the menu, bat was as tasty as Christmas turkey.

Lizards, on the other hand, seemed to be in endless supply. Unlike picking up a crayfish, catching these reptiles required some cunning. The ubiquitous land mullet in particular was fast and standoffish. I'd had some success with little spears fashioned in the fire and if I was quick enough I could occasionally run a lizard down with a rock. One morning I was trawling through memories and recalled that Uncle Robbie had shown me how to make a snare for rabbits in Oberon. It was a game-changer in the forest.

After a few months some nylon fishing line came into my possession, and I rigged the bush around me with little traps. I'd make a simple hangman's noose with the fishing line and tie it to a springy branch that I'd bend over and put tension on using a rock or another branch. With a nice fragile set, whatever walked through the noose would be snared and flipped up. The first time it worked I was elated. I was onto a whole new food supply which was a great relief. Contrary to popular belief, food isn't overly abundant in a rainforest. Occasionally, though, something to eat would literally fall – or slither – into my lap.

I wasn't exactly terrified of snakes, but I was never in a hurry to get too close to them either. So when I awoke with a mystery serpent squirming on top of me in the middle of the night I was more than a little dismayed. I had no option but to lie deathly still and hope to high heaven it wasn't a lethal species and that it didn't suddenly decide to strike. It truly was the stuff of nightmares, and those minutes before the massive reptile slid off me remain the longest of my life. Although I initially considered killing the diamond python something of a primordial triumph, I came to regret it pretty quickly. After I'd munched through maybe a quarter of a kilo of cooked snake steaks the following night I felt satisfied and tired. I stoked up the fire, lay down on my bed of ferns and started thinking about its blood.

I had carefully removed the python's skin: a beautiful latticework of glistening charcoal scales interspersed with mustard yellow markings. Then I drained its blood into an empty Sunshine milk can. I was set on keeping it and had to figure out a way to preserve it in the long term. I decided that the next day I'd tip some into a small brown glass vial I had and seal the top with wax from my candle. That way I'd be able to take it with me everywhere.

'Yeah,' I thought as I started to drift off. 'That'd work well.'

I had a strong instinct that the snake blood represented something more than just a means of transporting oxygen around a reptilian body; I felt the snake was imbued with a spiritual force. I thanked it again for its sacrifice and fell asleep.

In the very next moment I was shrieking in agony and pure terror. A sharp, burning stick tore through my leg. I screamed at the top of my lungs but no one could hear me. A malevolent, ancient entity pinned me to the ground while other demons ripped the skin from my limbs and pulled my muscles off my bones.

'Ahhh!' I was suddenly awake and the screaming was gone, replaced by the soft crackle of the fire. It took me a moment to gather myself and realise it had only been a nightmare. I calmed myself down and eventually drifted off again, though I'd come to wish I hadn't. Back in the land of nod, the evil continued where it had left off. I was skinned alive again and flayed by wicked beings. They fed me into a fire and a huge serpent appeared on my chest. It coiled around me and . . . 'Ahhh!'

It went on for weeks. A recurring nightmare. Every single night. The same horrors about snakes, demonic entities, fire and agony. Part of me worried it might never stop. 'It's just that killing it was taboo,' I'd reason to myself in the waking hours. 'Snake is taboo for you and the ancestral spirits want you to know it. It'll pass, OK?' Finally, after two or three harrowing, near-sleepless weeks, the night-mares gradually faded away.

I'd see other snakes from time to time after that – all kinds of interesting types – and I didn't feel overly nervous or bad about them. I learned to read snake trails and could tell a big one from a small one. I let the snakes do their thing and they left me alone. But I never con-sidered eating one again. They joined the crayfish on my protected species list.

20

HEATHER

Heather was the first witch I ever met. She was a blonde woman in her thirties; very attractive, very intelligent and she dressed like a hippy, with lots of flowing dresses and frills. On the day I first met her I was dying for a ciggie. I'd ventured along the trail out onto the road in the hope of somehow getting some tobacco. Heather had been coming the other way. She took one look at me and asked, 'What do you need?'

'Whatever,' I responded. I wasn't exactly Mr Have-a-Chat at the time but I managed to cobble together a half-polite follow-up sentence. 'Oh, I'm looking for some bread. Do you know where I can get some?' It turned out I was craving it more than nicotine.

'Sure, I'll find some for you.'

We arranged to meet again on Mill Road in a couple of days. When we did, Heather handed me half a loaf. And not just any bread; it was a dark, heavy rye the like of which I'd never had before. I broke a chunk off, tried it and fell in love with it.

'Thanks,' I said, still chewing. 'Hey, I've got this really cool snakeskin. Do you know where I can trade it?'

I found out later that, in addition to being a witch, Heather was a vegan. But she was sympathetic towards me and said she'd make some enquiries about who might want to trade something for my butchered diamond python. Again, we arranged to meet a few days later.

'I found someone who might be interested in your snake-skin. What do you want for it?' Heather asked.

'Tobacco, rice and milk.'

A couple of days later I returned with the snakeskin and Heather gave me the goods. When we exchanged I was so pleased, particularly with the tobacco. Finally, I could smoke again! But I was also stoked because it looked like trading might give me a longer-term future in the forest. It marked the beginning of my relationship (built closely around Heather) with the people who lived on the edges of the forest. I called them the fringe dwellers but they were really just the residents of the properties up on the mountain. It turned out that Heather lived in one of the shacks I'd passed on the day I walked in.

These were all baby steps and, for the most part, I remained a highly skittish human being. If I ever heard a car approaching I'd hide in a ditch on the side of the road until it passed. Over the years thousands of Australians would have driven past me in all parts of New South Wales and Queensland without ever knowing it.

I was afraid – I had been all my life, but now I had something to protect as well. Primarily I didn't want people to know I was living in the forest because I feared the authorities might come and make me move. As stupid as it sounded to me, I knew it was illegal to camp in there. People did know I was in there, though. Heather knew, the fringe dwellers knew. It wasn't that hard to figure out. Someone would be at their sink doing the washing up when they'd see a wild-looking man walking past in the direction of the forest. The local gossip would start.

'Have you seen that feral guy with the Akubra hat?'

'Yeah, I saw him last year. Is he still living in there?'

'Yep. Saw him yesterday.'

And so on. Eventually my signature Akubra rotted away and I got a new lid. It was a big black felt hat and I went to the trouble of sticking nine different coloured sewing pins into the brim to represent the orbit of the planets around my skull, thus reminding myself that I wasn't the centre of the universe. I had started to do some 'work' on myself in the forest.

In the beginning my contact with Heather occurred once every five to ten days as we established lines of communication and a bit of a rapport. After a while that dropped back to once every six to eight weeks, depending on what I needed. If I didn't bump into her I'd walk down near to her fence and say a cooee. I never just rocked up at her shack. It wasn't that kind of relationship. It was superficial and sparse – deliberately so. Even though she'd been nothing but kind to me, I trusted no one and I didn't want her to have too much information.

It wasn't so much that I was worried Heather would dob me in (after all, she was enabling my survival in the forest), it was more a case of wanting to protect her from me. She was a nice person and I didn't want to hurt her. She was always up for a conversation but I never wanted to talk much beyond our terms of trade. The old voice would start up in my head. 'If you get to know who I am you're not going to like me.' I was volatile and dangerous; a 100 per cent genuine, officially diagnosed sociopath.

So, naturally I was in a conundrum when Heather invited me to her house. 'Come around tomorrow and we'll sit down and have a smoke and a talk.'

I had trouble sleeping in the ferns that night. I really didn't want to go to Heather's house, but since she'd been generous enough to ask me, the respectful thing to do was accept. And so the next day I found myself sitting down sharing a joint at Heather's house. I realised it was a big mistake straight away. I was frightfully uncomfortable and hardly spoke a word. Heather told me a bit about herself; how she did volunteer work and handed out information pamphlets on HIV awareness at the Mullumbimby markets. She was campaigning for a needle exchange for intravenous drug users in Byron Bay Shire, too. Oh yeah, and she was a witch. 'A white witch, though,' she said with a reassuring smile. 'So, a good one.'

I sat and listened, terrified that she was going to ask me to share a bit about my life. We couldn't have that! So, after the shortest of visits I stood up and said I had to go, pretending I'd only dropped in on my way to another appointment. In all honesty, though, the only other thing on my agenda was throwing rocks at bats.

It had been weird sitting in someone else's home. The concept of 'home' had always been a difficult one for me. Exactly what was a home? Where was it? If it was a fixed, familiar surrounding where you felt safe then that ruled out where I'd grown up in Tamworth. Or was home a haven where you were given support, understanding and love? I'd heard people say, 'Home is where the heart is.' I strongly disagreed. I'd carted my heart 20,000 kilometres to every which where, only to find myself forever homeless.

But after more than a year in the forest it started to feel a bit like . . . home. I still didn't feel supported or loved but at the very least the forest was less chaotic than anywhere I'd ever lived and I felt safe there most of the time. I'd explored from my camp on the western ridge right across to the eastern bluffs of the mountain. I'd wandered along sun-dappled trails and sat on a mossy bank in a serene gully and marvelled: 'How rich am I? I have this all to myself!' I'd started to think of the forest as my personal domain and I carried on naming the places I discovered. It was helpful in terms of navigation but there was a definite element of sovereignty at play, too.

With Rome and Pompeii already accounted for, I named other places in honour of great ancient empires. An area near the entrance of the forest I dubbed Carthage because it was where I did trade with Heather. Alexandria was a regular resting spot that I named just to keep up the theme. I even had Hades – a horrible, rocky incline where I fell down and badly gashed my leg one dark, steamy, miserable day. If I suffered the same injury today, I'd go straight to emergency.

One of my happy places was a gargantuan prehistoric log. It was chest high, as long as a bus and wrapped in the thickest, greenest blanket of moss on earth. When it rained the carpet glowed luminescent and it was moist and cool to sit on. I could lounge on that log for hours knowing there was no rush, no threat and no need to pack up my things and flee. I was sitting on that fallen tree one day when it occurred to me I had completely reversed my primary instinct to be somewhere else. It felt like the forest wanted me to stay, too.

Caveman life at camp was ticking over quite nicely. I'd placed a couple of big rocks on top of each other to make a little workbench-cum-table and I arranged a couple of other rocks nearby for my chair. More stones were arrayed around the fire for cooking purposes. OK, the Flintstones would have done more with the place but it was refreshingly uncomplicated nonetheless.

My bed didn't really evolve much – it was still essentially a pile of freshly cut ferns stacked on springy tree branches. After a year I decided to get the Driza-Bone out and rig it up as a canopy and it worked amazingly well until it finally rotted away a couple of years later. If the Driza-Bone company ever want to make a testimonial ad they should come and talk to me.

With the raincoat roof gone I messed around weaving palm leaves together (another trick I learned from Uncle Robbie) to try to make a bit of shade and bedding. I even made a hat once and wore it into town. The more time passed, though, the more I grew used to just being rained on. Even so, I had a crack at building a bit of a shelter by laying thickish branches on top of each other lengthways and filling the gaps with dirt and clay I carted in from the main trail. Not so much a log cabin as a log wall. I ended up buying a small tarpaulin, too.

In time I untangled many of the mysteries of the forest. During the early days I used to get freaked out by a terrifying, high-pitched squealing noise that would keep me awake at night. These were unsettling sounds – very weird, otherworldly, sustained shrieks. I'd get up in the morning and obsess about finding the source. I spent days looking for tracks and trails left by the phantom creatures but I could never find a trace, until one day when I was walking along a trail I heard one.

I nervously pushed through the bush towards the source of the squealing and realised with a touch of apprehension that it was coming from overhead. 'It's gotta be an alien!' I lifted my head at the exact time the shriek pierced the air, only to see two tree branches rubbing up against each other in the wind. I could see where the dark wood had worn smooth and squeaky. It was a massive relief and I laughed out loud at myself. Over time I learned that different types of trees made different types of squeals and – just like the lizards rustling in the undergrowth – once I knew what it was I wasn't frightened anymore.

I also stopped catching and eating the creatures around me, particularly after I established a bit of trade through Heather, who became pivotal in my development as a hermit, finding all kinds of things for me, from food, tobacco and booze to useful odds and ends. I was getting to know the animals; I'd see them about the place, often at the same spots, and I developed a kind of kinship with them. At the very least I considered us all to be neighbours.

The last animal I killed was a little kangaroo that I used to see from time to time. Amazingly it got caught in one of my snares. I killed it and ate it and regretted it straight away. I was painfully aware that I didn't see it around the place anymore. That had a profound effect on me and I decided at that moment to become vegetarian, or at least try to.

For the first few months I'd have a meat pie on re-supply runs into Mullumbimby that were bankrolled by the sale of my collection of lizard skins through Heather. After a while this changed to a spinach and feta pasty or a vegetarian pie. I also found myself buying nuts, legumes and lentils from the health-food shop to cook in the forest. I'd snack on dried figs, dried apricots, dried apple and banana. The main problem with that type of food was that it went mouldy very quickly so I also started to eat a lot more rice and ended up creating my own signature line of homemade dampers:

INGREDIENTS
Sunshine powdered milk
Creek water
Flour
A bit of rice for body

METHOD
Mix ingredients in the Sunshine milk tin
Slam the lid on and toss into fire
When the lid pops off it's half-cooked
Finish on coals and serve with fingers

I started making the odd foray down to Byron Bay, too, another day and a half's walk from Mullumbimby. While trips to Mullumbimby generally accounted for six days (two to get there, two in town and two to get back), visits to Byron Bay could last eight to ten days, sometimes longer if I got locked up for drunkenness or fighting.

On the long walks people would sometimes stop and offer me a lift out of the blue, especially on lonely roads. Sometimes I'd accept, particularly if I was exhausted, but other times I'd say, 'Thanks but no thanks.' It depended on my frame of mind; I knew I was dangerous in a certain mood.

Partly these trips were about going on benders at the Railway Hotel in Byron or the Chincogan pub in Mullum-bimby, and partly to stock up on supplies. Because my memory wasn't as good as my forgetory, a shopping list was essential. The first thing I'd bought on my maiden run into Mullumbimby was a pencil (which I called my magic stick) and some paper. A typical early shopping list would be:

Drum tobacco x 2
Tally-Ho papers x 8
Matches x 3 boxes
4 litre cask wine x 1
Tea x 1
Can of Sunshine milk x 1
Can of baked beans x 2
Rope
Byron Shire Echo x 1
Can opener x 1
Fork x 1
T-shirt x 1
Bowl x 1
Pillow case (rag) x 1

On other trips I'd poke around the Mullumbimby Markets and pick up beads, knick-knacks and other little treasures. One day I ran into Heather down there while she was handing out her HIV flyers. We exchanged a bit of small talk but I got away from her as quickly as I could. People still freaked me out. I wandered over to a little stall instead and bought some marbles.

I'd purchased a small yellow canvas dillybag that was on my shoulder everywhere I went. Inside it I kept what I deemed to be the essentials: magic stick and paper, a candle, a box of matches, tobacco, Tally-Ho's, hash pipe and a feather. I added the marbles to the dillybag. I used to say it was so nobody could ever tell me I'd lost my marbles but I was only half-joking; there were times in the forest when I thought I might be going a teensy bit crazy and I'd get them out, just to steady the ship.

Sometimes I stayed away from town. I was prepared to go hungry rather than venture into society and interact with humans. Other times my clothes rotted away and I simply had to go. Whenever I needed clothes I'd hit Vinnies in Mullumbimby and pick up second-hand T-shirts and jeans for just a couple of bucks. After a while I switched to wearing combat-style pants – sourced from the army disposal store – because all the extra pockets came in handy. My basic outfit in the forest was army pants, cut-off T-shirts and lace-up GP boots. Ever since I tore the sleeves off my first forest T-shirt to make slings to hunt bats, I did it to every T-shirt I had after that. I was just more comfortable feeling the wind and sun and leaves on my arms.

I had developed other customs and rituals, too. After the great python visit I took to peeing in a giant circle around the perimeter of the campsite to keep any unwanted critters out. I always peed in a clockwise direction about twenty feet from the campfire and I reckon it worked. I never again woke up with a snake parked on top of me. Up until that point I'd sprinkled salt in a circle around the camp but it had no force-field properties whatsoever – the python being the proof of that.

The other important piece of apparel I took to wearing was the vial of snake blood. It dangled next to my heart on a cord around my neck. Combined with the fact I was a sociopath, the sacred blood imbued me with immense power.

21

BEER AND BUDS

Apparently the blitzing of backyards and doing anything remotely horticultural was all the rage. I didn't have a TV but from what they tell me I could have given any celebrity gardener a run for their money. I'd collected seeds from the various deals of pot I'd bought or been given and figured the rainforest would be a great place to start a crop of my own. I planted my seeds about 200 metres upstream of camp – close enough that I could keep a good eye on them but far enough from home base that I wouldn't be guilty by association.

I usually started off with twenty to twenty-five seedlings, but by the time harvest rolled around in late May to early June I'd have five to seven plants left. The attrition occurred through the process of eliminating the males because only the females go on to develop the prized heads, or 'buds', packed with the cherished active chemical THC.

Once the males were dispatched, more foliage would be lost as I plucked plants clean to give me something to smoke while I waited for the rest to mature.

Still, the harvest was usually pretty decent. I'd end up with full plants that had quite a bit on them – maybe three-quarters of a pound in total. I could never be sure because I didn't have any scales. I think that was part of what made my barter and trade so strong: I tended to guesstimate an ounce and give overly generous deals.

While I might have been unselfish in that regard I was hyper paranoid about who I traded with. To begin with the only people I sold or traded pot with were introduced to me by Heather. It took a couple more years before I really established a regular customer base, mainly due to being so untrusting. Because I was heavily into addiction myself, I could easily pick who was a drug user and who wasn't. There wasn't much chance I was going to get busted selling to an undercover cop, but paranoia is paranoia.

Perhaps the most challenging part about cultivating and dealing pot from my base up on the mountain was working out how to preserve my supply through the winter months. I had to figure out preventative steps otherwise the per-ennial mists and humidity would turn my mega stash into blackened, decayed mush within a few days. Months of work would be lost. Once again, the mighty *Byron Shire Echo* came to the rescue.

Even though I was growing and selling and trading in drugs, I never viewed the process as a means of making money per se. It wasn't an 'enterprise' or business. For me it was purely about survival, managing trauma and providing some comforts and quality of life for part of the year, be it alcohol, food or a tarpaulin. I was hardly Pablo Escobar with a mansion in the mountains and a private plane to whisk me down to Mullumbimby and Byron. But, like Pablo, I was well aware it was a criminal activity and I was suitably security conscious. Fortunately, I had a pretty good idea of who was coming and going in the forest, right down to which trails people would take.

The biggest threat would arrive out of the blue every other year or so in the form of a police air-wing patrol. Whenever their helicopters clattered into the canyon below I'd become incredibly anxious. The fire would be extinguished and I'd scatter leaf litter and twigs over any bare patches of the lava rock. From the air, bare rock beneath trees would be a sure sign of human activity and grounds to search the area.

I'd go to great lengths to camouflage myself against airborne surveillance. Everything at the camp would be dismantled and carefully hidden in the undergrowth. My tarp, backpack and cooking equipment were all strategically stashed, and whenever the chopper came anywhere near I'd dive beneath the bushes too.

For some reason, the coppers tended to concentrate their efforts down in the canyon rather than up on top of the mountain where I was up to no good. Sometimes they'd buzz the cliff top, and every now and then they'd get so close that I could clearly see the people inside from my little hidey-hole in the scrub.

My luck held for years and my crop was never discovered, unlike Pablo Escobar. In truth, cultivating marijuana in the forest was a comparatively carefree exercise and I have to say mine was a well-tended crop. The TV gardeners would have been impressed.

In the beginning I used the offal from whatever animal I'd killed as fertiliser, particularly the land mullet. Later, after I went vegetarian, I sourced guts and fish heads from shops in Brunswick Heads and Byron Bay. I even once traded a couple of ounces of mull with Heather in return for some big bags of Dynamic Lifter. After a couple of seasons I had the growing of dope down to a fine art and I became quite attached to it. One year, when the forest was particularly parched through drought, the creek dried up and I had to carry water in a plastic shopping bag from a water hole thirty metres downstream. I did whatever it took to look after my plants.

During my expeditions across the mountain I discovered there was a good reason why the police conducted aerial patrols. I was hardly the Robinson Crusoe of local drug growers in that neck of the woods. My policy, whenever I found someone else's plantation, was to strip one plant of all its foliage, leaving a bare stem and all the other plants untouched. That way the growers knew that their crop had been found, but it wasn't under threat from raiders or the police. It was more like a reassuring wink: 'Oi, I know you're here but there's nothing to worry about.' The last thing I wanted in the forest was other growers hunting down thieves. Besides, I knew how I would have felt if someone had robbed me. I even felt retrospectively guilty about the plants I ripped off in Bowen with Danny Doyle.

*

I had my pot sorted, but there was still one quandary I had in the forest: how to get access to alcohol. For as long as I'd been homeless I had been a chronic alcoholic. While most people use alcohol for recreation or social occasions, I used to drink with one primary aim in mind – to kill the pain. But there was no way I could carry, or even pay for, enough booze to keep the wolves from my mind. It was OK to go to town on a bender every now and then, but the cost of staying drunk was pretty high. With no other options, I'd bring a couple of 'silver pillows' of cheap cask wine and sometimes a bottle of mead or – very, very occasionally, bourbon – back to camp with me. These would last a few days or maybe a week if I was very sparing. It just wasn't good enough really. The cheap production of booze was inevitable.

I concluded that I needed to make my own grog during one miserable night of forced abstinence by the fire. Although I knew how to spoil Dad's home-brew, I had no idea how to conjure alcohol. Before long I was standing in the hardware store in Mullumbimby asking the bloke behind the counter for a few tips. Given that I wasn't going to be hanging in my shed after work lovingly crafting home-brew in funky brown bottles, I'd have to go basic. They call it the open brewing process.

I bought a large green plastic garbage bin to use for the wort, a thermometer, a clean sheet from Vinnies, a DIY Coopers Brew Kit and some sugar, and lugged it all back to the forest with amber bubbles in my eyes. Sterility is of the highest importance when brewing beer, which was going to pose a few problems for Mr Troglodyte. I had to rely on creek water to clean everything and also for making the brew itself.

I collected what I estimated to be twenty litres from the creek and separately mixed the contents of the home-brew kit with sugar and two litres of water boiled over the fire. I blended it all in the wort and stirred it with a big stick. The temperature had to be twenty-five degrees Celsius, which is where the thermometer came in. Once satisfied, I covered the wort with the sheet, which I washed in the creek every day, and left the contraption to do its thing.

Three or four days later I dipped an enamel cup into the garbage bin, scooped out some 'beer' and downed it. 'Bleargh!' It was wicked stuff and I nearly vomited it straight back up. The desire to kill the pain, however, trumped any issues of taste and self-preservation. And kill the pain it did – the familiar woozy warmth and light-headedness welled up inside me and the following mouthfuls went down a little easier. I wasn't going to win any awards for flavour but I'd successfully turned my little creek into a river of alcohol.

From that moment on I spent the vast majority of my time in the forest either drunk or stoned – usually both. Depending on the time of year, a brew could last me up to two weeks, but by that time it was pretty terrible stuff and I really had to force it down. Sometimes I'd fill my canteen with green beer and take it on adventures with me, but I'd get so smashed on the stuff that I'd have to lie down in the undergrowth and sleep it off before I could lurch back to the safety of camp.

Whenever I lifted the sheet off the wort I peeled the lid off my inner turmoil. Drinking on one's own can intensify shame and self-loathing, and that's precisely the downward spiral I entered. I'd get very drunk, very stoned and very depressed. I was constantly battling gastro problems in the forest, too, and I imagine my creek-infused ale was the main cause. I'd get terrible stomach cramps and diarrhoea that lasted months – years – but staying drunk took priority. Nausea and depression be damned.

During the fateful dry season when the creek slowed to a slimy trickle I was forced to brew beer with stagnant water fetched from the water holes upstream near the dope. It certainly wasn't the best vintage but I still drank it and paid a heavy price with an excruciating bout of gastro-enteritis. It's hard to believe that I actually acquired a taste for the stuff and looked forward to the evil flavour. It just goes to show you how far off track a life can go.

Being drunk was only half of my pain-management program. The other key ingredient was dope. The thing with pot is that you can eat it fresh off the plant all day long and never get stoned. Tetrahydrocannabinol (THC) is only soluble, and thus absorbable in the human body, in fats or alcohol. That's why people make dope cookies and cakes – the THC is activated in melted butter during the cooking process. The alcohol method is much more involved but just as effective in making hash oil and cannabis extracts.

I didn't have the wherewithal to do either of those things, so I figured I'd cut corners and use my own stomach as a THC processing vat. I'd drink green beer for breakfast and wolf down a handful of buds from the crop. It worked like a charm. The dope would dissolve into the alcohol in my gut and leave me deeply stoned. Soon, green beer and green buds became the basis of my daily diet. And I smoked it during the day as well.

I wasn't always completely smashed out of my head. It was all about finding that sweet spot. There was no consistency or rhythm in how I approached each day – it was quite whimsical really. I could wake up and think, 'It's a really beautiful morning, I'm going to try not to get too wasted today. I'm going to get a great supply of firewood instead.' I might go down to the orchard to see if there was any nice fruit down there, or some eggs, or I'd start collecting the night's bedding.

These tasks could account for a couple of hours. I'd be drinking and eating and smoking pot all day, but at the back of my mind I'd be trying to keep the pain deadened while keeping the brakes on. It was a fine line and sometimes I sprawled right across it. That used to scare me. I was well aware that I lived near the edge of a 400-foot cliff and I was a long, long way from help.

I was always more likely to get right out of my skull when I was in town. If I fell over there it would only be into the gutter or onto the sand. Then again cops lurked in the towns, and apparently they were out to get me.

22

MAKING A WILL

If I was feeling pretty strong, which was rare, I could walk from camp to Mullumbimby in sixteen to eighteen hours. Not that I really counted it out. I realised that I only developed measurements for things I valued so I had no real concept of time. Sometimes I'd go into a pub and say, 'Are we still in 1994? Oh yeah? What month? What day is it?' It was only by going to town that I came to understand how much of a time warp I was living in out in the forest.

The lure of town was generally threefold: I'd need supplies, I'd want to go on a bender and I'd be hungry. Sometimes I'd wake up in the forest absolutely starving (not peckish), so I'd start off towards Mullumbimby dreaming of the garbage bins I knew were waiting behind the pub, the cafes and the bakery. I could usually find a feed in one of those. The only other option for free food was the soup kitchen that sometimes operated in Mullumbimby. I only went there once because they'd expect you to sit there and listen to them preach on the Bible in return for the food. No thanks, I'd rather scavenge.

Although I'd lost my grip on the passing of days I had gained an incredibly heightened sense of smell out there in the time warp. I even had a special bench in the middle of Mullumbimby I called the 'smelling chair'. I'd sit there with my eyes closed and inhale the scent of the people passing by. It was amazing to me that I could smell individuals within the crowds. I could tell the difference between female and male; between blokes who washed and blokes who didn't. I could smell people who ate garlic the night before; frankincense, musk, different soaps, different colognes and perfumes; even the items people were carrying.

After a while there were three or four people I could identify purely by their odour. My favourite was a particularly fragrant female whose perfume I loved. Since I kept my eyes closed I have no idea what she looked like, but in my mind I conjured up a tall, long-haired brunette with soft skin. She had sharp facial features and was very Celtic looking. I tilted my head backwards whenever she walked by. Mmmm.

There was a flipside, though: some blokes stank so badly it just about made me gag. Ironically, I knew I reeked as well but I couldn't really smell me; it was the lived-in scent. Fortunately, Mullumbimby's sizeable alternative population tended to leave me alone. A wild-looking man with a jet-black beard, beads in his hair and a homemade solar system on his head didn't look out of place sniffing the air among the street dancers, fire-twirling and the hoopla.

My parents on their wedding day in 1954. After the girls and I came along there was hardly a whiff of friendship in the air, let alone romance.

From left to right: Twins Lynette and Louise, Glenda and me. We may have presented well to the outside world, but underneath our outfits we were often black and blue.

We six children were all sardined into a narrow two-bedroom house that my grandfather owned in North Tamworth. Here, I'm protectively holding my baby sister, Roma, and behind me from left to right are my sisters, Wendy, Glenda, Louise and Lynette.

St Patrick's Orphanage, Armidale, where I was sent when I turned ten. I thought I was going to visit my Aunty Muriel.

My father (*left*) with Tom and Eileen Winters and their daughter, Gwenny. They briefly fostered me, but made it clear that the arrangement was a burden on them. There was no warmth.

As an adult I retreated into the forest and started to do some 'work' on myself. I stuck coloured pins in this hat, representing planets. It was my way of reminding myself that I wasn't the centre of the universe.

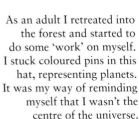

My former campsite as it is today. Here, you can see my little workbench-cum-table made out of rocks, which lies undisturbed, save for the dead tree that has fallen across it.

Standing at the edge of the waterfall where, twenty-eight years earlier, I felt a relief and calmness settle for the first time in my life.

The forest was in drought when I visited it in late 2016, but this water hole is indicative of the stagnant slosh I brewed my creek beer with one season. No wonder I got so sick.

The views north-west up the canyon from the campsite.

Receiving my PhD from Nick Burton Taylor, the Chancellor of Southern Cross University, in 2016.

As I had never celebrated my birthday before, Leanne's mother, Bev, organised a surprise dinner to celebrate the many birthdays I had missed out on. *From left to right*: Dr Sandy Darab (who took me under her wing at university), Leanne Maynard (the amazing woman who stood by me even at my very worst), me and Dr Yvonne Hartman (who also guided and mentored me at university). What a night!

My beautiful daughter, Katie. Nothing could have prepared me for the feelings that welled up and exploded in a supernova of gratitude and wonder the day she was born.

Leanne Maynard, who went through the highs and lows of my gaining an education.

Simple friendships. My two dogs Cherie and Yashi have taught me so much.

At night-time I'd go to the Chincogan pub and get slaughtered before crawling back to my park bench up the road. Other times I'd get a nice cup of coffee and a croissant, or a spinach and fetta pasty, and go and sit quietly by myself. I never had enough money to buy food after a night on the drink – I had a knack of always having the perfect amount of cash with me at the pub. If I arrived with $50, I'd spend exactly $50. If I arrived with $500, I'd spend precisely $500. Uncanny, that.

If I went to the markets I might vaguely bump into people I 'knew' – hippies who'd moved there for the lifestyle, drifters, some locals. My version of getting to know someone wasn't very intimate, it just meant I noticed something about them: maybe a red tie in the hair, a scar, a shaved head, a tattoo or some other feature. If I saw the red hair tie again I'd think, 'Oh yeah, I know you.' The only time I'd hang around for a chat was on the odd occasion I'd run into Heather in town. Even then I'd keep it brief.

I discovered after a while that I liked watching people as much as I did smelling them. I'd make trips to town especially to do it. I wouldn't have any creek beer that day and instead would take some pot and a bottle of water, and go and sit at the markets or on a bench and simply watch what people did. I was a bit like Sir David Attenborough observing the hippy wildlife. 'The female adorns her head with flowers while the male tries to attract her attention by doing a special dance.'

I'd study the way people talked to each other, the actions they used, the way they mingled and had fun. 'How do they manage that?' I'd puzzle. 'How do they have fun?

What is fun exactly? Why am I so alone?' But I knew the answer. To me 'fun' was sitting in the sun with my eyes closed smelling strangers. Hardly a communal activity. Hardly that much fun.

Nobody knew my real name, which was a good thing because I hated it. I hated Peel, I hated Smith and I especially hated 'Smithy', because that's what Dad used to get called and I hated him. Although I quite liked Gregory, people inevitably shortened it to 'Greg', which I also hated and still do. I'd tolerated 'Beardy', but it had been a long time since anyone had called me that, so, on the forest fringe and in the towns, whenever anyone asked my name I'd tell them it was Will.

I'd taken on my alias years earlier during a stint sleeping rough in Sydney. After I'd recuperated from my disagreement with the Branxton Railway Bridge, I drifted back to Kings Cross and into the abyss of drink and homelessness. At the time I was living in a park underneath the railway overpass at Woolloomooloo, but I'd still go to Matthew Talbot's for a bit of food and shelter now and then. One freezing Sunday morning I hit Talbot's for a cup of tea and a bit of breakfast. I was sitting around feeling sorry for myself when some reasonably well dressed people started to arrive. It was an Alcoholics Anonymous meeting.

A big, slow-moving guy lumbered around handing out cigarettes from a carton tucked under his arm. When he finally got to me I reached out and snatched a greedy handful. He just smiled and said, 'Have some more.' So I did, but I'd sussed out that they probably wanted me to stick around in exchange for the smokes. 'OK then,' I thought. 'I'll stay and listen.'

When the anonymous alcoholics started talking, they came out with the scariest things I had ever heard. They went on about unfounded fears, about things that happened inside their minds, about self-loathing, child-hood trauma, emotional pain, guilt, shame and internal wounds. I started looking desperately at the door. Then someone stood up and held forth about 'will power' and how the power of the will doesn't work for alcoholics. 'Yes it does!' I thought, defiantly. 'I've got plenty of will power! And it works!' I made a resolution then and there that I would never be like that bunch of losers. I would go my own way with my will power and I would be OK. So, off I went to fight my battles and I lost them all.

But I kept the name William H. Power.

Will Power.

The H is for 'Higher'.

Up in the Byron Bay Shire, Will was the crazy wild man with the excellent pot. Sometimes, if I was too tired to walk to Mullumbimby or Byron Bay I'd range southwards to the tiny Hamlet of Federal. I liked getting a couple of long-necks of Coopers Pale Ale from the general store. It was the real stuff, not my creek water Coopers – this was a beer with flavour! Luxury! I'd offload a bit of pot in Federal to finance the gourmet beverages, and buy some tobacco. The next trip might be to Byron Bay.

You can't just stride into the main street of Byron and start selling dope, but there are ways to do it. The old piggery-cum-backpackers camping ground came in handy because it was full of little burrows and hiding places. It was also full of young hippies and travellers – a good place to show up with a bit of green for trade and sale.

I never wanted people to know I was arriving in town so I'd usually walk out of the forest at night. I trusted no one, but I'd established a couple of relationships. Sometimes they'd buy a bit of pot, other times they'd trade. Putting aside the risk and the paranoia that went with it, it was a relatively easy way to provide myself with some basic comforts and sustenance. I'd sit at a table at the Rails or in the park next door, and if one of the contacts I'd made wandered by I might say, 'Look, I've got a bit of mull, what've you got?'

'I can get rid of that for you,' they might reply. 'What do you want for yourself?'

'A couple of bottles of bourbon, some tea, milk and bread. How about you pay me at the backpackers?' I'd sometimes book in there so I could grab a (very rare) shower. They knew me there – I always signed in as William H. Power.

23

BUSH SPORTS

I was in control in the forest. It was my space, nobody knew it like I did and nobody could ever kick me out. Even if they'd wanted to, they would have to find me first. Plenty of people knew I was living somewhere in the Goonengerry mountains, but no one had any idea exactly where. I know this because they used to come looking for me. I'd always hear them – or smell them – long before they stumbled anywhere near my camp.

Very early on I'd worked out that the key to staying hidden in the bush came down to how well I could control my fire. Smoke was the anathema of secrecy so selecting the right wood to burn at the right time of day was crucial. Dead, hard, very dry wood was the best – essentially a smokeless fuel. Although it burned OK, wet or greenish wood sent up cumulus puffs of white smoke. You might as well drop a pin marker on Google Maps.

On misty or rainy days I could get away with burning a bit of greener fuel because the smoke would melt into the rainforest's natural fog. Keeping a fire going in the rain wasn't that hard, just a matter of leaning a big log over the top of it and stoking the flames underneath. The only other time I'd risk a smoky fire was after dark when it didn't matter. It had the added benefit of keeping the swarming mosquitoes at bay. Besides, I figured anyone who was in the forest at night was there for nefarious purposes and the last thing they wanted was to run into me.

In the event that someone did happen upon my camp, I had a series of secret escape trails. I was at peace with the idea of having to walk away. I was prepared in my mind to just pick up my dillybag and go. That was real freedom, I thought. I called it my Moscow Strategy, in honour of the slash and burn tactic used against Napoleon's army in the defence of Moscow. Until such time I was free to stay and set fire to as much wood as I pleased.

Smoke – but not the campfire variety – was often the first sign that people were looking for me, or at least roaming close. Eau de ciggie carries a long way in the bush and my half-man, half-marsupial nose would twitch at the first distinctive hint of Winfield or Benson & Hedges, even before I heard any voices or blundering footfalls on the forest floor.

I strongly suspect these intrepid explorers were fringe dwellers. They'd have seen me walking along Mill Road towards the main trail; or they'd have eyeballed me in Mullumbimby or Byron Bay, or seen me trudging along on the outskirts of town. It wouldn't have been too hard to make the association. Nine times out of ten it would be a couple of young guys who'd chance their hands and attempt to find the Bearded Bunyip.

I didn't mind at all. In fact, I quite enjoyed it because it gave me something to do. I liked to play games with them, only they didn't realise they were playing. There were a lot of trails in the forest. Some were wide and some narrower, other tracks were barely perceptible and some – the ones that I made – well, you couldn't see them at all. The trick to covering your tracks, I had worked out, was to never walk in a straight line. If I wanted to make a pathway from the creek to my camp, for example, I would never just plough straight into the bush at a right angle to the creek. Such a clumsy approach would be obvious and visible straight away.

Instead, I'd make an oblique path at a thirty-degree angle to the creek. But after five metres or so I'd stop and head back in the opposite direction, still at a thirty-degree angle of progress, for another five metres. Then back and forth and so on until I ended up with a zigzagging track that was completely invisible from the creek. You could be standing right in front of it and never see it. Or I could be hiding in there watching you and you'd never know it.

I could arrange the forest like a human chess board, and my favourite game was designed to mess with the heads of the little pawns who'd come in search of the king. Not unlike the rest of the country, it was a sport played mainly on weekends.

Though I generally never knew what day it was at any given time, I could pick out Saturdays and Sundays or holidays because that's when more people tended to come into the forest. For the most part the mountaintop was tranquil, but on weekends, depending on the time of year, it could get a bit louder. Chainsaws, motorbikes, 4WDs, voices. All the noises that rubbed me up the wrong way.

I'd prepare for their arrival by making big, obvious trails designed to send them away from the vicinity of my camp. On the opposite bank of the creek I'd stomp out obvious tracks that led uphill and deeper into the forest. Once I'd gone, say, twenty metres, I'd stop dead and carefully walk back out. The result was a phantom trail that plunged meaningfully into the heart of the forest and then abruptly stopped dead for no apparent reason.

Whenever people walked down the creek towards my territory, I'd have already put my fire out as a precaution. I'd have heard them coming a mile off – or smelled their ciggies. They'd usually look around a bit, marvel at the view from the top of the waterfall and inevitably spot one of my bogus tracks on the northern side of the creek. I'd sit in a hidey-hole on my side and watch them disappear into the bush. After a while I'd see them stop, bewildered that the trail just ended. Sometimes they'd look straight up at the rainforest canopy. I don't know if they were expecting to see a spaceship or a drop bear but I found it tremendously amusing.

Sometimes, if I was feeling particularly fiendish, I'd whip up a set of baby tracks for the weekend warriors to puzzle over. These were easy to construct and they really screwed with people's minds. I'd make a fist and gently press it into the sand of the creek bank, leaving what looked like the curl of a human foot, only tiny. Using a finger I'd smudge little toe prints near the top and, with alternate hands,

I'd make a trail of little footprints along the length of the creek. Voila! Human baby tracks in the middle of nowhere! Freaky stuff.

It's not surprising, then, that I became the subject of wild rumours and local legend. Not that everyone was fearful of me. One day, after about four or five years, I found a note under a stone near the entrance of the main trail. It was written in pen on a single sheet of lined paper torn from a spiral notebook, and it was addressed to me:

To the Man in the Forest,
I have some accommodation on my property.
You'd be welcome to stay in it for free if you'd like.
It's the first gate on the left as you go down the road.
Please consider it and let me know if you'd be interested.

It gave directions and the address of the property on Mill Road. I knew exactly which one it was. The owner was a guy they called The Professor. He was a university lecturer, but he also had greenhouses in which he grew plants: palms, flowers and all manner of amazing flora.

He lived on a breathtakingly beautiful piece of land – a couple of hundred north-facing acres draped across the eastern side of the mountain. Unbeknown to The Professor, I went on a clandestine property inspection one day while he was at work. In one field, away from the main homestead, I found a roomy caravan with a large glass annexe built on the front of it. I assumed this was what he had in mind for me, and I have to admit it was pretty tempting. I visualised myself sitting in the sun with a joint, gazing all the way out over Brunswick Heads and Byron Bay. You could even see the lighthouse. Quite a domain.

The note had said to consider the offer, so I did. I thought about it for a good six months before I finally decided I'd pass. In the end I realised I didn't want to be obligated to anyone for anything ever, and it was just as well. About a year down the track I learned the reason The Professor had wanted me on his property. A myth had grown about a creepy man who lived in the forest and The Professor had figured if I was living on his land no one would go near it. Apparently he'd been losing plants and other property to thieves and he thought I might make a good guard dog. Thanks, but no thanks.

Perhaps this added to my mystique. The more they couldn't find me, the more people wanted to know who I was. This put me at an advantage, and I was quite happy to feed my own mythology. As with Byron Bay, whenever I went into Mullumbimby I'd usually walk there during the night and already be in town when people started moving about in the morning.

While it gave my reputation an edge, this nocturnal navigation also sharpened my sense of touch beyond anything I thought possible. The tactile sense was the only one I could confirm and trust implicitly in the dark. After a while I found that I could walk through the forest at night with my eyes closed without breaking a spider web – just by feeling my way. I could sense the nanosecond a web brushed against my face and I'd stop, adjust course and keep moving. Whenever people asked me how I was feeling I'd reply, 'With my hands.'

In all those years I never ran into another person in the forest at night. Probably a good thing; I might have scared them to death.

Yet the irony of people being afraid of me was almost comical: after all, I was frightened of them. If an amateur weekend search party *had* managed to find me up there, and maybe turned the tables and watched me through the bushes, perhaps their fears would have been replaced by pity. I was totally alone and my day-to-day life was pathetic. If I wasn't drinking green poison out of a garbage bin for breakfast or eating fistfuls of dope, I was scrounging up firewood and ferns to sleep on, or scraping together meagre rations to eat with my filthy fingers. I'd sit for hours and stare into the canyon while I contemplated the tattered story of my life. The drunker and higher I got, the more I gibbered and mumbled to myself. Not so scary after all, just sad.

In the beginning I occupied myself by setting tasks to pass the time, even if they seemed impossible. For a long time my only tool in the forest was my pocket knife. It had a lovely stainless-steel blade, maybe seven or eight centimetres long, which folded out of the handle. I discovered I could move a two-tonne fallen tree using that knife. I just had to think like an Egyptian.

I read somewhere that the ancient Egyptians had built the pyramids using pretty simple rules of physics and engineering. I didn't have any giant stone edifices to move but there was a massive log near Rome that I'd started to obsess over. It was at the bottom of a long, steep section of the main trail and I became fixated on getting it to the top, simply so I could roll it all the way back down again. The problem was that it was huge – about three metres long and as high as my waist.

Slowly, my inner-Ramses came to the fore. I used the knife to sharpen some smaller branches in order to jam them in under the fallen tree. Using these as levers, I was able to shift one end of the log a little, then wedge in a rock to hold it in place while I went and moved the other end with another stick. Up the hill it went – wedge by wedge, inch by inch. Three days later I stood triumphant at the summit with one foot on the fallen tree like a wrestler standing over a hapless foe. With a thrust of my boot I sent it thudding down the hill, kicking up leaves and clumps of dirt from the trail before it careened off into the bush with a satisfying crunch.

With no TV or even a radio, little projects like this occupied my head and distracted me from my myriad problems. After a few years I guessed it would be worthwhile trying to keep track of time. Rather than buy a watch I looked around the forest. I soon found what I was looking for: a very straight stick of uniform width around fifty centimetres long. I sharpened one end and shoved it into the dirt at one side of my campsite, supporting it with rocks at the base so it wouldn't budge a millimetre.

Although it started as an attempt to make a sun dial, the stick took off on other journeys in my mind. I would watch it every day, and before long was marking the ground around it with little sticks and rocks of different shape and colour. I had rocks to chart the sunset and sunrise, others to mark the zenith of the sun on particular days. Other rocks and sticks related to the moon cycle. I started to plot the solstices and the equinoxes, the changing of the seasons, and I'd mark them out with little stones, too. It ended up being more of a universe dial than a sun dial.

I left that stick in the ground for years. It gave me something to think about, and I didn't have to put a lot of energy into it. All I had to do was stare at it, which became a ritual. But I also became fascinated with the piece of wood itself. If you leave a stick in the ground and watch it for long enough, you'll see it as a tiny pin upon which the entire planet spins.

I played other games, too, with my candles. I constructed little moulds in the dirt and attempted to make different shapes – little animals and the like – by dripping wax into them. Sometimes I'd spend hours simply picking up dirt and separating out the silica. After a few hours I'd end up with just a handful of the sparkling mineral, like Blackbeard of the bush with his treasure. And I would explore. I roamed all over the forest and I knew all of its secrets and riddles.

There was one place, however, that was strictly off limits. Although I often toyed with the idea, I never climbed right down to the bottom of the waterfall into the valley below. I was extremely wary of the cliff top, particularly given how wobbly I'd get on dope and my creek juice. Sometimes I'd clamber down a little way to see how far I could comfortably go, but mostly I treated the cliff with respect. I didn't realise it until later but this showed me that I didn't really want to die.

I also had the fire for entertainment. A good campfire beats a flat-screen TV hands down – even watching

Inspector Gadget on Tryptanol and cones. After a while the fire became more to me than just a bush television and means of cooking and keeping warm – it ended up at the centre of my spirituality. The most incredible things started to happen around my campfire. Amazing conferences and gatherings that would eventually save my life.

24

MAGICIANSHIP

There were a few people around Mullumbimby whose brains had been short-circuited by magic mushrooms. One guy in particular was hard to ignore. He had eyes like dinner plates and if he wasn't gibbering to imaginary mates he'd be performing some bizarre dance routine in the middle of the main street. He used to terrify me, not because he posed any kind of threat but because he made me wonder how long it would be before I joined him.

One of the convenient things about 'shrooms, gold tops or whatever you want to call them, is that they're 100 per cent free. Just like ye olde faithful marijuana, they literally sprout up out of the ground. Even so, finding them can be a bit hit and miss. When the season and the conditions were right, I'd hike into the paddocks and fields that skirted the mountain to try my luck. Sometimes I'd come back empty-handed, other times I'd have enough hallucinogenic fungus to stage a remake of Woodstock. Back at camp I'd make a big brew of soup using fresh mushrooms, and spread out the remainder on the lava rock to dry in the sun before wrapping them in strips of the *Echo* to keep for a rainy day.

The 'magic' in magic mushrooms is a psychedelic compound called psilocybin. It can rearrange your brain chemistry in the most spectacular way. Tripping on mushrooms can also be quite unnerving, and even though I knew that people sometimes didn't come back from a trip (like Old Mate in Mullumbimby) I bloody loved it. Tripping is an eye-opener at the best of times. Hallucinating when you live in a rainforest is something else again.

By the time I started munching magic mushrooms I'd been in the forest long enough to know that there wasn't too much in there that could hurt me. I was the apex predator, which meant my mind was at ease when it came to the scarier realms of paranoia. This made it easier to cope once the mushrooms kicked in and I started seeing amazing critters out of the corner of my eye.

I was convinced otherworldly things were following me; exotically strange little creatures that would hide behind trees or dart into the ferns as soon as I caught sight of them. Intrigued, I'd double back to look for them all over the forest. I'd try to trap them but they always managed to slip away just as I got close enough. Finding these bizarre animals became an obsession. I'd have a nice big breakfast of hot mushie soup and head off determinedly along the trails in the hope of a close encounter. I'd spend hour upon hour quietly creeping through the palms and the undergrowth in an attempt to take them by surprise.

When the mushies started to wear off I'd realise what was happening. 'I hallucinated them!' I'd laugh out loud, and shake my head at what a silly sausage I'd been. 'That was really good! Ha-hah! Can't wait till the next time I'm on mushies!' Had anyone observed me during one of these screwy missions to find the fugazi fauna in my head, they'd have thought I was insane. Maybe I was, just a tad.

I used to love tripping at night, too. Especially under a full moon. I'd get suitably ripped on magic soup and walk for miles and miles through my enchanted woods. From high up on the eastern ridge of the mountain I could see the lights of hinterland towns spread out towards the coast like diamonds scattered on a black sheet.

I'd become a student of the lunar cycle and knew when the moon would appear at its biggest and brightest. One time, when a monster moon was due, I decided to have a bowl of mushie soup and make a night of it. As the psilo-cybin went to work on my synapses, I set off from camp using a stout eucalypt branch for a walking stick. I must have been a sight with my wild hair, massive beard, hat with the coloured pins and wizardly-looking walking staff, stalking the trail like a drug-fried Gandalf.

A year or so earlier I'd discovered a little spot on a fence near The Professor's property on Mill Road, where at night, if I swept my gaze from north to east, I could see everything from the twinkling lights of Tweed Heads up near the Queensland border to Ballina and every town in between: Ewingsdale, Brunswick Heads, Byron Bay, Mullumbimby. 'My kingdom,' I'd muse as I looked out over the inky landscape. 'Sleep, my subjects. Sleep.'

I figured this would be the perfect spot to watch the

moonrise while tripping. I climbed to the top of a massive fence post for maximum vantage and waited for the moon to appear over the Pacific. I was excited and mightily stoned. 'This,' I assured myself, 'will be awesome.' Soon a glint of white light spilled over the horizon and lit up a shimmering shard on the black skin of the ocean. 'Awww!' I was really starting to trip hard. The moonrise had become the most intense interplanetary spectacle in the history of the universe. 'Wowww!'

Without warning, global catastrophe struck. The moon started sinking back below the horizon. 'Argh! Oh no! I've upset it. Please don't go down. Please come back, moon! It's OK. I'm sorry!'

I was shattered. Everybody down there in the towns was going to know it was me who'd broken the moon. Everyone on earth would know I wasn't a good person – that the moon went down because it just wanted to get away from me. My intense high of a few moments earlier had twisted into a devastating low. And then things got worse. A teeming plague of tiny mice crawled up my legs and spread out all over my body. They bit me everywhere. 'Oh no! The people are punishing me already! They've sent mice to attack me! Argh!'

I started swatting them off me. I must have looked a sight; like a drug-fried Gandalf losing the plot.

In the next breath I was flooded with relief as the moon started to rise again. 'Oh, thank the spirits for that,' I gasped. 'Whoophh. It's OK. It's gonna be OK.' Except I could still feel the evil miniature mice nipping my body. They were biting harder, too. With the moon back in the sky I looked closer and saw I was in fact covered in hundreds of big ants. I'd been standing on top of a huge nest the whole time.

I leapt down and brushed the ants off me, and when I looked back to the east I noticed a bank of clouds out towards the horizon. I realised that the moon hadn't gone down after all, it had just slipped behind the clouds for a minute or two and the magic mushrooms had done the rest.

Fortunately, I never made a return to a psych ward, nor did I wind up singing songs to myself in the middle of the traffic, but magic mushrooms definitely had an impact on my brain function for quite a long time. I'd be in the middle of a sentence, for example, when I'd just seize up mid-syllable, completely unable to speak or move. Or I'd be about to put some food in my mouth and I'd suddenly freeze like a statue. I could be stuck fast in these moments for what seemed an eternity, but eventually, like the Tin Man after a few squirts of oil in *The Wizard of Oz*, I'd loosen up again.

The next time I'd be in town and I'd see someone whose mind was in permanent disarray I'd wonder why I kept rolling the chemical dice. My own insanity lurked just around the corner.

25

THE BIG SMOKE

Despite the continued debauchery, by the mid-1990s I felt I'd gained some semblance of control over my life. Although it was little more than a collection of rocks and branches, my camp had become my single most enduring address since childhood. I had a cash crop for income, I was producing my own alcohol, I was secure and my perimeters were set. I understood tracking and I knew where people were and how to avoid them. I was also more and more confident about going on my little adventures into the towns to offload pot, which in turn gave me enough money to go on benders and keep living in the forest.

By then I'd become pretty good at cultivating dope up on the mountain, but success posed a problem for me: I could never hope to store the yield of a crop (usually close to a pound) at the camp without it being destroyed by mould. Consequently, whatever I grew I needed to dispose of reasonably quickly. Selling a pound's worth in Byron Bay would be a fast track to arrest and gaol. So, I figured I'd take the bulk of it into a city where I could flog it in one go and undertake some serious partying in the process. Brisbane was a hell of a lot closer, only 150 kilometres away, but I chose Sydney, mainly because I had this romantic idea that I could reconnect with Meredith. Seeing her would be worth the extra 630 kilometres.

Once the crop was dried I packed it into green garbage bags and wrapped the lot up in a blanket I'd bought from Vinnies in Mullumbimby. I stuffed this into my green army haversack along with some spare clothes, and hit the road. I walked for about six hours before I scored a lift with a fringe dweller all the way to Uncle Tom's roadhouse on the Pacific Highway, the mighty bitumen river that flows all the way down the coast to Sin City.

I decided to sleep on the roadside and start hitching south in the morning. In all my years thumbing rides, it's worth noting I was never picked up by a beautiful blonde or a mum taking the kids to soccer. It was mostly truck drivers. I saw a lot of Australia from the passenger seat of interstate semitrailers. If it wasn't a trucker it would be a tough old bloke or a really cool, tolerant person. Years earlier I scored a lift with a guy at Telegraph Point and we hit it off so much I went back to his place and spent two weeks mulling up and drinking on.

My first lift the next day wasn't that extreme, but he was a pretty good guy. He drove me all the way to Port Macquarie, nearly 400 kilometres. I told him about my life in the forest and he was fascinated. So was I – it was the first time I'd confided in anyone about my secret life as a hermit. It felt sort of good to let it all out to a random stranger.

I asked him if he smoked pot. 'Sure do,' he said, so we stopped a couple of times along the way for a sneaky joint. We said our farewells at Port Macquarie, his destination, but not before he bought fifty dollars worth of the mull, which gave me some running money. I was tired so I looked for somewhere to sleep for the night. I ended up crawling underneath an old church just off the highway. I started out early again the next morning and scored a ride further south to Maitland.

At the end of the second day, I arrived in Sydney and booked into the Astoria guesthouse in Darlinghurst. I'd stayed there once years earlier and knew I could rent a room by the night on the cheap. The Astoria was infamously sleazy and dingy, and the rooms smelled of urine, spilled alcohol and stale cigarettes. On the upside, there were no questions asked. I paid in advance for four nights with the option of extending and went out in search of Meredith.

She no longer lived at the stinky unit in Darlinghurst, and after two days scouring various haunts where I hoped I'd see her strolling the pavement or glimpse her reflection in a street window, I gave up.

I was a little crestfallen but now I also had to find another fence for my crop. I took a sample up to nearby Kings Cross to see what I could do. I'd spent plenty of time in Sydney's infamous red-light district and I knew quite a few of the homeless and dependent types who crammed pitiful lives into its crevices. It wasn't long before I bumped into a guy I knew named Kim. I offered him a smoke and he couldn't have been happier. We had a few joints back at the one-room apartment he shared with his girlfriend, and exchanged notes on life. I felt comfortable enough with Kim to ask him if he knew anybody who wanted to buy a pound of dope.

'Probably. I'll get back to ya.'

I left and returned that evening with another sample. Kim scurried off with it to some place that must have been pretty close because he was back in thirty minutes. He said his contact was interested and wanted to meet. We did so shortly afterwards and the deal was done for $900 within twenty minutes – with an invitation to do the same the next year if I was of a mind.

I gave Kim an ounce for his troubles, put the cash in my pocket, thanked everybody and left. Back at the Astoria I hid the money under the carpet in my room. That night Kim treated me to a couple of lines of speed and we went on an almighty tear through the Emerald City. I ended up at one of my old haunts, the Taxi Club, and when I staggered out I was very, very drunk.

I stayed in Sydney for another week drinking, smoking pot and partying on. By the time I was ready to head back to the forest I had about $600 left. I thought I'd give the interstate truckers a rest and instead treated myself to a train fare north. I grabbed some supplies at Mullumbimby on the way back to camp, and when I walked into the forest I was feeling happy and contented. Sydney had been a great success overall but I was glad to be home. When I harvested my crop the following year I did it again, except I caught the train both ways.

On every one of those nights in Sydney I'd secretly hope to walk around the next corner and straight into Meredith.

I'd imagine what I'd say, how I'd smile at her and show her a good time. But each time I'd leave disappointed. Who knows what becomes of heroin-addicted drug dealers? I really hoped she'd survived. I really hoped I would, too.

26

JESUS CHRIST!

'Come and listen to this! Come and listen. You should hear what he's got to say! Hey, man, it's Jesus! He's back!'

I was sitting in the park next door to the Railway Hotel at Byron Bay delivering a sermon. Or, to be more accurate, I was sitting in the park drinking port, smoking pot and talking philosophy with a bunch of Indigenous people and hippy backpacker types. Apparently I was making quite an impression.

I'd been fumbling about and making a mess of myself up in the forest for five or six weeks when I decided it was time to head down to Byron with an ounce of pot to trade. I made a beeline for my favourite pub, the Rails, and settled down for a good session on the Coopers Sparkling Ale. I had a nice little system going: I'd sink a couple of beers and then duck out into the park, have a few pipes of dope and head back to the bar. On one such pipe run I bumped into a group of people who were just settling in at the park for some storytelling, so I decided to buy a bottle of port and join them in a circle on the grass.

It was just on sunset and there was a nice vibe in the air. Everyone was happy, enjoying the evening as loose threads of blues guitar drifted across from the pub. True to form I didn't start any conversation, I just sat and listened, but after a while the port changed my mood and demeanour. I started chiming in with pearls of wisdom here and there, and with every gulp of the sickly sweet wine I grew steadily more philosophical. I had large things to say about what the others were discussing and I made my own reasonably considered contributions about life, spirituality, politics and everything under the sun.

I pulled out some dope and asked, 'Who'd like to roll the joint?' I dunno, maybe they thought I said it with my palms outstretched and in a deep, messianic voice: 'Who among thee will rolleth the joint?' But I don't think I did. There were a couple of volunteers and I handed it to the woman sitting next to me. She twisted up a couple of spliffs and everybody mellowed even more as the philosophy-inducing herb worked its magic. Drunk, stoned and wrapped up in the moment I really let loose with my penetrating insights on the cosmos. Before I knew it I was the only one doing the talking. Everyone else was either asking me questions or listening to the answers. That's when the pretty young woman on the other side of the circle piped up earnestly, 'Hey, are you Jesus?'

Well, who was I to say? For the time being I decided it was best to play along. After all, she was quite attractive and perhaps there was a chance of a bit of nookie for

Jesus, so while I didn't say I was the Son of God I didn't say I wasn't, either. It was one of those situations where I found myself a few steps ahead of everybody else and I was able to tap right into the heads of those hippies late into the night. I suspect some of them were running with it too and maybe wanted to believe something special. Either way, the response was amazing. 'Where do you get all this knowledge from, man? How do you know all this stuff? You're amazing. This is magic. You *are* Jesus!'

But I guess if I really had been the Second Coming I wouldn't have crashed out face first in the sand outside the public toilets down at the beach like I did later on. The next day I booked into the backpackers for a couple of nights so I could have a shower and get some proper rest. I was much more comfortable being plain old William H. Power than I was being Jesus H. Christ.

While I was only a god for one night, there were plenty of other times I found myself around a fire on the beach with a group of people letting my inner guru out. The dope would flow and people would inevitably start sharing their thoughts on the deep stuff. Metaphysics is big in Byron Bay. Time and time again I'd be the centre of attention, holding the group in my thrall with the added drama of being able to see my mountain from the Byron Bay beach.

'Oh yeah, wow. Tell us another story!' my disciples would plead.

'Nah, the sun is coming up, man. I've gotta go,' I'd respond, gesturing allusively to the north-west. 'I've got to get back up to my mountain.' Then I'd disappear into the wild until the next time I popped up in town.

As much as I liked to fly under the radar, I didn't always manage to keep out of trouble. After all, I was still an unhinged, dangerous and violent alcoholic, and while I might have had my moments of being cool and spiritual, I was just as likely to get in a vicious fight or say something that would frighten the life out of someone. I guess that's why people called me Charles Manson, too, and sometimes I felt I possessed that kind of darkness. I'd walk past punters in the street and think, 'You people don't realise how close to danger you are.' I'd feel my vial of snake blood dangling around my neck. 'You don't know the powers I have. You people have no idea who you're dealing with.'

On occasion I could just be plain offensive. I was tripping on mushrooms one morning when I mooched into the health-food shop at Mullumbimby to pick up some dried fruit and lentils. There was a well-dressed lady being served ahead of me and she seemed to be taking hours. She was asking the shopkeeper all kinds of questions and then placed an order, only to change it. It was probably only a few minutes, but in my drugged-out state it felt like half a day had passed. Finally, I could wait no more. 'Excuse me,' I interjected.

She turned around.

'If you don't hurry up, I'm gonna throw up all over you.' Classy stuff.

While the risks were different from the ones I faced in the forest, I was well aware that danger lurked in the towns, too. If the biggest threat in the forest was getting drunk and falling off the cliff, the biggest threat in town was getting drunk and winding up in the Byron Bay police cells overnight. Fights on their own posed no real danger – that was just disrespect for myself. Being locked up was another thing altogether. I hated it. Because I was a messy and annoying public drunkard a lot of the time, the local copper, Sergeant Bates, would have no choice but to throw me in the clink for my own safety.

One morning, as he rattled the key in the cell door to let me loose on the world once again, he fronted me. 'I know what you're up to. I know where you go and what you do and one day I'm going to catch you.' The way he said it made me think he must have known I lived up in the mountains somewhere. Maybe he knew the coppers at Mullumbimby and maybe they knew I lived up there? Whatever the case, Sergeant Bates never caught me doing anything – certainly not trading in pot – and he was too busy looking after the town to drop tools and go bush in search of me.

Noted, but relatively unchecked by the authorities, I had become a mercurial figure in Byron Bay Shire. I was always the outsider. I was just occasional. You couldn't rely on me. No promises. What you see today is what you get today. I could be different tomorrow. No guarantees. No real relationships.

I did have one mate, though. Binjina was an Aboriginal man from Mossman in Far North Queensland. I met him while sitting in a park in Byron Bay one afternoon and we just hit it off without really talking. For the duration of our time together we never spoke more than a few syllables to each other. The day we met he sauntered up and sat next to me on the grass. I said, 'Where ya going?' Binjina just pointed up towards my mountain. 'OK,' I said. 'Let's go.'

We walked all the way back to the mountain in silence. Binjina lived up in the forest for about three months.

He had his own place where he did his own thing and he never came to my camp. We'd mind our own business but catch up on the main trail every few weeks and walk back down to Byron together to get on the drink. We were strikingly similar people when it came to basic needs.

Binjina took me to a party once with some Indigenous people at Upper Wilsons Creek near Mullumbimby. An elder of the mob took a shine to me and presented me with a didgeridoo. I was so honoured I told him I wouldn't sleep until I could play it. He just smiled and went inside to drink more booze and smoke a joint.

Binjina showed me how to put beeswax on the didgeridoo, make a mouthpiece and seal the leaks and splits in the wood. He explained the principles of the didge and then went in to join the party, too. I sat outside by the fire, obsessively trying to master circular breathing in order to play it properly. In the small hours of the next morning I was still sitting there trying to play it. By that time I had some semblance of circular breathing happening, but I could only play for three to four minutes at best. The next day the elder was impressed and named my didgeridoo 'Short Story', because I could only use it to communicate in tiny snippets. Little did he know that was the story of my life.

Because we had pot, Binjina and I would get invited to a lot of parties in town. We'd sit around in someone's house handing out drugs and getting free booze in return. If it wasn't for the alcohol I wouldn't have gone to parties. I never attended a bash where it was all about playing music – I'd only go if people were sitting around talking. I had a lot of trouble with music. It grated up against me in the most uncomfortable way. The Catholic Church and the Sisters of Mercy had taught me that music was evil and, for whatever reason, I had taken that to heart. There were two notable exceptions – Tchaikovsky's '1812 Overture' and Queen's 'Bohemian Rhapsody'. I loved the enormity of the overture and the way it told of Russia's refusal to be overthrown by Napoleon's raiders 200-odd years earlier. I loved 'Bohemian Rhapsody' because it's one of the most beautiful songs ever written and, as far as I was concerned, it was all about me. Just like the poor boy in Freddie Mercury's imagination, I also sometimes wished I'd never been born at all.

Although thirty years had groaned past since my time at St Patrick's, in a way it might as well have been thirty minutes. The physical bonds were cast off long ago. Hell, I'd been running away ever since. But the mental prison that Sister Winifred and her cohorts had slapped, screamed and shoved me into remained as rigid as ever. I may have been surrounded by immense beauty in the forest, but part of me was still locked under the stairs in Armidale. 'Why did they need to break the spirit of a child so that the spirit of the Lord may enter?' I'd wonder as I downed another cup of poison-beer. I could sit on a log and think about that for days only to decide, 'They didn't break me enough. The Lord never entered me because I'm a terrible sinner. I have lied and cheated and stolen and hurt.'

Binjina drifted out of my life forever before long, and I was completely alone once again. In my head, though, it was getting pretty crowded. Mum and Dad had always spent a lot of time with me by the campfire. Oh, how I hated them and delighted in telling them so. While they came in for special attention it seemed there was a cast of thousands living with me: Aubrey, kids at school, the priests, all the wardens, nuns, shrinks, doctors, cops and my ancestors. The forest could sometimes fall deathly silent, especially at night, but the commotion between my ears never stopped.

And then there were those who were absent: my daughter and my sisters. Six little girls who I never got a chance to know. My sisters had an inkling I was living in the Northern Rivers somewhere, and when our mother had died way back in 1992 they'd asked the police to see if they could find me. No one ever did, so Sergeant Bates and the rest of them clearly never had a clue where I was, or even who I was.

That was about to change.

27

BEING ME

Around 1997–98 William H. Power started to run really low on will and power. I was coming apart at the seams both physically and mentally. My diet, if you could call it that, had led to alarming weight loss. I was emaciated, exhausted and becoming stooped over. Years of malnutrition and the middle finger I'd given to my general health had had a karmic consequence: my teeth rotted away in my skull. Whenever I'd feel a molar grow loose, I'd reach in with thumb and forefinger and pluck it out, roots and all. I was down to my last three – my other teeth were scattered like stones across the top of the mountain.

Even by my own low standards I was in steep decline. I'd stopped exploring the forest and it had been a long time since I'd done anything fun like leaving trails of baby footprints around or lying on my back in the creek. Heather had long gone, having fallen in love with a great man and moved away to have some babies. At least, that's what I liked to think.

Most of my time was spent slumped around the campsite drunk and stoned or recovering from the latest inebriation. I'd often lie all day on the rotting foliage I used to call a bed, only getting up late in the afternoon to force myself to go and get some firewood. The first thing I'd do before I dragged myself off the ferns was have a couple of pipes. The second was drink some putrid booze.

I was forced to make the occasional trip into Mullumbimby for supplies and I never passed up the opportunity to get on the drink in town. I was sitting in the pub one afternoon ordering a few of my latest tipple ('Bourbon and bourbon, thanks, no ice') when I felt the need to step outside for a joint. I shuffled around the corner to what I thought was a reasonably out-of-the-way place and sparked it up.

'Oi! You can't do that here!' a voice beside me bellowed. I hadn't seen the copper and he startled the daylights out of me. My adrenaline was pumping but I just gazed at him blankly, the way one might look at a speed camera. I dropped the joint on the pavement, crushed it under the toe of my boot and walked away. Although the policeman had essentially let me off, I spent the rest of the day stewing about what I perceived to be an outrageous injustice and a gross indignity. By sundown my lifelong contempt for authority had focused into a searing laser point, and I directed it all towards one perfectly reasonable country cop.

I drank myself into the usual oblivion that night and slept on my regular park bench up the street from the pub.

The next morning I was still boiling with resentment for being told by some upstart that I couldn't walk around in civilised society smoking drugs whenever I felt like it. Fair dinkum! Who did this copper think he was? After some breakfast (the remains of my takeaway bottle of bourbon) I decided I'd launch a high-profile protest action. I rolled a massive scoob, walked about 200 metres over to the Mullumbimby Police Station, sat on the front steps beneath the coat of arms and started puffing away. 'Up yours, you mongrel copper,' my silent choofing screamed. It was pure arrogance.

The cop wasn't nearly as cool about it as he'd been the day before, and I wasn't the fastest rabbit in the pen that morning either. He arrested me and locked me in the cells without any resistance or fanfare. So much for my demonstration on the barricades of dope-smoking decency.

'What's your name?' he asked.

To this day I don't know if it was because I was full of indignation or because I was befuddled by bourbon and pot or because, deep down, I knew I could die up in the forest and was subconsciously preparing to re-enter society. Whatever the reason, I didn't respond with the usual 'William H. Power'.

'C'mon, mate, what's your name?'

'Gregory Peel Smith.'

By uttering those three words I suddenly had a history again. I'd been tethered to society all along by my driver's licence number. It had been years since I'd renewed it but the New South Wales Police Service and the Office of Debt Recovery had been happy to wait for me to pop up again. It turned out I had warrants outstanding relating to unpaid traffic violations – just over $2100 worth. I either had to pay the fines (fat chance) or serve time in Grafton gaol to clear the debt at a rate of $100 a day (let's go). When the cop filled out the paperwork necessary to have me imprisoned I noticed he didn't charge me with smoking drugs on his front step.

The entrance to the 140-year-old Grafton gaol looked a little like the front of St Patrick's Orphanage. It was all archway and dark brickwork. I was still wearing my army pants, T-shirt and GP boots when I was led into the processing centre. I had to hand over all of my clothes, the boots and the dillybag I had with me when I was arrested in exchange for prison greens and thongs.

There were two stages of incarceration at Grafton: for the first week I was placed in a cell with just one other bloke and after that I was released into the general population for the remaining fourteen days I had to serve. Grafton is a medium-security gaol so I was alongside proper crims who were doing proper time. I sat around in the yard being my usual antisocial self, watching the other guys while they watched me. Being a bit of a connoisseur, I detected fairly quickly that some of them had a bit of home-brew going. They'd made it using potato peelings apparently. I also caught the occasional whiff of pot.

'What's that stuff you got going?' I inquired at one point.

'Not enough to share with you,' was the gruff retort. I just shrugged. That night some of the inmates were playing cards and instead of gambling money they were betting cones of marijuana. Naturally, I wanted to join the game.

One of them, a guy named Phegan, put his palm up and said, 'Well, hang on, what do you have to buy in with?'

'I've got a whole heap of pot.'

'Oh yeah? What do you mean you've got a whole heap of pot?' (Suddenly a bit more polite.)

'Just what I said. I've got heaps of it. It's stashed in the toe of my boots.'

One of my favourite TV shows of the 1960s had been *Get Smart*, which starred the great Don Adams as bumbling Cold War spy Maxwell Smart. Among other ridiculous gadgets, Agent 86 had a secret telephone built into his shoe. When I became a drifter I appropriated Max's spy-craft into my own subterfuge and constructed a secret compartment into the tip of my boots. I'd always buy them one or two sizes too big so I could comfortably stuff half an ounce of pot (or money or whatever) into the toes. Then I'd insert a piece of cardboard between the stash and my digits so that if someone stuck their hand in there to search it they'd think they were feeling the end of the boot.

The only problem was that my boots were in the store-room where the screws held inmates' belongings until they were released. 'That doesn't matter!' said Phegan, who was fast becoming my new best mate. 'Because you're only in for the short-term you're allowed access to your clothes so you can launder them ahead of your release.' The things you learn in prison!

The next day I followed Phegan's advice. Sure enough, I was allowed to wash my clothes in the prison laundry and sort out my boots. I returned with half an ounce of my finest forest buds stuffed down my jocks.

Over the next two weeks I was treated like royalty by

Phegan and the other prisoners. They were polite and attentive towards me, they cooked my food and shared their tobacco with me. In return I kept them all as stoned as buzzards. When it was time for me to leave they were sad to see me go. I gave them the remainder of the pot and promised that I'd return with more. The plan was for me to throw tennis balls stuffed with weed over the yard wall. Great thinking, 99! A week later several ounces of dope sailed high through the night air and landed in a quiet corner of Grafton's exercise yard.

Keeping my word with the convicts in Grafton gaol exacted quite a physical toll. I hitchhiked from Grafton to Lismore and walked the remaining day or so back to the forest. When I reached the mountain I was so exhausted I could barely put one foot in front of the other.

28

INTERVENTION

By the time the aliens came for me I was in a pretty bad way.

Physically I was a wreck and my mind was unravelling at a rapid rate, too. Paranoia was the order of the day. Excursions into the towns were fewer and further between but that didn't mean I was lacking company. I'd spend months at the camp drinking and smoking, and thinking that every unexplained sound was someone sneaking up on me. Strangely, though, I never saw them. I was pretty sure they were aliens and I suspected they had a base down near Federal. I even went looking for them there a few times when I was on mushrooms, but I was never able to pinpoint their location. They were clever buggers.

Eventually I did get to meet them. It was some time in 1999. I was having a couple of pipes and polishing off a cup of creek beer when two of them appeared on the other side of the fire. I wasn't that surprised. After all, they'd been creeping around the camp for months. I didn't say anything, I just stared at them until one of them spoke. 'So, you've been looking for us?'

I denied the accusation point blank. 'Nup. You've been sneaking around watching me.'

'Yes, we have been watching you, but we haven't been "sneaking around".' As one of the aliens spoke I noticed it had no hair and its skin was gothic white, including the surrounds of its mouth – I wouldn't call them lips, they were more like very thin, smooth plastic tubes.

'Then how come I couldn't see you when I heard you?'

'You weren't looking.'

'Yes I was.'

'You were looking for something you weren't sure existed and therefore you couldn't see us. You can see us now only because you know we are here.'

The aliens seemed genderless and were dressed in very fine cloth that looked soft and comfortable compared to my filthy army pants and rotting T-shirt. Their arms and legs appeared to be exceptionally thin and long, though it was difficult to tell because of their loose-fitting clothes which extended to the bottom of where their wrists and feet would be. They looked so clean and well and smooth.

They asked me how I was doing.

'Good, fantastic, brilliant. Nothing wrong with me,' I assured them. Furthermore, I added, I was as tough as nails and if they wanted to find out just how tough, I would accommodate them. Fortunately a fireside brawl with the aliens wasn't necessary. They said their philosophy was premised on gentleness and understanding.

'You can't survive without hurting things,' I countered.

'Yes, that is true,' they said soothingly. 'Survival is challenging by its very definition. That's why we live our lives without the need to survive.'

'Oh yeah? How do you do that?'

'We are very organised. Planning, organisation and discipline are very important in living a balanced life.'

'I like my life the way it is,' I said, staring into my empty cup.

'No, you don't! Your fathers and mothers have told you that you are sick. Why do you argue with them?'

I looked up. How did they know about my ancestors? Those were private and intimate conversations.

'So, you know my mothers and fathers?'

'Yes.'

'But you're not them?'

'No.'

I was on to them now. I knew what they were doing. 'You're trying to lure me into that conversation about leaving here. You've been talking to them. You're on their side.'

'We do not do "sides",' they responded. 'We do not have to talk about anything you do not want to talk about.'

'Good, leave me alone then.'

'We will come and sit with you at the fire tomorrow and we can talk about anything you like.'

'Can I stop you?' I asked, but I knew the answer already.

'Probably not.'

'OK then.'

The following day I sat at the camp trying to process the visit. 'Who are they?' I pondered. I concluded that they were aliens, just as I'd suspected. 'How did they get here without getting wet or dirty?' It must have been because their feet didn't touch the ground. I'd noticed that when they moved it was as if they just glided, though they still made quite a lot of noise in the bush. 'Where did they go, since I didn't see them leave?' Answer: they just weren't there, like when they were suddenly there. They were like my fathers and mothers only different. In fact, they must have sent them.

'I'm not moving,' I decided. 'I'll die here. It's safe and it used to be quiet. It's more like Central Station these days. A population explosion. There won't be enough room on the mountain for all of us soon.'

Later in the day they came back. This time I was slightly more civil. 'So, where are you from?'

'A different place.'

'What do you mean by place?'

'Place is a construct and can be anywhere and any time and not necessarily of this world.'

I sighed. 'Don't piss me off with existential philosophy. Where do you go when you're not here?'

'We are always here. We have always been here and we will always be here.'

I pretended to busy myself with the fire, poking it with a stick as I gathered my thoughts. 'OK. Let me put this really simply: when I can't see you, where are you?'

'The answer is just as simple. Wherever you are, so are we.'

'Wherever I am so are you? So you are me?'

'No, we come through you. You are the window which allows us to come through.'

I put down the stick. 'OK, that'll do. What do you want?'

'You came looking for us. Should we not be asking what it is that *you* want?'

'Good question and I have the answer. I want to be left alone!'

I turned my back on them but they didn't seem to get the hint. 'You are never alone,' they continued. 'You have to live with the spirits of all the animals you have killed. They will never leave you. They will always be with you. Perhaps it is them we came to share time with and you just happened to be here.'

Guilt. Shame. More guilt. I moped around for days thinking about what the aliens had said. 'I've stopped eating meat anyway!' I thought. 'I haven't eaten meat for years. That kangaroo was the last thing I killed, and I said sorry to its spirit. The bloody aliens just float around looking at me. What are they waiting for? Are they talking to the other spirits? I can't hear them. I wonder if they'll still be around when I get back if I go down to town?'

Fed up with the aliens' cross-dimensional meddling, I dragged myself out of the forest and set off for a bender in Byron Bay. I spent two nights there drinking cheap wine in the park and at the beach. I ran into some Indigenous people I knew and they were kind enough to share some pot with me. They even gave me some to take back home (which went straight into the toe of my boot). On both nights I got so pissed I passed out. The first morning I woke up in the sand dunes. The second day I came to in a laneway near the Rails. I counted myself lucky that Sergeant Bates didn't find me because the last thing I needed was a night in the cells followed by his snide comments in the morning. I was getting enough of those from the aliens.

I hitched a ride from Byron to Mullumbimby so I could stop and get some supplies – two casks of wine (one for the walk back to the forest and one for the camp) plus rice, flour, powdered milk, dried peas, dried fruit, nuts and pasta. With the shopping done I started shuffling painfully out of town past the golf course, when I got an unexpected lift from a familiar face. He lived near Crystal Castle and drove an old yellow Ford 250 truck. He'd given me the odd ride to and from Mullumbimby over the years and the only question he ever asked was, 'Wanna lift?' Nothing else – not even, 'How ya doing?' Probably because the answer was so obvious.

The bonus was that I got back to camp with almost two silver pillows full of wine. It was a new moon so it was pitch black by the time I arrived home, and as soon as I got there I kicked the fire into gear and got stuck into the vino, helped along by mouthfuls of poison from the wort. Although I tried to make the wine last, I drank myself into a near-legless state and stayed like that for two days straight. Not once did I see a sign of those two pests.

A couple of nights later I was lying in the ferns feeling pretty rotten when I heard a voice from the other side of the fire. 'So, how is your head?' I looked up. It was them again.

'My head's fantastic. Great. Not a problem.'

'Do you know what self-honesty is?'

And so the discussion would begin, and go on and on.

The truth is I'd been talking with my ancestors for maybe a year before the aliens started sniffing around the camp.

Although psychosis had clearly set in, I was well aware that I was becoming frightfully physically ill. Deathly ill. We all knew it.

Looking back, the decision I'd made in the early years to stop killing animals and go vegetarian contributed to my health failing over the long run. I had no idea how to go about being a vegetarian while maintaining a proper standard of nutrition. With a steeply diminished amount of protein going into my system, I was already out of kilter and low on pep. But by adding to that copious amounts of crude alcohol, all manner of bacteria from the creek, hallucinogenic drugs, raw cannabis, smoked cannabis, tar and nicotine, low nutrition, exposure, sporadic eating, chronic gastroenteritis, insomnia (not to mention a history of long-term homelessness, violent physical and sexual abuse, and not once seeing a doctor in the decade I'd lived in the forest), well, it was no wonder I wasn't feeling my best.

By my tenth year on the mountain, in the common era of 1999, I couldn't walk without the aid of a stick or branch to hold me up. If I had to put a percentage on the amount of time I spent sober or straight in that decade it would be seven to ten per cent. For years there had been no rhythm to life whatsoever. I might sleep drunk during the day and be awake all night for a week, and then suddenly do the reverse the next week. Along with my mind I'd also fractured a lot of ribs, fingers and toes since I first walked in. The ancestors were really worried about me and they told me so. I didn't really want to talk about it, so we spent a lot of time on other subjects instead.

Like the aliens, my ancestors just turned up one day at the fireside. I'd fallen into a very dark state. I'd become closed in at the camp and I didn't like to leave it anymore. If I wasn't sitting around staring into the canyon or at the fire I'd be focused on weird, obsessive little projects like whittling and shaping sticks, trying to bind them with twine or shaping stones. I'd started to think I was an amazing artist who created miniature masterpieces. In reality they were just the pathetic doodlings of a demented mind.

One day I looked up from fumbling with some twig or other and there they were. There were four main beings that day, but sometimes there were fewer, sometimes more. We didn't need any introductions. I knew who they were – they were me. They were me from a thousand years ago. They were me from a hundred years ago. They were me from the beginning, from the very first life. They were all of my mothers and all of my fathers, all the way back. I could look into any of them and see me. Inside each one of them there were a thousand other people. They were pure wisdom and knowledge and power. Above all, they were pure love, and their purpose was to help me love me.

Some of the ancestors were Druids and some of the more ancient ones had pieces of metal in their hair; adornments made of lead, tin, copper and bronze. They appeared as real as any human being I'd ever spoken to, but they cared about me more than any single human possibly could.

'The problem is people don't like me,' I told them early on in the piece.

'Have you ever given people a chance to like you?' they asked. 'Do they really know who you are?'

'Of course I've given them the chance! I've lived out there with them in their towns.'

'Were you living with them or just living among them?'

I didn't always have an answer to their questions, and while they gave me a lot to think about, I preferred to talk about subjects other than me. A lot of our early chats were around the rights and wrongs of the world and society. Christianity and Catholicism were hot topics of discussion, although whenever religion came up it tended to be a case of me talking (complaining) and them listening. We spoke a lot about ethics, morals and values – subjects that could get quite in-depth. There was no way we could get through them all in one sitting. I'd fall asleep and sometimes I wouldn't see them for a few days or weeks.

Fast forward and I'd be struggling back into camp with some wood and they'd be sitting there quietly by the fire, so we'd pick up where we'd left off. We had an exchange about the virtues of the Catholic faith that extended over months in that fashion. The ancestors were patient with me. I wanted to explore the notion of confession; specifically how anyone thought it absolved a perpetrator from committing acts of theft, sexual abuse, emotional cruelty and so on. We also talked a lot about fire; how important it was in supporting human existence; the cleansing effects of smoke and fire; the ability to cook, keep warm and to look into the dying embers and behold a ballet in flames; the pure meditation of fire.

We discussed the Spanish Inquisition in some depth, and explored the cruelty of colonisation and slavery. We had exchanges about equity, compassion, life and immortality. They showed me where I was positioned in the overall scheme of my DNA sequence (I was a simple but important link in life's trajectory). They pointed out to me that how I represented myself was my responsibility.

The ancestors indulged me on one of my pet hates: plastic and the disposable society it represented. Other topics came up off the back of that. What were my values? Did I have problems with the values that I had? We explored my anger and my hatred of my father and my mother. We talked about them a lot. Eventually the ancestors helped me see that hating my parents was consuming me. It would continue to create barriers and destroy any ambitions I might have. It was a limitation to anything I ever wanted to do.

On my now rare re-supply trips to Mullumbimby I always accepted a lift when it was offered because it was getting hard to drag one foot in front of the other. I'd purchased books from Vinnies and some of them informed the discussions back at camp. My favourites included *Jung and Tarot*, *The Holy Blood and The Holy Grail* and Douglas Adams' *Hitchhiker's Guide to the Galaxy: Trilogy of Five*. When we were done with that we talked about the Knights Templar, we explored the idea that it was not Jesus that was crucified but rather his brother, we explored how to move heavy objects with leverage. I told them about the time I rolled the log down the hill.

Eventually we ended up talking more and more about the elephant in the room, or the hermit in the forest as it were. 'We're really concerned about you, Gregory. If you stay up here you could die,' they said. 'It's time to leave and explore the world anew. You need to see the wider world as a forest and learn how to live in it.'

They insisted that I had enough wisdom and knowledge and that I had worked on myself enough to go out into society. I said I had no idea what they were talking about and that I'd rather die in the forest than go back. Before much longer it became obvious that that was exactly what would happen if I didn't do something soon. We agreed that death in itself wasn't a problem. The concern, they pointed out, was held in the hearts of others. I still had sisters somewhere who I didn't really know. I had a daughter who I hadn't seen for so long. These were major issues – hopelessly loose strands of emotion that I could never hope to tie if I just lay down in the undergrowth to die and decay in the mist. I was confused and frightened about how I'd ever deal with putting any of that back together.

'It will be OK. We just need you to go.'

I didn't answer.

'It's time, Gregory.'

I remained silent. The ancestors just looked at me with love. In the end I had no choice: there was no rational argument for staying in the forest; no compelling reason to die.

'Rightio,' I finally murmured. 'We'll go.'

In choosing to give society another chance I would have to close the door on the strange, sad, ridiculous, lonely, crazy and magical world I had created for myself at the top of the mountain. But before I could leave my forest I needed to untangle myself from it. This took a week or two. I scoured every square centimetre of the campsite and surrounds, slowly removing everything that didn't belong there – the garbage bin, cans, cups, tins, lids, tarpaulin, bottles, bottle tops, clothes, books, thermometer, bags, scraps of cigarette paper, burnt matchsticks, strands of rope, and bits of fishing line, rubber and newspaper. Everything that had been put down, dropped or fallen off me over ten years was painstakingly collected and carried back out. It was highly symbolic, and crucial that I was thorough. When I'd finished the cleansing, only the structures remained: the chair and work table I'd made out of rocks, and the ring of stones around the fire.

The effort took all my remaining strength and caused a rip to open up in my failing mind. I recall glimpses of the last days out on Mill Road when I was carting rubbish out to put into bins. As for the final time I limped out of the forest and back into the 'real world'? Just me, my didgeridoo and my dillybag? I have no memory of it. I don't even know if I said goodbye.

29

EPIPHANY

I was right back where I'd started – alone and slumped on a park bench in northern New South Wales. I even had a bag full of booze and drugs with me. It was as though I'd entered the Goonengerry time warp and been spat out ten years later fundamentally unchanged.

I'm clueless as to how much time had elapsed since leaving the forest. Maybe a few weeks or a couple of months. I don't recall how or why I ended up in Tweed Heads either, but I can make an educated guess. I assume once I left the forest I was either offered a lift or I hitch-hiked to Lismore or Byron Bay. Either scenario would have put me alongside the traffic estuaries that flow into the well-populated Tweed Valley 100 kilometres to the north.

Somewhere along the line somebody was alarmed enough about my appearance, my behaviour, or both, to take me to the emergency department at Tweed Heads

Hospital. It's possible I went there of my own accord, but given my track record on health it's unlikely I suddenly felt it was time for a check-up. The truth is I just don't know. In addition to malnutrition, exhaustion, the loss of my teeth and the fact I weighed just forty-one kilograms (less than half my normal weight) my mental state was frightfully feeble. The complete absence of memory around this time was as disconcerting then as it is today. It's as if pages were torn from my life story and scattered to the wind somewhere in the Northern Rivers.

I can verify that I received hospital treatment and that my identity and bona fides were established. I was given a Medicare card, processed for welfare assistance and given access to a disability pension. This unexpected injection of funds is how I came to be sitting on a park bench behind Tweed Heads Hospital alongside a new backpack. I'd taken myself shopping and filled the bag with the essentials I deemed necessary to build my life anew:

1 x 750 ml bottle of bourbon
1 x 4 litre cask of Fruity Lexia wine
1 x packet of Drum tobacco
2 x packets of Tally-Ho papers
1 x $100 bag of hydroponic marijuana
1 gram of cocaine

I'd been on the brink of death when the ancestors intervened up on the mountain, and although they saved my life by convincing me to leave the forest, I felt they'd given me scant advice on what I should do with it once I'd stumbled back into society like a lost, near-skeletal sheep. I understood that I was supposed to give the world a second chance and to treat society like a different kind of forest, but that was easier said than done. I hadn't the foggiest idea how to get started, let alone make progress. In a vacuum like that, old habits die hard.

Traditionally when I'd re-supply with illicit booty, my modus operandi had been to hike back up to the mountain, kick-start the fire and get busy obliterating my brain cells and emotions. Now that the forest was over for me, and with nowhere else to go, my homing beacon went haywire and charted a default course for my most recent location – Tweed Heads Hospital.

The occasional medico and hospital visitor walked past me as I sat alone in the stretched-out afternoon shadows trying to figure out where I was going to get drunk and crash that night. I felt completely lost, and the tragic banality of my predicament overtook me. 'I lived ten years as a hermit and nothing has changed,' I thought bitterly. 'Not a single thing is better or even different. I'm still homeless. I still have nothing. I still have no one and I still have nowhere to go.'

In that moment I felt more alone than ever before, which, for the world's loneliest loner, was saying something. There were twenty-odd million people in Australia, billions more around the world, and I didn't know any of them. Not one. It was a profound and devastating realisation. 'If only I had one person to tell all my problems to,' I pondered as tears pooled in my eyes, 'then things might be okay.'

When I'd been a boy I'd nurtured a fire in my belly; a passion that burned inside me in spite of all the pain.

Now, with one arm wrapped around a bag of cheap alcohol and contraband, only the very faintest flicker remained. I felt like reaching inside and extinguishing it forever when, out of nowhere on that sunny afternoon, a mist swirled around me.

It began as a fine, grey haze but quickly thickened into a soupy cloud that was so dense I couldn't see an inch in front of my face. I became spooked and hyper-vigilant. Suddenly I was standing in a fighting position. My mood had swung from sorrowful to angry and I was waiting for the next battle. Slowly, the fog began to recede and I saw my hands were gripping the handle of a large double-edged sword. I held it up, ready for the inevitable.

As the fog receded further, I saw devastation and chaos all around me but not a single soul to fight. I was shocked by the scale of the damage that had already been done. The park bench and the hospital were gone and instead I stood alone in the middle of a smouldering battlefield. 'OK, it's coming.' I keyed myself up. 'This is definitely where the next fight is gonna be.'

I stood rigid in the field for a long time – legs firmly planted on the cold, muddy ground, shoulders cocked, and itching to swing that heavy blade at the first attacker. I waited for the onslaught. And waited. And waited.

Eventually the mist disappeared altogether, leaving me with a clear view across a scorched and broken landscape that stretched all the way to the horizon. It was an appalling scene of devastation. Under an oily grey-brown sky, I gazed across ground that was cracked and blackened. Muddy craters were scattered with rubble and the smoking remnants of shattered rocks and splintered trees. It was silent and the air stank of decay.

I gripped the handle of the sword even tighter. 'Come ON!' I taunted my enemies. But there still wasn't a soul in sight. Nobody charged at me, no one tried to hurt me. And that's when it struck me: all of this chaos and destruction was the wreckage of my life. And I had created it all by fighting myself. There had never been anyone else. In all those miserable, messed up years *I* had been the enemy. 'It's me!' I gasped. 'It's always been *me*!'

I tried to drop the sword, to fling the damned thing on the ground, but it stuck fast in my hands as though an extension of my body, my psyche and my soul all rolled into one. As quickly as it had started, the vision was over and I was on my backside once again on the park bench with my head hanging low. Strangely I wasn't the least bit frightened or confused, just relieved and deeply grateful for what I had been shown. It was as if a cell door had been unlocked and I was welcome to walk free, should I choose to. 'Thank you,' I whispered into my lap. 'Thank you. I don't want to fight anymore. I won't fight anymore.'

For the first time in my life I felt at peace. I had no desire to blame anyone, no need to be angry at the human race and no impulse to judge myself or anyone else. I had no fear, and at long last I knew with absolute certainty what I had to do. I stood up, slung my trusty dillybag over my shoulder, picked up my didgeridoo and walked away leaving the backpack full of liquor, mull and $200 worth of cocaine on the bench seat.

Each step away from it was a giant leap along a brand new pathway, away from the destructive influence of drugs and alcohol. The painkillers had been killing me all along. I even left the ciggies behind; smoking tobacco was a vice of the past. So too was any kind of deceit or act of violence. From now on I would choose wisdom over waste, love over loathing and empathy over enmity. I would forgive myself. I would forgive everybody else in my life, and I would strive to honour my ancestors and humbly take my place among them.

I passed the entrance to the emergency department where I'd been delivered cursed, broken and poisoned only a month or so earlier. I never once looked back, but I did wonder who might end up finding that backpack. They were either going to get a nasty shock or a pleasant surprise.

As I walked along the banks of the Tweed River I slipped my hand into my dillybag to check on my few remaining possessions – my matches and a candle, my magic stick and notepaper, some stones I'd souvenired from the forest and my marbles. I caressed those precious glass balls with the rough tips of my fingers.

I slept rough in a park that night but for the first time in many, many years I was 100 per cent straight and sober. That's probably why it took aeons to drift off. When I did, it was a shallow, fitful sleep, the first hurdle in a long, exhausting journey to sobriety and abstinence. I was about to learn that the best things in life never come easy.

Even when I'd been paralytic drunk and stoned out of my cranium in the forest, it remained the single most beautiful place I had ever seen. By contrast I considered the towns and cities to be crowded, polluted monuments to ugliness and mass consumption. Society was home to so many things I abhorred: industry, shopping centres, choking traffic, police cells, plastic, suburban sprawl, churches, orphanages and human beings.

Attempting to avoid ugliness was a major reason I'd turned to drink and drugs in the first place. Ironically I used mass-market pollutants like cask wine to try to inoculate myself against the repellent things that existed in the world and inside of me. Now that I'd left my lovely mountaintop home and shut off the chemical taps I had used to try to stay numb, I was out in the open, completely vulnerable and totally terrified, but I was ready to face the greatest challenge of all. Life.

I felt a little like the lizards that darted about in the forest. I wandered around the Tweed Valley for a few months, easily startled, studiously avoiding humans and scurrying into sand dunes and parkland to hide away and sleep. Now and then I'd venture north across the once fabled Queensland border to seek sanctuary on the warm, world-famous sands of the Gold Coast. I used the pension money to get public transport and buy food, but I also relied on soup kitchens for a bit of shelter and sustenance, even if it meant occasionally putting up with the religious ravings of whatever suburban zealot had the microphone that week. When you're hungry, you're hungry.

As much as I tried to push it down, another appetite gnawed at me constantly. Every single day I craved alcohol and – surprise-surprise – nicotine. For quite a while whenever I felt the chemical itch I gave myself a mental kick for abandoning the backpack. My mind would slip into the well-worn grooves of the long-play record that spun out of control in my brain. 'Do it. Do it. Do it,' the old Gregory implored. 'I don't drink and I don't do drugs. I don't drink and I don't do drugs. I don't drink and I don't do drugs,' the new me would stonewall in response. It was a tiring back-and-forth but it was a conversation I had to have. Now and then, it would fall blessedly silent for half an hour or so – the fragile beginnings of clarity.

After a couple of months on the wagon something lovely started to occur. As my mind gradually sharpened, I began to see beautiful things; *really* see them. At first it was gardens. For so long I had only beheld beauty when it was reflected in the glorious chaos of the rainforest.

In society, however, order was prized. There were carefully planned pathways, manicured lawns, neat rows of flowers, paved courtyards, trimmed hedges, straight edges and palm trees that grew obediently in the middle of highway roundabouts. For some people such humdrum suburban arrangements might seem unimaginative and pedestrian, but to me they had taken on a beguiling beauty. I would stop to admire council parks or a garden bed outside a block of units. Sometimes I'd be so enamoured that powerful emotions would spill into parts of me that had once been flooded by green beer. Mostly the feeling was of gratitude.

My emotions weren't the only things in bloom. Faculties were coming back to me, too. My memory was beginning to outperform my forgetory, and my resolve to live a better life was hardening into real ambitions. I was thankful to be supported by a pension but I desperately wanted to get a job, keep it and use it to build the foundations of a brighter future. Although I now had the advantage of being sober, well intentioned and motivated, I was still a haggard, homeless sociopath with a short fuse and an extremely limited education.

It was time to get busy.

30

PLANET GREGORY

For years people had crossed the street when they saw me coming. Ladies would clutch their children's hands a little tighter and vector them clear of my flight path, or people would suddenly step into a shop front or random doorway they obviously had no business going into. Anything to avoid the scary man. It wasn't a good feeling but it was slightly better than being invisible, which is how I'd felt during my desperate days hanging around Matthew Talbot's in Sydney. There I'd learned what it was like to be nothing; to have fellow human beings look through me as though I didn't exist.

In my newly sober state I started to understand why a mother might not want her kids running smack-bang into me. My clothes were beyond shabby and my hair was several feet long, matted into dreadlocks in parts with some lengths still wound tight by twine and beads from

Mullumbimby Markets. My prodigious beard, which had once been jet black, had developed a grey streak down the left side that made me look like a feral male version of Morticia from *The Addams Family*.

I knew my appearance was confronting to a lot of people and I realised I didn't smell terribly fragrant either, particularly on hot days. In the forest I didn't care about my body odour, but now that I'd undertaken to participate in society I was becoming self-conscious about it. Just caring about how I presented was a massive turn-around, and I found myself asking different questions. There was less, 'Why don't I just get one bottle of bourbon?' and more, 'How do I want to be perceived in society? How do I want to be received? How do I go about it?'

It was becoming clear that something had to change if I was going to fulfil my end goal of gainful employment, and – the Holy Grail – a place of my own. Sometimes I'd talk to outreach workers in the soup kitchens about my ambitions and they'd offer a bit of encouragement. One day, though, a counsellor took me aside and laid it out pretty bluntly.

'You need to clean yourself up,' he said. 'You're going to have more luck in the world if you're tidy and presentable.'

I nodded in silent agreement.

'So maybe you should get a haircut and have a shave.'

WHAT?!

That terrified me. It wasn't that I was wedded to my 'look', or was in any way vain. I was simply mortified that people might see the person who was hiding in the undergrowth wrapped around my head, myself included. I just knew I was the ugliest person on earth. I was Pus Head, the grub who should do everyone a favour and just piss off. At least the beard and hair partly obscured my hideous visage. But then again, I desperately wanted a job so I was faced with a dilemma. In the end the decision came down to the fact I had given my word that I'd strive to be the best person I could be, and if getting a job required a haircut and a shave, then I would do it.

A day or two later I stood naked in the bathroom of the cheapest motel in Surfers Paradise with a pair of scissors. The scariest part of the process was forcing myself to look in the mirror – something I had studiously and success-fully avoided most of my life. During the split seconds in which I dared to make eye contact, I was shocked to see a frightened, toothless and sallow man peering back at me. I raised the scissors to expose him even more.

I didn't just hack away at my hair, I took it slowly, cer-emoniously. I carefully snipped each length and set them aside. When I was done, I tucked one of the matted bangs that had formed into a dreadlock into my dillybag. The skunk-striped beard was next, but I didn't keep any of that.

When it was over I felt alien and vulnerable. There were no more furtive glances in the mirror. I was done with mirrors. I stood in the shower for a long time afterwards and counselled myself that it had been the right thing to do. I reminded myself that I was absolutely determined to do the best I could to be 'part of'. Sprucing up by way of scissors and soap was testament to my willingness to change.

In the morning I checked out of the motel and resumed life on the street. Yes, I was still sleeping on benches and beaches but at least I didn't look like a hermit-wizard anymore, and I smelled pretty good too. Apparently, though, I still appeared somewhat haunted. A few weeks after the haircut I was sitting on a bus threading through the Coolangatta traffic when a dude dropped a sachet of pot into my lap. 'You look like you could use this, brother,' he said with a wink and a solemn nod. I thanked him all the same and handed it back, but I did half wonder whether he'd found it inside a backpack on a bench at Tweed Heads Hospital.

As part of the rebuilding process I visited a dentist and dental technician and now had teeth. Even though I could finally chew properly, I still had trouble building up my weight. Given my allergy to reflections I was spared the shock of seeing my naked form in a mirror, but in hospital they'd told me I weighed just over forty-one kilograms, which must have been the full tare of my skin, bones and internal organs. Since I was still living a nomadic existence and not eating properly, I was struggling to bulk up. Around ten months after I left the forest I decided I had to address the emaciation, and resumed eating meat mostly by way of takeaway hamburgers and pies.

While I was undergoing a major metamorphosis, I noticed there had been some changes in society during my ten-year hiatus, too. Out on the street and on public transport people were carrying what appeared to be miniature walkie-talkies in their pockets. They not only held these little devices up to their ears and spoke into them – USUALLY IN A VERY LOUD VOICE FOR SOME REASON! – they sometimes held them in the palm of one hand and stabbed away at buttons with the other.

When someone explained that they were mobile phones I was blown away. As a kid I'd seen the hard-bitten police detective Dick Tracy speak into a phone on his watch, but Dick was a cartoon character. It was fantasy! Not anymore. These mobiles were the real deal. 'What planet *is* this?' I marvelled.

I'd entered the forest circa 1989 – years before mobile phones became ubiquitous, even before the boom in personal computers. Given my mid-1960s primary school education, I was daunted by the technology of the twenty-first century. During my years of hibernation the world had moved on in leaps and bounds. The human race was beginning to communicate by 'text message', even the mail had become electronic, and people expended 'giga-bytes' while 'surfing the internet'. Meanwhile, on Planet Gregory, I still had trouble writing legibly with my magic stick.

I doubled down on my job-hunting efforts and spent my days sitting in soup kitchens or on street benches as I combed the classifieds. Since I didn't have a mobile, I fed coins into payphones to call potential employers, only to be knocked back from every single position I applied for. It's not as though I was aiming too high; I didn't apply for any gigs as a senior account manager or a CSIRO lab technician. I was angling for gardening jobs, warehouse work, cleaning positions and general shit-kicking. More often than not the rejection was accompanied by the same six words: 'Sorry, but you've got no experience.'

Sometimes the voice at the other end of the phone would ask for my address. I didn't have one but I couldn't rightly say, 'Well, tonight I'll be on the sand up near the dunes at Duranbah Beach. I'm not sure of the cross street, but it's down at the south end.' After the third or fourth such stand-off, I got myself a post-office box in nearby Coolangatta. It was the first real address, as opposed to a campfire, that I'd had in well over a decade.

Even though I now had a hole in the wall outside the local post office, I couldn't get an interview. I was trying my hardest to step up and take part in the world but I wasn't being invited to even put my case. I was frustrated and angry, and at those times the drunkard-druggie part of my mind would swagger in with a bourbon in his hand and a joint in his gob to give me a slap for leaving that bag of booze behind. 'A few drinks and a couple of pipes would hit the spot right now, you idiot,' he'd sneer.

On the days I ran out of avenues to look for work I'd wander around the streets simply concentrating on not getting drunk. One afternoon I was sitting at a fish and chip shop at Tweed Heads when I became fixated on a construction crew hard at work at a building site across the road. For no particular reason I felt compelled to find out what they were making. I put down my piece of battered hake and strolled over.

'So, ah, what are you guys building here?' I asked the young bloke in a hard hat and a flannelette shirt who was operating a stop/go sign at the main gate.

'It's gonna be a university actually, mate.'

'Oh yeah? Good one.'

I walked back across the road to finish off my fish and chips, unaware that a seed had been sown. Over the next few weeks, as the rejections for job interviews stacked up, my mind kept drifting back to one word – university. 'Exactly how do people get to go to university?' I wondered. I had no idea. I reckoned you probably had to have really nice clothes and a lot of money. At the very least you'd need to have finished high school.

It was becoming depressingly clear that my plan of getting an entry-level job and working my way up the ladder, as I had at the flour mill back in Tamworth all those years ago, wasn't bearing fruit. It was time I sat down and asked myself some hard questions, like: 'What skills do I have?' and, 'What can I offer a prospective employer?'

'Okay, let's see,' I thought. 'I can knock a bat out of a tree with a slingshot. I'm a pretty good tracker and I can light a fire in the middle of a rain storm.' While these were all excellent skills, and essential had I been applying for a position as the Wild Man of Borneo, I couldn't imagine an employer throwing their arms wide and saying, 'Wow! You can stone a bat! When can you start?'

It was obvious that if I wanted to get a job I needed to acquire some skills. To do that I would need to educate myself.

31

HUMPTY

I had always been different. This was partly because of the way I communicated with people. I'd never learned the usual conventions of conversation and civil discourse so I made others feel uncomfortable without really trying. On top of that, my natural default was towards arrogance, confrontation and obnoxiousness. I was an awkward, big mouthed, sharp-elbowed know-it-all who made everyone squirm.

People avoided chatting to me because I could talk them out of anything. I could make a logical argument to support any proposition in any situation. I could make an ironclad defence of the fact that blue is actually purple and also silver, and you'd have no choice but to believe me. People used to tell me I could sell ice to the Eskimos. I'd never even been to the snowfields but I could certainly sell dope to the hippies, so who knows?

By the time I was in my forties I also knew I could generally out-think most people. I'd have them figured out after a minute or two and know exactly what they wanted, what they didn't want and how to work things to our mutual advantage. Ironically this used to bug me because I found people boring. I was like a kid who'd worked out the Rubik's Cube on the first go; it wasn't a challenge after that. Unfortunately this didn't make me particularly smart or interesting, it just made me conceited, because I had no frame of reference or even a place in the world. I'd certainly never had anyone to help me develop whatever intelligence I might have possessed.

Although I was smarter than people had ever given me credit for, I struggled to convert that into a tangible benefit. After all, I couldn't even convince someone to interview me for a lousy job poisoning weeds and mowing lawns. Although I was confident I'd made the right decision in abandoning job hunting in favour of pursuing an education, I knew that consigned me to homelessness for the foreseeable future. People didn't get rich being students. In fact, studying was likely to cost me money. But the decision had been made and a student I would be.

My first step was to phone the campus of the NSW North Coast TAFE at Kingscliff (noting for the first time that TAFE stood for Technical And Further Education). I explained my situation to the lady at the other end of the line: I was a mature-aged person who was eager to do a course.

'OK, is there anything in particular that you're interested in studying?' she asked.

'Something that's for a beginner,' I said. 'Kind of entry level.'

'Let's see . . . we offer a six-week computer course. Is that something you'd be interested in?'

'That sounds perfect. Can you tell me how much it costs?'

She paused while she looked it up. 'That particular course is free, actually,' she replied.

'Even better.'

In the winter of 2002, using my Coolangatta post-office box as my home address, I filled out the paperwork required to commence studying Certificate 1 in Information Technology. It would be my first foray into the education system since 1968 (not counting my heroin-blurred stint at Ultimo TAFE back in the 1980s). I was sleeping in the sand dunes at Coolangatta, a solid two-hour walk to the TAFE campus at Kingscliff on the southern shores of the Tweed River, and two hours back at night. This gave me some good thinking time.

I turned up on the first day looking neat and present-able. I was excited and scared stiff. I couldn't quite believe that I was a student at a college and that I was about to apply myself to understanding the computer gizmos that now seemed to rule the world. I'd never sat at a PC, let alone a laptop, and I'd only just purchased my first mobile phone – a brick of an Ericsson that I'd acquired in order to chase work, though ironically I now had no one to call.

I had geed myself up during the long walk to campus that morning. 'Computers! Cutting-edge technology and I'm going to learn how they work. Woo hoo!' Compared to sitting in a soup kitchen circling ads in the newspaper this was thrilling stuff. I felt as if my life had suddenly shifted gear; I'd turned a corner and embarked on a thrilling intellectual odyssey. 'Yippee! Day one at college, here I come!'

By the end of day two, I hated computers with such venom that I wanted to smash one. I might as well have been Gronk walking out of the jungle in 3000BCE to try to understand the combustion engine. I could not get my head around the silly machines no matter how hard I tried. I was not on an arc of incremental learning like everyone else in the class. For them, learning computers was an organic extension of what they were already familiar with. For me it was a case of:

Tutor: 'So, here is a computer, Gregory.'

Me: 'A what?'

What's more, the course wasn't designed to teach us how to use computers – the purpose was to teach us what computers were and how their various components worked together in order to, you know, compute. 'Gah! My HEAD!' But as much grief and anguish as the machine and the course were causing me, I stuck it out. I developed a simple five-word mantra to deal with the situation: 'Be there at the end.' In other words, my quitting days were over.

'Be there at the end,' I'd counsel myself on the long walk back to my camp in the dunes. 'No matter what happens, don't drink – and be there at the end.'

Six weeks later I was there at the end to complete a Certificate 1 in Information Technology. Aside from proving to myself that I possessed the depth of commitment to finish what I'd started, I learned two very important things at Kingscliff TAFE. One was that I hated – utterly hated – computers. The other was that I loved to learn.

Learning gave me new things to think about. OK, I didn't like computers but I understood that trying to unlock their mysteries took my thought processes away from other places; particularly from the dark realms where trouble lurked.

I can't overstate the impact that first TAFE course had on me, and it chimed perfectly with the awakening I was experiencing as a result of not drinking and drugging. There had been a paradigm shift and the momentum was starting to gather. I could feel a touch of wonder coming into my life. The ember in my belly was glowing again and I could feel other, long-dormant coals starting to catch alight, too.

I'd walk around Tweed Heads and Coolangatta and have some 'wow' moments. One day I stopped in the street to read a little notice that had been put up outside a church. 'Now is a gift,' it read. 'That's why they call it The Present.'

'Oh wow. WOW!' I marvelled. 'That is just *profound*.'

I fixated on that for a week. I processed it and analysed it, flipped it over and checked it right out. 'The gift. The Present. The now. The power.' These were the building blocks of my existential awakening. I worked at embedding them into my psyche and focused all of my energy on appreciating the value of now.

But as much as I tried to enjoy unwrapping my new presence, old thoughts would still call out and try to drag me backwards. Insidious ideas about sabotage, mostly. A little voice would pop into my brain and remind me how good it was to sit in the sunshine with a full body-stone and a nice drink. It was a constant battle and it was driving me nuts. I understood the importance of interfering with thought processes and disrupting their influence. Studying how computers worked had left little time for my mind to drift to my old, wicked ways. Now that the course was finished I had to come up with a proxy subject to fixate on in order to run a mental counter-insurgency against addiction.

I have no idea why I chose Humpty Dumpty, that clumsy egg, or whatever it is, but every time the voices of vice started up in my head I decided I'd recite the nursery rhyme over and over again. I'd get lost in a maze of questions about Humpty Dumpty: 'Who or what he might have been. Who was the king at the time and why did he give a stuff about Humpty? And what about those horses? Was this the royal court? What role did Magna Carta play in the tale of Humpty? Were the king's men knights of the round table? Who were the square heads? Who were the round heads? What about Cromwell?' And on and on until, soon enough, the craving would pass and I wasn't thinking about alcohol or drugs anymore.

I started to develop a mental role model, too. I don't know whether it flowed from my Humpty Dumpty obsession, whether I planted the seed while reading about the Knights Templar in the forest or whether it was a hangover from wielding the double-edged sword in my park-bench epiphany, but I chose a valiant knight as my spiritual ideal. One in shining armour, no less. I liked the idea of a brave man who roamed the realm; a protector and champion of the people, causing no harm and being chivalrous and gentlemanly along the way.

Episodes of clarity would arrive in my head like sunny periods on a cloudy day and I soon developed another mantra: 'Just be the best person you can be today. That's all you have to do. Just get through today without hurting anyone, including yourself.' That was a massive break-through. I didn't want to hurt *me* anymore. I had finally started to outsmart the old Gregory – the one who wanted to hide in the forest, hate the world and tear me down. I did it by implementing a simple management strategy.

1. *Get sober*
2. *Sing Humpty Dumpty*
3. *Be the best person I can be*
4. *Be there at the end, no matter what*

These were deliberate and considered steps I had to take to break the cycle of destruction. It was like a cheat sheet for the game of psychological chess I was playing against the flaws in my character and the horrors of my past. Sometimes I had pretty fiery exchanges with my inner-de-mons. They'd make some venomous little suggestion like, 'Let's just go and get drunk for one weekend. No one will know about it and you can start over being sober again on Monday.' But my knight would shout them down. '*I* will know about it, and I know it will destroy me. You won't drag me down with you.'

Slowly, clarity started to settle on me, rather than just pay fleeting visits. Green shoots began to show and the conversations I had with myself were changing. 'You're worthwhile. Don't let those demons in here. They feed off seeing you writhe around in pain and anger. Don't let them win. They won't win anymore. Just be the best person you can be now. Take that responsibility. Own it. Be it.'

I wasn't trying to be perfect – there's no such thing. But in the past when I made mistakes I used them as an excuse to give up. In trying to stay in The Present I came to realise that if I stumbled it was okay, it was just part of life. I just needed to get up, dust myself off and be the knight. I had to put my armour on every day and learn about the things I didn't know. Learn how to be a person in this new world, in this new forest. Learn to hunt. Learn to understand. Learn to read the signs. Learn to be. Just learn.

'I'd like to get my School Certificate. Is there a course for that?' I was back at Kingscliff TAFE and eager to tick an educational box that had remained empty my whole life. In truth, it was an opportunity that had been stolen from me by Dad when he pulled me out of school in second form. In my mind, the School Certificate – or leaving certificate – had always been the pinnacle of academic success. In Tamworth loads of kids left school at sixteen after gaining their School Certificate. They'd go on to do trades, apprenticeships, work in the public service, join family businesses or whatever their futures beckoned them. Leaving school at fourteen, as I did, was uncommon and it didn't give you many options. In fact, I carried it like the mark of Cain. I don't think it even occurred to me that there was a Higher School Certificate and something beyond that called tertiary education. To me, the School Certificate was it, and it represented complete validation in the world.

'No, I'm sorry but New South Wales TAFE doesn't offer the School Certificate,' the student advisor replied.

Instant deflation.

'But I believe Southport TAFE up on the Gold Coast offers a similar program,' she added, and handed me a card with their phone number.

Instant excitement.

I phoned Southport TAFE and, yes, they did indeed offer a course that might cater to me. I made an appointment to speak with a student liaison officer and caught the next bus north. The following day I was sitting down with her.

'I rang up about the School Certificate. Apparently you don't do that but you said you had another program?' I began hopefully.

'Yes, that's the tertiary preparation course,' she said. 'That's better than the School Certificate. If you pass that you can apply to attend university.'

Better than the School Certificate? Apply for university? My ego revved into the red. 'Yes, that sounds right for me,' I said. 'Is it free?'

'No, it costs $750.'

'I don't have that much money,' I said, deflated once again.

'Don't worry – we can talk about that. We can organise for you to pay it off. Come in on a Monday and pay us twenty-five dollars and we'll teach you for the week.'

'I can do that,' I said, glad to be heading back to TAFE. 'Twenty-five dollars I can definitely do.'

32

THE GREAT-ISH PRETENDER

The tertiary preparation course at Southport TAFE ran for eight months during 2003, and not one of my lecturers or classmates had the faintest clue that I was homeless for virtually all of it. As usual I was withdrawn, and anxious to shield myself and everyone else from the uncomfortable reality of who I was.

If you passed me in a corridor or happened to line up behind me in the cafeteria you'd be completely unaware that I was an uneducated, highly dangerous, ex-forest-dwelling sociopath who slept on a public beach. I may have shaved and cut my hair but I was still a 'vagrant' – riffraff with no fixed address. My short back and sides were just a disguise. Where I used to hide behind a beard, my clean-shaven face was now my mask. I was hiding in plain sight.

I had purchased an old Mitsubishi L300 van and moved my camp from Tweed Heads thirty-five kilometres up the Gold Coast Highway to a quiet nook in the dunes near Southport Beach, in order to be closer to TAFE. My first day was nerve-racking. There were twenty other students (mostly well-dressed types) and true to form I could barely bring myself to say a word to any of them. Everybody else seemed to like a chat, so I quickly had to master the tactic of diversion. I'd give superficial responses to people's questions and deftly redirect the conversation back onto them.

Although it was odious to me, most humans are generally happy to talk about themselves. Many of my new classmates had specific ideas about why they wanted to go to university.

They were keen on business, making money, doing research or serving the community in one way or another, so it wasn't hard to get them talking. If ever someone posed a tricky question to me like, 'Where do you live?' I had a prefabricated response ready to go. 'Oh, I'm down at Tweed Heads.'

'Yeah? Whereabouts in Tweed Heads, Gregory?'

'Just a place down near the beach.'

While fending off such inquiries had become second nature, studying in the hope of attending university was an altogether tougher proposition. The course was designed to teach the basic building blocks of academic pursuits, such as how to write an essay, how to do research and how to use a computer (as opposed to how they were built). It was daunting, particularly considering I was coming off a frightfully low academic base. My last educational assessment had been when I was eighteen and locked up in Yawarra, and it stated:

IQ range: 81–93
Reading age: 10 years, 2 months
Spelling age: 10 years, 6 months
Gap reading comprehension age: 9 years, 5 months
Mathematics sample: Early 5th class skills

Thankfully, the teachers at Southport were patient and tolerant. One of the first things they focused on was teaching us how to write properly. What is a sentence? Generally speaking, every sentence needs a verb and a noun. What is a paragraph? Paragraphs have three parts: an introduction (topic sentence), two or three supporting evidence sentences (this was the big challenge for me) and a concluding or linking sentence.

When it was all broken down like this, I felt I had a chance. It wasn't rocket science after all! Suddenly, learning wasn't about being 'smart' – it was largely about following a formula. I'd learned to formulate beer in a bin in the bush, without textbooks and tutors, so I was confident I could figure out how to write too.

Next we probed the question of, 'What is an essay?' An essay is a series of paragraphs that construct an argument. That confused me. 'An *argument*?' My idea of an argument was different from TAFE's. Their arguments resulted in marks and grades; my arguments resulted in pain and blood. Once again the teachers were patient and accommodating of my needs. And again, it was all about steps and formula.

Soon we were given an assignment to write an essay on a subject of our choosing, so I had the opportunity to put my powers of non-violent argument to the test. I chose to write about the life and legacy of Queen Hatshepsut, the second female pharaoh of Egypt. Don't ask me why; the lady just fascinated me. She was possibly the richest woman in the world and yet today, more than 3500 years later, she's little more than a name to most people. Her story reinforced in me that the only things I truly own are my name and my achievements, or my word as a man. Everything else, in my view, was superfluous.

I poured a lot of effort into my dissertation on Queen Hatshepsut, which was reviewed by a tutor named Janet Diehl. 'This is a really good essay, Gregory,' she began. 'It's a very logical essay. But where is your evidence?'

'What do you mean "evidence"?' I responded.

'Well, where did all this information come from?'

'It's all my opinion.'

'You're not qualified to put your opinion in an essay,' Janet explained gently.

'What do you mean? It's *my* essay, isn't it?'

'You need to have academically peer-reviewed empirical evidence to support your essay.'

'Oh.'

'You need to be published to be able to do that – you can't just have your opinion.'

'Right.' I thought about this for a moment. 'Well, one day I'm going to be published, Janet, and I'm going to call my book *My Considered Opinion.*'

Janet laughed. She was lovely. We had a long conversation about what empirical evidence was and why it was important to establish an argument. I returned to the subject of Queen Hatshepsut and wrote the essay properly. I used empirical evidence and I researched it all using a computer and the vast resource that is the World Wide Web. What do you know? I was actually beginning to learn.

While things were progressing reasonably well in the classroom, life outside was still a battle. Even though I had the L300 van, I still slept on the beach as it was ten times more comfortable than a car seat. While making a bed in the sand isn't as bad as some other options (mainly because you can mould the ground to the shape of your body), it can be very loud if a big surf is running, it's wet when it rains and there's always the threat of being moved on with a baton in the chest or woken with a kick in the mouth.

I discovered, too, that Gold Coast beaches were a magnet for all kinds of nutty carry-on after dark. Boisterous drunken people loved to hit the beach at all hours of the night, it was a go-to place for late-night spliff smokers, and I even became familiar with one Gold Coast couple who liked to make love on the sand whenever there was a full moon. The werewolf lovers.

Because the local economy is built on neat stacks of tourist dollars, rangers and cops on the Gold Coast put a lot of effort into making sure homeless people don't spoil the vibe. Really, who wants their Queensland holiday ruined by the sight of some hobo studying in the sand dunes? To stay one step ahead of eviction I kept my camp deliberately small. At night I'd pore over my notes and textbooks while sitting on the beach, and in the morning I'd always beat the rangers out of bed.

Most days I'd rise before the sun and sneak into a nearby caravan park to grab a quick shower in the amenities block. Sometimes I had to go without washing, depending on whether the park manager had locked the gate. If a gate was locked, then it was locked – I didn't want to break in because that would cause trouble. I was done with trouble.

I had to be wary about caravan parks for other reasons, too. Some of the residents were fringy, unhinged types, and I could sense there were drugs and alcohol seeping out of the vans and cabins. So, I'd have my shower and be halfway down the street before anyone was the wiser and I'd arrive at TAFE early in order to type up my notes from the night before. Sometimes it seemed the only thing that was getting any easier in my life was the typing part. I was determined to learn the correct Q-W-E-R-T-Y method and although I ached for a few months as the muscles and tendons in my fingers stretched to match the task, I became quite a proficient typist. Tick!

As part of the assessment for the tertiary preparation course, we were required to keep a personal diary. That sounds easy enough, in theory, but I really struggled with it. Just writing was hard enough, but sharing details about my life? That went against all of my instincts. I knew, though, that if I was going to make my way in this new forest, I was going to find it uncomfortable – just as I'd had to get used to discomfort when I first went to live on the mountain at Goonengerry.

I was agonising over what to write in the diary during a stroll along the Southport foreshore one evening, when I picked up a pristine bird feather that was lying on the grass. I marvelled at its green and yellow hues, and later that night I twirled it between my thumb and forefinger and contemplated what an education might mean. How might it change me? What might my future look like? 'A bird can fly anywhere it wants,' I thought. 'That's freedom.

Real freedom.' And that's what I figured an education might give me – the freedom to go where I chose and be who I wanted to be. I slipped the feather into my TAFE diary as a bookmark and a constant reminder of a yearning to spread my wings and fly with whatever birds I chose to.

Down on terra firma, however, I was spending a lot of my time in the company of Humpty Dumpty, and although by now I was comfortable with him and all the king's men, I was still struggling with actual human beings.

Like me, Karen Wise was a mature-age student at Southport TAFE. Unlike me she was chatty, upbeat and asked lots of questions. I found her irritating at first, which says everything about me and nothing about her. Karen was also the very first person I ever joined for a cup of coffee. Obviously, it was her idea.

We'd been exchanging small talk after a class one day when she asked me if I'd like to go downstairs with her to the TAFE cafeteria. 'Um,' I gulped. 'Yeah, sure.' The proposition absolutely terrified me. I felt the same way I had when Heather asked me to drop by her place for a joint.

Coffee? *With another person?*

We paid for our respective brews and sat down at a table in the same manner hundreds of millions of people do every day the world over. Except to me this was a giant leap forward. I might as well have been Neil Armstrong and the cafeteria the surface of the moon. Karen was a really pleasant lady – a great conversationalist and very inquisitive. I told her I lived at Tweed Heads ('You know, just down near the beach') before swinging the conversational spotlight back onto her. Although I was frightened, I was also thrilled. I felt as if I were at some funky little cafe in Paris exchanging thoughts with an intellectual peer. I felt sophisticated, engaged and 'part of'. I had made it.

But it didn't take long for the voice to start up. 'If only Karen knew who I really am.' Not only did I suddenly feel like a freak and a loser as I sat there, I was beginning to feel like a complete fraud as well. I had no business studying at TAFE or trying to enter university. Who did I think I was kidding? I was a complete and utter –

'I'm thinking of having a barbecue and inviting a bunch of people from the course,' Karen said, unwittingly inter- rupting the torrent of self-loathing that was gushing through my mind. 'Do you think you'd like to come, Gregory?'

Whoa! A freaking barbecue? Coffee was one thing, but I was pretty sure I wasn't ready to stand around with other people for more than a few minutes! I politely told Karen that I'd have to get back to her. I explained that I was pretty busy 'with study and a lot of other stuff', but if I could make it I would, although it would depend on whether I wasn't caught up doing all those other things in my busy schedule that I had to do.

Karen was cool about my non-commitment, but a few days later she gave me a date for her get-together and, after much anguished consideration, I decided I would go. It was what a valiant knight would do. I liked Karen and we were becoming friendly, so I rang her up – my first ever social call on my first ever mobile phone – and graciously accepted her kind invitation.

The barbecue was held on a Saturday at Karen's place in nearby Carrara. I recognised all the faces in attendance:

three men, including me, and five women. I was extremely tense and on-guard. I stuck close to the blokes and talked solely about TAFE, curriculum and assessments. The booze flowed and when I thought an appropriately polite amount of time had passed, Humpty and I made our excuses and were the first to leave. Karen told me later that they partied until late and that I had missed out on a great time. 'No I didn't!' I thought. I'd had a good time sitting in the sand dunes back at Southport Beach working on my assignment. Until it started to pour with rain.

33

THE 'BURBS

'I'm homeless and I'd like some help to find a place to live.'

I was sitting in an office at the Southport TAFE campus talking to a student counsellor, but I may as well have been speaking to a brick wall. 'OK, what you do is you go to a real estate agent or look in the newspaper or on the internet and find a place you like and tell them blah-blah-blah-blah-problem-solved-go-away.'

I sat there feeling defeated and totally misunderstood, 'I know all that!' I thought. 'What I'm saying is I need someone to help me *do* all that stuff.' I wasn't as social-ised as the average Joe so it was no surprise the counsellor didn't realise I hadn't the faintest idea how to take the simple steps everybody else took for granted. I walked out frustrated and angry.

A short time later I went on a long, restless walk and ended up on Chevron Island, a suburban atoll in the middle of the Nerang River that flows through Surfers Paradise. Overcome with frustration and despair, I sank onto a park bench and began to weep. I'd come so far since leaving the forest, but for all my efforts and the hope and ambition I had for a better life, here I was, still homeless. With my face in my hands, twenty-five years of sorrow welled up and spilled out of me. I could not stop myself from crying.

'Are you alright, love?'

I looked up and squinted into the sun. A heavyset grey-haired woman in a floral dress had appeared and was standing right in front of me. She looked worried.

'Are you alright?'

'No, I'm not,' I sobbed.

'What's wrong? Tell me what's happening.'

To my amazement I opened up and told the lady everything. How I'd been homeless for years but now I was trying to study for TAFE. How I'd been to see the counsellor and he didn't understand what I was saying. How no one seemed to understand me. How all I wanted was to get a safe, dry place to live in so I could study in peace and go to university one day. How I needed someone to walk me through it.

She gently took me by the arm and ushered me to my feet. 'OK, we can do this. Let's go for a walk. How much money have you got?'

By living on the beach and not drinking, smoking or doing drugs I'd managed to amass about $1000 thanks to the pension. The lady reckoned it would be enough to get me started in a place of my own. We walked to a real estate agent in a row of shops on Chevron Island. There were places to let advertised in the windows, and a stack of pamphlets in a wire stand out the front with other properties listed in them. The lady waited patiently as I looked at the options.

'See anything you like?'

I jabbed my finger at the cheapest unit in the pamphlet. 'Yes. This one.'

'OK, so now all we have to do is go inside and talk to someone about renting it.'

Once in the shop, though, the agent pulled that patronising 'Gee, I wish I could help you' face, and pointed out I had no recent rental history. But my grey-haired guardian angel wouldn't hear of it – she argued my case, and within an hour I was standing alongside her, inspecting the unfurnished one-bedroom unit. The building was a single-storey, 1960s affair comprising three flats. Mine was at the back, hemmed in and shaded by two multistorey apartment blocks. It was a tiny, dark, horrible place – and I loved it.

'So, what do you think?' my angel asked.

What did I think? I still couldn't believe that this amazing woman – a stranger who didn't know me from a bar of soap – had taken time out of her life to help put mine on track. I told her I loved the place and she took me through the process of signing the lease papers. I picked up the keys about four days later and when I turned up to move in, there she was, eager to show me how to get the electricity connected. I thanked her profusely and never saw her again.

For the first time in my life I was alone in a place all of my own, not counting the mountaintop and my post-office box. It was completely empty save for me, my dillybag, my backpack and a computer floppy disk. I sat on the floor and took it all in. Suddenly, I was scared. 'What on earth do I do now?' I figured I needed a bed, and maybe a chair as well. It dawned on me, as I sat there on the bones of my backside, that I'd swapped the soft sands of the wild for the unyielding, albeit carpeted, floor of suburbia. Some renovations were necessary.

That night I liberated ten milk crates from the laneways and alleys of Chevron Island, carried them back to the unit and started interior decorating. Using my pocket knife I unscrewed the bathroom door from its hinges and laid it atop six milk crates. Voila! A bed! I had always preferred, where possible, to sleep off the ground away from the creepy-crawlies. It was no different in the unit.

The next day I went to an op shop and scored some second-hand blankets. I bought a brand new pillow, too. With my bed sorted I turned my attention to a desk and chairs. In the end the solution was simple: each morning I'd dismantle the bed, arrange four stacks of two milk crates on top of each other, and lay the bathroom door across them. Voila! A desk! With a milk crate or two left over to sit on I also had a chair. Honestly, Ikea is thoroughly overrated.

There was only one thing missing. The following night I went out for a walk and quietly prised the bowl-like hub cap off a busted-up Volkswagen Beetle I'd seen parked a few streets away. Back in the unit, I filled it up with some sticks I'd collected and soon had a nice fire to sit by. A campfire had become central to my spirituality. After all, that's where I'd met my ancestors – it was as if they'd been attracted to the flames. It was also in the glow of the flickering light that my whole new understanding of who I was had started to come into focus.

The weeks were ticking down to the end of the TAFE course, and with a roof over my head and desk to work at I was able to concentrate a good deal better. I soon had a flatmate, too. He definitely wasn't the youngest cat I'd met. He had numerous battle scars and looked like he was pretty hungry. A fellow traveller.

He turned up out of the blue one day and parked himself on the mat I'd not long purchased for the front sliding door. He was obviously homeless and neglected. At first I tried to shoo him away because he'd get tangled up in my feet as I was trying to unlock the door after TAFE. Before long he cheekily barged past my legs and into the unit where he made a bee-line for the kitchen and generally got in my way.

After the third or fourth time I nearly tripped over him I called him Doofer, because he was always due for something. I was never quite sure if he was due for a pat, a scratch or dinner. I'd throw him out in the mornings and go about my routine at school. When I came back in the evening he'd be there on the mat with a look on his face that said, 'Go on then. Open the bloody door, will ya?'

Somehow, in a moment of weakness, I cracked open a can of sardines I had in the cupboard, found him a bowl and gave him dinner. The next thing I knew I was stopping at the supermarket on the way home to buy more sardines. Doofer a feed.

I was in my own place, I was studying, I was sober and I had a furry little mate.

Cat or no cat I was still haunted by a lifetime of trauma, addiction and abuse. I grew increasingly antsy during the final weeks of the tertiary preparation course because there was talk that some of the students were looking like they would indeed have a future at university. Apparently, I was one of them. As we were waiting for the final assessments to come in I became obsessed with my results. I decided, unilaterally, to sit for the STAT (the Special Tertiary Admissions Test). It's a scholastic aptitude exam that people can take to gain entry into undergraduate courses at Australian universities. I wanted to make sure I was up to the task. I told my tutor, Janet Diehl, about my plan. 'Oh, don't bother with that. You don't need to do it, Gregory!' she assured me. 'The tertiary preparation course is all you need and you're almost finished. Just relax.'

Fat chance. I went ahead and arranged to sit the STAT, and three weeks later, when the results arrived in my post-office box, I was devastated. I had scored less than three per cent. I was beyond upset. I had devoted the best part of a year to trying to get into university. It had been a dream ever since I saw the men building a campus at Tweed Heads, and all along I'd been wasting my time! Three microscopic per cent? How pathetic.

I took the letter to TAFE with me the next week, sat down in Janet's office, handed it to her and burst into tears. 'I'm not smart after all,' I bawled. 'In fact, I'm really, *really* dumb. Less than three per cent, Janet! *Less than three per cent!* You need eighty-six per cent to study at university.'

She leaned back in her chair and started laughing. 'Gregory, don't be silly!' she said. 'You don't understand. The STAT is designed for people who have been educated in a certain way – in what's considered the normal way. You're not normal. You think way outside the square. Your understanding of things is acutely different. Really, don't worry.'

Looking back I believe this is what the tutor at Ultimo TAFE had been trying to tell me in 1987. 'Don't give up on your education.' He saw beyond the junkie to someone whose intellect was apparently unique.

I wasn't at all convinced Janet was right, though, and I continued to fret. I was, however, slightly chuffed that the only answer I got right in the whole STAT exam was, 'How many books are there in *The Hitchhiker's Guide to the Galaxy* trilogy?' Too easy: there are five. Douglas Adams had been a favourite of mine up in the forest, so I had learned something useful during those crazy years after all. What's more, I'd proved you didn't necessarily need a babel fish in order to speak to aliens.

There was a much simpler grading system for subjects in the tertiary preparation course. You either scored one, two or three. If you got a one, you failed. A mark of two was a pass and if you scored a three, that was essentially a high distinction. When the results came in a few weeks later I got threes right across the board. The next time I saw Janet she just smiled. 'Told you so,' she said.

For the second time in two years I'd been there at the end.

*

The graduation ceremony – the first I had ever attended – was held inside a large auditorium at Southport TAFE. 'I shouldn't be here,' I kept telling myself. 'If only they knew who I am and where I come from.' When my name was called over the PA I froze in my seat. It was only after I was nudged by the classmates on either side of me that I managed to stand and walk onto the stage. The mayor shook my hand and presented me with my certificate. As I shuffled off stage I was so overwhelmed that I started to weep.

My body was there but my mind had switched off, which I'd find out later is called a 'dissociative episode'. My brain had trouble processing the events of the day. It wasn't so much the big room, the crowds, the formality or the mayor – it was the fact I was being acknowledged. Little time had passed since I had been a drunken homeless man who slept on the floor of a Sydney toilet block while four million people looked the other way. Only a couple of years prior I was hiding in a rainforest, drinking moonshine and eating magic mushrooms and dope for breakfast. Now, here I was on a stage in an auditorium shaking hands with the mayor while people cheered and applauded.

I resumed my seat in a daze. Then my name was called again and it was announced that I was being given a special achievement award. And the day became a blur that only got blurrier.

When it was all over I had time to reflect. Rather than feeling proud of my achievement, graduation day left me mired in even more self-doubt and a conviction that I had earned none of it. There had to be some mistake. Surely it would be just a matter of time before people found out who and what I really was.

34

TREVOR

Having yearned for so long to have a roof over my head, it was ironic that only a month after moving to Chevron Island I began to feel that very roof caving in on me. The walls started pressing up close and the windows grew smaller. It was dark, stiflingly hot and claustrophobic. The massive apartment blocks that dwarfed my building hummed with dozens of noisy air-conditioners that constantly whirred and sputtered in my general direction.

After a few months I hated every minute in that unit. So, when a new friend called Leanne invited me to stay with her, I jumped at the chance. I'd met Leanne through a mutual friend at TAFE and we seemed to click straight away. Leanne lived in a bright and breezy unit with her son, Daniel, a little way down the Gold Coast at Mermaid Waters, and we were gradually becoming an item. I must have told her that I was getting jack of my tiny microwave oven of an apartment.

'You can come and stay with me,' she said.

I really liked Leanne and it seemed like a great idea. My only misgiving was leaving my pal Doofer to fend for himself.

It was around October 2003 when I packed the last few things into the L300. I went back inside the unit and gave Doofer one final tin of sardines. As I farewelled him I hoped he might somehow find his way to the doorstep of the grey-haired lady in the floral dress. She knew how to look after busted-up blokes like us.

It was starting to dawn on me that my successful completion of the tertiary preparation course had truly opened up the door to university. It was a big deal, not just considering the challenges I had overcome to get there, but because as far as I knew I was the first in a long line of Smiths, stretching all the way back to the great William Joseph, to attend university. Now I just had to figure out what I was going to study.

As I researched university degrees that might interest and suit me, one word – sociology – kept leaping out of the booklets and brochures. It became lodged in my brain. Intrigued, I looked up the definition in the dictionary:

Sociology – noun: the science or study of the origin, development, organisation and functioning of human society.

Oh yes, indeed! That was for me. I would study human society. I would learn everything there was to learn about it, and I would finally come to understand why I had never fitted in. I would unravel and examine society in minute detail in order to comprehend why I hated it so much and why society hated me right back.

I discovered that sociology was offered as a major at the School of Social Sciences at Southern Cross University, which had campuses in Tweed Heads and other parts of northern New South Wales – what I considered to be my neck of the woods. It didn't take me long to commit. Towards the end of 2003 I went through the application process and soon accepted an offer to start studying at the university in the New Year.

In February 2004, having sold the L300 in order to buy textbooks, I found myself on a bus heading south for my first day at SCU's campus at Tweed Heads. I stepped off the coach and straight into my past. 'I'm sure I've been here before,' I thought. 'Maybe it was in a dream?' Then it dawned on me: the last time I'd walked towards those gates the place had been a building site and I'd just wiped fish and chip grease onto my tattered jeans. 'It's gonna be a university,' the workman had told me back then. And now it was – just in time to receive me.

Although faintly reassured by the familiarity of the location by the Tweed River, I otherwise felt naked and vulnerable. The campus was full of people – most of them far younger than me – but I felt like I was the only one there who was desperately trying to be someone else. I persisted with the short hair and shaved face but the bullshit mask was beginning to suffocate me.

I had no idea what to expect at my first lecture. About forty of us were milling outside the classroom when a little old guy wearing a red and white polka dot bow tie came bustling down the hallway with his arms full of what appeared to be junk from a science lab. He opened the door and we all filed in while he set about dumping the bits and pieces all over the desk. There were half a dozen pairs of spectacles, a small telescope, a medium-sized telescope, different types of magnifying glasses, some looking glasses and a few pairs of binoculars.

'Where is this going?' I wondered. It was supposed to be the first lecture of our core unit, 'Approaches to Social Science', not 'Introduction to Optometry'. When we were all seated our lecturer had our undivided attention. 'That,' he said, gesturing to the assorted clutter strewn on his desk, 'is social science. It's the ability to look at society through different lenses.'

It was a powerful, perfectly distilled message delivered with such simplicity and elegance that I was floored. From that moment on the lecturer had me. It was so simple and clear – everybody has a different take on the world. Sister Winifred's views on orphanages, for example, were totally different yet no less real than mine.

Next, the lecturer said something else that had a profound impact on me. He'd been talking about empirical evidence – what you can and can't do in terms of citing facts. He said you can't, for example, make the ironclad statement that all crows are black. 'What happens when an albino crow flies past?' he asked. 'Authority is undermined and then you're stuffed. Better to say something like, "Most crows are black."' It was another important lesson – never make assumptions.

I was daunted during those first weeks at university and there were days I'd need to spend time with Humpty Dumpty to stop me throwing it all in and disappearing into a bottle down by the banks of the Tweed. I was skittish, awkward and anxious, and I felt I was masquerading in a world I had no right to inhabit.

'Be there at the end.'

About a month into the semester my latent volatility burst to the surface in a spectacular display of classroom pyrotechnics. I'd been seated in a semicircle of students during a unit called Interpersonal Communication that was being convened by a very nice female tutor. In one of the exercises she asked us to, 'Think about a happy experience from when you were a young child and share it with the group.'

I was on my feet in a furious flash. 'There's an assumption in that!' I exploded as I pointed accusingly at the tutor. It was a spontaneous eruption – I had no control over what I was doing. 'You people have got no idea, have you? What makes you think everyone had a happy childhood, eh? Fair dinkum.' I turned and stomped out of the room; each footstep like an angry exclamation mark.

Outside I gulped in some fresh air and calmed myself a little. The next thing I knew, another lecturer – a fellow named Trevor Lucas – had sidled up to me. 'Are you okay?'

'No! I'm not!' I was ropeable. 'That tutor is making assumptions in there!' I told him what she'd said and why I was so upset. Trevor listened to me quietly and asked if I'd mind if he made a suggestion. 'How about I point out that assumption to her after the workshop?' he offered. 'And how about at any of the future lectures or workshops we let you know in advance if there's any content that you might be uncomfortable with?'

I thought that sounded reasonable. I could see he wanted to make an effort on the university's behalf. 'OK, yeah. That would be great. I'd appreciate that.' From then on, each week before lectures and tutorials in that unit I got a quick briefing on what they were going to be about.

As much as I was learning and enjoying the units in the Social Sciences, I still didn't really understand what a degree was or what I would do with one once I had it. I'd hear students talk about units, electives, majors and having to make decisions on directions or pathways of study, but it was pretty much Swahili to me. I was flying blind, tiptoe-ing through each lecture, workshop or tutorial each day, week by week and month by month, not really knowing what I needed to do next.

Slowly, however, I learned that my degree consisted of twenty-four units. A major area of learning consisted of six units in the same field of study, each one complement-ing and building on the knowledge of the others. Two major areas of study were required to form an under-graduate bachelor degree. It was also possible to include a minor area of study. A minor contained four units in the same field.

I started by taking a couple of counselling units as electives alongside the compulsory core units, with the view that I might get a degree in counselling and help other damaged people understand and deal with their problems. It wasn't much of a plan because, in truth, I didn't really want to listen to other people's problems when I could barely address my own – most notably of late a severe inferiority complex and a strong, inexplicable sense of shame. Still, with nothing else in mind and knowing that I wanted to get a job when all was said and done, counselling was it.

In the next semester I started a sociology unit called Deviance in Society and my lecturer was Trevor Lucas. He was very middle class – open collar, neat slacks and polished shoes. I had given up my ridiculous mask and returned to wearing my hair and beard long. It made me feel quite headstrong in his class. On the first day he asked us to introduce ourselves. Generally it went: name, degree, how far into the degree, what we might like to do when finished. When my turn came, I sat back in my chair with my arms folded. 'My name is Gregory and I'm here to learn.'

I didn't reveal any of my past experiences to him but for some reason Trevor took an interest in me. After a couple of weeks he buttonholed me after class. 'What's your pathway in university, Gregory?' he inquired.

'I don't know,' I answered honestly. 'I'm not sure.'

'Would you like to come and talk about it?'

'Yeah, OK.'

A few days later we were sitting in his office where he introduced himself properly. 'My background's in criminology and I have a history of working in the Victorian juvenile justice system,' he said. 'Over the years I've had a lot of experience working with what people like to call "problem children".' He put inverted commas around 'problem children' with a wiggle of his index fingers. I liked him straight away after that. Here was a man who had empathy; a man who got it. Trevor held up a printout of the academic units I'd completed and the ones I was enrolled in for the following semester, including my two counselling units. I'd begun a major in sociology and was grasping at what to do next.

'Just from watching you, it seems like you're developing an orientation towards a counselling major?' Trevor ventured.

'Oh yeah, maybe,' I conceded.

'You'd probably make a really good counsellor but think about this: every now and then someone comes along who can make a difference.'

'Make a difference how?'

'If a clock gains five minutes every few days and a counsellor has to keep coming along and putting the clock back on time – well, that process just goes on and on, doesn't it?'

I nodded. 'Yes, I suppose it does.'

'But every now and then someone comes along who can learn about how the mechanism of the clock really works. They can go in and fix that mechanism or make changes to it so that the clock doesn't gain time anymore. Maybe you're one of those people.'

I sat there and took it in. Or at least I tried to. It sounded really weird but he still had my attention. 'I'm not exactly sure I follow what you're saying, Trevor.'

'Sometimes,' he said, leaning towards me, 'the problems are more about social policies and educating the policy makers than they are about the people who are experiencing poor outcomes.'

He described how, during his time working in juvenile justice, he became frustrated with the lack of empathy officials showed towards children who clearly had underlying troubles caused by family problems and out-of-home care. 'One of the best ways to address this,' he said, 'is to help policy makers understand the ongoing issues that are faced by these care leavers.'

Ongoing issues. I could write a book about that, I thought.

From that moment onward, my path through university was clear. Following Trevor's advice I ditched the counselling units and instead continued with Sociology and planned majors in either Human Relations or Community Development, plus a minor in Indigenous Studies.

Trevor, more than anyone, helped shape and focus my long-held desire for an education and gave it a real purpose – a *mighty* purpose – beyond just getting a qualification for a job in an office tower somewhere. He convinced me it was possible to make a difference in other people's lives by changing the way people think and how laws and institutions operate.

This realisation also helped me to start owning my past, to know that I didn't have to feel ashamed or fearful of being judged – that my life experience gave me something unique to offer. My perspective was an important lens through which society could be viewed. Today I wish Trevor could see how far his advice and counsel have taken me. When I met him I had no idea he had terminal cancer. The world lost him just over a year later, but he remained right by me throughout my entire education. He's still with me today.

35

NOT FORGOTTEN

The process of learning at university level started to re-shape me and the way I presented to the world. At times I felt like I was acclimatising through osmosis as I became more used to campus life and interacting with people in general. Being involved in tutorial discussions, and researching and writing essays on a range of socio-logical topics not only gave me a deeper understanding of how Australian society functioned but also of my place in it. And my place in society was rapidly changing.

I decided to do my second major in Community Development. The caveat being that it was taught face-to-face at the Coffs Harbour campus nearly 300 kilometres away. By now I had been living with Leanne for several months but, not surprisingly, it wasn't all smooth sailing. After all, I had lived as a hermit for more than a decade and wasn't used to sharing a space with another human being, no matter how fond I was of her. I made a snap decision to prioritise my education over my budding relationship.

When I stepped off the bus alone in Coffs Harbour a few days later I hadn't the faintest idea where I was going to live, but I had resolved that I would do whatever I could to avoid sleeping rough ever again. I wandered over to the information kiosk at the bus stop to find it manned by three elderly ladies. 'Hello, I've just arrived in town to start studying at the university and I'm looking for a place to live – a cheap place,' I explained, before adding rather hopefully, 'I don't suppose you know of anywhere?'

Luckily I had chanced upon the best, most impressively staffed public information booth in Australia. The ladies fussed and clucked, and before I knew it I was handed the address of a house only a few suburbs away whose owners were renting out a granny flat for a very reasonable price. I thanked the lovely information gurus and hailed a taxi. The place turned out to be a neat, two-room affair with a tidy kitchenette and a nice, homely vibe. It was also quiet and tucked away at the back of a property owned by a couple called Robert and Glenys Cowin. I slept well that night and woke early to give myself time to walk to my new campus. That's when I learned that it was a solid one-hour hike away.

I'd spent much of my life travelling by foot, and the older I got, the more walking seemed to sap me of my energy. In the forest I put it down to malnutrition, drugs, booze and cigarettes. But now that I was taking care of myself, I figured grinding fatigue was just the price I had to pay for a hard-lived life. Still, the loping biped movement provided a good tempo for meditation and processing whatever I had learned or was wrestling with each day. The only time walking was a pain was when it was raining, and I had arrived in Coffs Harbour right in the middle of a particularly biblical wet season.

After one depressingly sodden week I trudged back to the granny flat on a Friday evening to find a couple of items had been left outside for me. The first thing I noticed was the nice big umbrella leaning against the screen door; the second was the plate on the front step piled with roast lamb, mashed potatoes, baked pumpkin and carrots. Beautiful people, Robert and Glenys. After a couple of months spent walking back and forth to uni a fellow student, Lynda Lloyd, suggested that if I was on the highway at a certain time each day she would pick me up. Great! Pre-planned hitchhiking.

The further I progressed with my undergraduate studies the more confident I became in myself and my world view. Where once I would hide at the back of the class and scurry away as soon as it had ended, I became more willing and able to participate in conversations.

Although I had spent a lifetime resenting society, I was coming to realise it stemmed from never having really understood it. Now, by studying it and unravelling how it worked, I found I hated society and the people in it far less. I began to see society not as a machine that chewed up and spat out people like me, but as an incredible organism made up of billions of precious little components at the mercy of myriad variables – political, class and caste systems, policy decisions, religious doctrine, poverty, racial tension, tribal rules, traditions, cultures, substance abuse and a thousand other lenses you cared to look through.

My lifelong resentment had also been caused by my having no understanding of myself. Now, through the processes of education and sobriety, I was offered an opportunity to introduce myself to me. Once I developed that relationship, I found I was able to start getting to know other people, too. Not only that, I started to realise I really liked other people. Leanne re-entered my life and joined me in Coffs Harbour, and I also found myself becoming friendly with a man named Dr Richard Hil.

The first time we met was at a tutorial he was facilitating at Coffs Harbour. Richard had been called on to teach a unit called Advocacy and Change, and another called Evaluation and Social Welfare. Richard's a brilliantly entertaining lecturer, but these were not his areas of expertise and he would be the first to admit it was a pretty dreary session. As he paused to gather his thoughts on the topic in the quiet lecture room I called out in a loud, clear voice: 'I used to be a werewolf but I'm alright *now-OOOOOW!*'

The class broke up and so did Richard – an adulthood echo of my second-form science teacher's appreciation of the rotten-egg gas gag. I think Richard knew I was hinting that, yes, he was boring us, but also that it was nothing we couldn't have a laugh about. After the class had finished, Richard collared me and introduced himself. He was a sweet and engaging man who was a bit older than me, and with the good looks of a young Rod Stewart. 'I'm glad you used to be a werewolf,' he said. 'I was dying in there.'

'Ha ha! No worries.'

Richard smiled. 'You seem like an interesting bloke, would you like to get together for a coffee and a chat one of these days?'

'Sure thing, that sounds nice.'

We left it at that, with a loose understanding we'd see each other around the traps on campus and find time to catch up. In the meantime I took it upon myself to do a bit of reading up about Dr Hil. It turned out that he was Polish-born but British educated, and that he'd written a book with a couple of other academics about children in care homes, the effects on children in State care and so on. I decided to speak to him about it at his next tutorial.

'Hello, Richard, I read that book you wrote about children in care.'

'Really? So what did you think?'

'I think you've got no idea what you're talking about.'

He was taken aback, and so I suggested that if he wanted to know the real story he should read *Forgotten Australians*, the 2004 Senate report on people who had experienced institutional or out-of-home care as children. I just so happened to have a copy of it with me and gave it to him.

'Thanks. Do you want to have a coffee and talk about it?' Richard asked.

'Yeah, I'd love to – *after* you've read the report.'

A week later I bumped into him again. 'Would you like to have a coffee?' he asked.

'Have you read that report yet?'

'No, I haven't yet, I'm afraid.'

'Well, I'm afraid I still don't want that coffee.'

It went on like that for a long time. Richard told me later the report sat on his bedside table while he ploughed through all the other books he had to read. 'It was so thick, Gregory,' he complained jokingly. 'And it looked like a bloody boring government report!'

I had come across the Senate report quite by accident while sitting in the university library doing some online research. When the words *Forgotten Australians* first appeared in my Google search I thought it must have been about soldiers or the Boer War or something. But I clicked through anyway and started reading the executive summary, which described the 'more than 500,000 Australians [who] experienced care in an orphanage or other form of out-of-home care during the last century'. It read:

> *Anecdotal evidence has shown an abnormally large percentage of suicides among care leavers. Care leavers harbour powerful feelings of anger, guilt and shame; have a range of ongoing physical and mental health problems – often directly associated with beatings or lack of health care as a child; and struggle with employment and housing issues.*

My hands trembled and I started to weep in the quiet of the library. Then I began to feel sick. I wanted to heave my guts out then and there but the nausea was accompanied by a strange feeling of relief, too – like a light had been shined into the darkest corners of my world. It was ugly, but at least I could finally see.

I had spent the best part of half a century wandering the world alone. I had always felt like a misfit, a freak, a loser, a sinner and, worst of all, that no one on earth could possibly understand me. Yet here was a report that described not only what had happened to me, but how and why it happened, and that I was not the only person it had happened to. Half a million others had suffered. The report *understood* me, to a degree. It made sense of me. A watershed moment.

After a while I had to stop reading. It's not a pleasant report and it took me a few months to finish it. Then I sent away to Canberra for a hard copy, which ended up lying dormant on Richard's bedside table.

Finally, Richard picked it up. Within a week we were sitting down over coffee at the campus cafeteria. 'I couldn't believe what I was reading,' Richard said with a grave shake of his head. 'I opened it up on the summary page and I was stunned. It was unbelievable. And it just got worse from there.'

Richard – now a professor – is a world-renowned academic who has taught at universities in the UK and throughout Australia. He has a keen interest in society's mistreatment of the disadvantaged and vulnerable and has written and read widely about such abuses. 'I knew all about the gross mistreatment of migrant children, the Stolen Generations and so on,' he confessed, 'but I had never heard a word about the Forgotten Australians. That's half a million kids who I knew nothing about. The first question, of course, is, "Why and how on earth could I not know?"'

At least he now knew one of those kids – me – and over time I was able to help us both understand the general ignorance around the Forgotten Australians. I'd experienced precisely that abuse myself and I'd seen others suffer around me, but until I read the Senate report even I didn't know how widespread and thoroughly systematic the gross mistreatment of children in out-of-home care was. It was shameful that it had gone undiscussed and undisclosed.

There was something else troubling about the report, framed by the fact I had found it completely by accident. How come I – an actual Forgotten Australian – didn't know this whole process had taken place? Senate hearings, investigations and reports? And if I didn't know how many other people whose lives had been ruined didn't know? Even today many people affected aren't aware there is help available for them.

Richard and I became firm friends and the more I told him about my own life, the more outraged he became about the hardships those early injustices helped create. A few years later we co-authored a chapter for a book called *Surviving Care: Achieving Justice and Healing for the Forgotten Australians*. It was a critical appraisal of the New South Wales Government's 2005 apology to the Forgotten Australians. As far as we were concerned, the apology was inadequate.

Richard became something of an academic champion of mine, but also a great supporter as a friend. I found him fascinating, witty and excellent company, and it was largely through him that I finally started to feel 'part of'. After a lifetime spent looking for a place to fit in, I would never have imagined that that place would be among academics.

Talking with Richard was good for me, too. He asked a lot of questions about my life, as a reporter would do.

It made me think about things I hadn't faced up to in years and didn't necessarily want to think about. As much as it helped me, though, it was becoming obvious that I required much more intensive professional therapy than chatting with my mate. I'd begun to 'zone' out and lose all perspective on where I was.

I was by no means a well person.

36

TRUE NORTH

As a Forgotten Australian I was told I qualified for some psychological help and was put in touch with a practitioner called Christina North. Christina admitted that she didn't know anything about the Forgotten Australians when I first met her, but added that she was willing to learn, which I thought was refreshingly honest. She seemed eager to expand her expertise and to go on the voyage with me.

Christina may not have worked with Forgotten Australians prior to me but she was no stranger to dealing with people who'd suffered trauma. Still, during our early sessions I was cautious and guarded about how much I told her. Over the years that followed, however, Christina became an important lifeline for me. She gave me a phone number I could contact her on twenty-four hours a day, and there were times I did.

It was Christina who formally diagnosed me as suffering chronic severe Post Traumatic Stress Disorder, severe depression and social anxiety. Sometimes these would manifest in episodes of dissociation (the zoning out). It was likely, she said, that I'd had these mental problems since childhood. For decade upon damaging decade.

It's even likely I'd experienced dissociative blackouts for most of my life, but – through either drunkenness, drugs or mental discombobulation due to my shambolic and chaotic existence – I never recognised them for what they were. Now that my fragmented mind was healing, the long-term, untreated symptoms of trauma and abuse were becoming more apparent to me.

Whenever I was dissociated, I would be physically present but have no idea where I was, much like the out-of-body experience on my TAFE graduation day. Then it started getting a bit weirder. I'd be in a supermarket and have no clue how I got there or what I was doing.

She taught me techniques to centre myself by focusing on familiar things around me. If I was at home it could be by placing my didgeridoo in the middle of the room and homing in on that. If I was out, my fingers could always reach for something else familiar, like my marbles in the dillybag.

Over time I recognised that my dissociative episodes tended to happen when I was highly stressed, got angry or in instances where, in the past, I would have lost control. I could black out if someone was rude to me or if I really wanted to just smash someone in the face. I consider myself extremely fortunate to have had Christina's help to navigate me through it. Others weren't so lucky.

*

Four of my sisters were Forgotten Australians, too, and although we had been estranged and scattered for many years, we had not forgotten each other – not that our memories were necessarily pleasant. Years could go by between phone calls. When I had been living rough in Brisbane in the period before I entered the forest I rang Glenda, the eldest of the five girls, out of the blue. She was easy to find because she'd always lived in the same house and had the same phone number and, like me, she never, ever rearranged her furniture.

I don't remember the precise reason for the phone call, but it ended up with me whingeing, hissing and slurring all manner of bitterness about my life. 'The problem with you, Gregory,' Glenda cut in, 'is that you're a very intelligent man but you have absolutely no common sense.'

I slammed the phone down. 'How dare she?' I fumed inside the steamed-up phone booth. 'I've got all the common sense I was born with. I just choose not to use it because I never know when I'm going to need it all.' I had the shits with her so badly that it was another five years or so before I called again. I was living in the forest at that point and I rang her from a phone booth in Byron Bay. That's how she knew to ask the cops to go and look for me the year that Mum died.

After I came out of the forest I kept up a bit of phone contact with Glenda, but had almost nothing to do with my other four sisters. On Christmas Day in 2004, I was having lunch at one of the local soup kitchens I now volunteered in, when my phone rang. I fished it out of my pocket but didn't recognise the incoming number.

'Gregory, it's your sister Wendy,' a voice said. 'Glenda

gave me your number. I heard you got off the drink a few years ago.'

'Yeah, that's right.'

'How did you do it? I need help. Can you help me?' she pleaded.

I wasn't sure I could, but I would definitely try. Wendy was working pumping petrol at a service station on the Gold Coast and she was hitting the bottle hard. She had pain from carpal tunnel damage in her wrists and a permanent ache from emotional damage to her soul. We chatted on the phone a couple more times and soon agreed to get together. It was a Sunday afternoon when we met in the shade of a big tree down by the water at Paradise Point, south-east of where she lived in the suburb of Coomera.

'There's something different about you,' she said as she peered at me quizzically.

'I reckon there would be,' I said. 'I've been through a bit since I last saw you. When was it? The eighties?'

'No, you've changed,' she said. 'It's in your voice and in your face.'

'Y'know, your life doesn't have to remain the way it is now, Wendy,' I said. 'You can take some control over the direction of it each day.'

Wendy didn't look convinced. 'I really hate my job.'

'Trust me, you can do something about that as well.'

A week or so later Wendy invited me over to her place for dinner. A couple of weeks after that her son, Scott, phoned me. His mother was drunk, going 'off her nut', he said, and he was worried that she was going to cause some serious damage or hurt herself.

'What's she drinking?' I asked.

'Um, scotch, I think.'

I headed towards Wendy's place but stopped at a drive-through bottle shop along the way and bought some cheap whiskey. When I got to Wendy's she was already pretty messy and pretty angry. Seething, in fact. I sat down in her lounge room and put the bottle in the middle of the table. 'Go on. Have some more,' I said.

Wendy poured herself a glass and launched into a bitter tirade about things that had happened when we were little. Each sip of whiskey was sprayed back out as a mouthful of bile. There were accusations, character assassinations, grievances, resentment, judgements and tearful retellings of Mum and Dad's heinous crimes. I just sat there and let her go for it.

'Here, have a bit more scotch,' I said, and Wendy refilled her glass. By now she was on her feet, yelling and screaming about how shit her life was, why we were so screwed up and what had she ever done to deserve all this bullshit when all she wanted was a normal childhood, a normal family and A BLOODY NORMAL LIFE?

'Have another one, Wendy,' I said, nudging the bottle across the table towards her. The next glassful brought out the violence. She picked up a chair and smashed it hard into her living-room wall, splintering the wood and putting a gash in the plaster. From there on it was no holds barred. Over the next little while Wendy ranted and screamed and tore her house apart. I sat and watched in silence as she flung appliances, lamps, furniture – anything she could lift – into the walls. Lights were smashed and the gyprock was pockmarked by the hail of flying objects.

Finally, I stood up and spoke. 'Wendy, I think you

missed a spot over there,' I said, pointing to an unmolested section of wall and offering the chair I'd been sitting on as ammunition.

Crash. She didn't miss that time. It was an exclamation mark at the end of a nerve-wracking night. Emotionally exhausted and blind drunk, my poor, tortured, beautiful little sister staggered into her room and passed out. I slept on the couch that night surrounded by the detritus of Wendy's anguish until the early hours when I heard someone moving about. It was Scott. He was gingerly picking his way through the debris like a salvage worker cleaning up after a cyclone.

'What are you doing?' I asked incredulously.

'I'm cleaning up,' Scott said. He said he always did after his mum carried out a spontaneous renovation.

'No-no-no-no-no. Put that down. Don't move a thing. Leave everything exactly where it is. She needs to see it.'

When Wendy came out of her room later that morning with bloodshot eyes and regret written across her face, she took a long, silent look around. Then she looked at me. I looked back at her. She hasn't had a drink since that day.

37

MERCY MISSION

Although my first marriage had been a train wreck, I decided to give love another whirl, and on Thursday, 20 July 1989, I got hitched for a second time. My bride was a lady by the name of Christine Ann Harlow and we tied the knot at the registry offices in Sydney. Christine was born in Calcutta, India, but had been living at Dharruk in the hardscrabble western suburbs of Sydney when we wed. As shown on our Certificate of Marriage, I'd moved up in the world and was ensconced in fashionable Pennant Hills in the city's north-west and working as a store manager. Living the dream again.

Dad had died by then, but, strangely, I can't remember if Mum attended the ceremony or not, and I don't recall whether Christine and I held a reception afterwards either. I can't put my finger on the name of my (second) best man, or if I even had one. I can't describe Christine's dress, or whether she was tall or short, a redhead, brunette or blonde. I don't know the colour of her eyes or the lines of her smile. In fact, I don't remember Christine at all, and I sure as hell can't think of a time I ever lived in posh Pennant Hills.

This ghost marriage to a phantom woman was just one of many bizarre and nasty surprises that leapt off the page when I was granted access to my government-held records after I put in a Freedom of Information application in the winter of 2006.

To have no recollection of it – none whatsoever – made me question whether the episode ever actually happened, but there it was in black and white, dated, stamped, signed by the registrar and filed in the Births, Deaths and Marriages archives. Within a year of this wedding I was well and truly living in the forest and waking up with a snake rather than a woman. I have no idea what became of this Christine Ann Harlow, only that she has long since divorced me.

My records offered a weird window into a turbulent past. While the marriage was perplexing, much of the other material was depressing. When I first read the court papers and psychological reports of my youth I was saddened by the things that had been catalogued about the sad, skinny little boy I used to be. I was also ashamed about some of the things he'd done. It was a lot to digest and I could only bear to read it a morsel at a time.

On subsequent reviews, however, I grew angry about the things that happened to me that didn't appear in my records. I had applied separately to the Gunnedah Congregation of the Sisters of Mercy to access the files they held about me and the sixteen months I spent in their 'care'.

The substance of the document they sent me comprised less than fifty words. The longest sentence related to my father's address, and that was because two places of residence were listed. The rest simply noted my name, my date of admission, my date of birth, my supposed religion, Mum's name, Dad's name and my date of discharge.

It was a classic example of why people like Richard Hil had no idea about the existence of Forgotten Australians for so long. Largely unregulated institutions, homes and orphanages had conveniently 'forgotten' to keep records of what they did to children. Or, if they did record and archive their evils, care leavers like me and the public at large weren't privy to them.

By contrast, the records relating to my time in juvenile detention – where there had been a certain level of oversight and accountability, or at least the appearance of it – betrayed a different kind of clerical amnesia. In boys homes, the written accounts of my progress were such a silly charade they bordered on pantomime: 'Hey, Gregory's an awesome boy! He's coming along just fine! He responds well to being locked up and is a healthy and active participant in our kiddie prison program of sports, fun and games. We'll just keep him here for a few more months to make sure he's the best, most well-adjusted sociopathic juvenile offender who ever walked the earth.'

In the punitive system, they didn't forget to make reports and keep records, they just forgot to be honest in them. And in the absence of any other documentation, the courts and society have taken those 'records' as gospel. Just as the psychiatric report Dr Freeman used to write me off as a sociopath for all those years, such papers carried weight.

I found his letter buried among the pile of Freedom of Information documents, preserved in my files forever like a DNA swab that never matched my profile in the first place. Even then, though, I still believed him.

Three years later Richard Hil and I were on a road trip to Sydney to watch the then Premier Nathan Reece deliver an updated and upgraded apology to the more than 200,000 former residents of institutional care in New South Wales. We weren't the only ones who believed the government's 2005 apology just didn't cut it, so after a sustained campaign Reece made amends. On the long drive back to Coffs Harbour I handed Richard a manila folder containing my records.

'What's this?' he asked.

'Don't say anything, just read it for a while.'

Richard pored through the wad of A4 pages as we motored north. He read the social workers' accounts of my childhood home, the portrait of my father as a vicious alcoholic, the dismissals of me as a dullard with an embarrassing IQ, the cringe-worthy retellings of my teenage crimes, the psychological evaluations, the court decisions and the detention centre 'progress' reports. When he finished he looked over at me, speechless. 'Well,' I said, 'what do you think?'

'What do you mean "What do I think?" I don't know where to begin,' he replied.

'Do *you* think I'm a sociopath?'

Richard's shoulders slumped and he let out a sigh. 'No, mate,' he began gently, 'I don't. What I just read was violence on top of violence. You were placed in a system that should have given you love, care and affection, and treated you with the respect that you deserved. Those looking after you should have fully known about the implications of your background.

'What you got was anything but. Then you've got this Freeman guy who had the audacity to describe you as a sociopath, which is one of the cruellest things you can do to another human being. So, no, Gregory Smith, you are not a sociopath – *they* are the fucking sociopaths. It's a sociopathic system that denied you love. Denied you the care and dignity you needed.'

I respected the hell out of Richard, but I still wasn't convinced.

'Do you think she might still be alive?' Richard was appalled by my stories about Sister Winifred and her Catholic cohorts. The beltings, the belittling, the locking of frightened children in the dark, my smashed mouth and her litany of casual cruelty. A slightly disgusted look would come across his face whenever her name came up. 'If she's alive,' he said, 'we should go and see her.'

Taking part in such a showdown had never occurred to me, but I said I'd try to find out about Winifred's state of existence. It was the summer of 2009 when I telephoned the Congregation of the Sisters of Mercy. Their archivist, a lady by the name of Judith Carney, informed me that, yes, Sister Winifred was indeed 'still with us'. She was a grand ninety-four years of age, retired and being looked after in a nursing home in the North West

Slopes town of Gunnedah, about an hour's drive from Tamworth.

'Oh, mate, we've got to go and pay her a visit,' Richard responded with an almost boyish curiosity when I told him this news. I, however, wasn't quite so convinced. Did I really want to be in the same room as that snarling ogre from my childhood? What would I say? How would I react? What would be the point? I didn't respond to Richard's idea to begin with, and mulled it over for a few days instead. Finally, after trawling through my cata-logue of painful memories about Sister Winifred, I realised Richard was right; I most certainly did want to have a word or two with her.

Not long afterwards, the good professor and I plotted a 740 kilometre round trip from Coffs Harbour to Gunnedah. Richard's vision is so poor that he's legally blind, but I didn't mind doing all the driving. After a lifetime of walking I really enjoy time behind the wheel. There are a lot of long highways and byways I motor down nowadays and recognise places where I once trudged or slept.

We decided to take our time and soak up 'the sights' along the way. We did a lap of Tamworth (the first and last time I'd been back to my home town since Katie was born in 1986), dropped in to see my sister Lynette and checked out some of my old haunts. We also admired the snowy oceans of cotton fields that lapped at the highway along the road to Gunnedah.

When we finally pulled into the car park of the nursing home, my heart started racing and my mouth went dry. We approached the neat-looking reception desk topped with a vase of fresh-cut flowers. 'Hello. We've come all the way from Coffs Harbour to see Sister Winifred,' I said halt-ingly. By now I was scared stiff. I didn't know if I'd have to face some cloaked Catholic gatekeeper, produce some secret visa or state the reason for our unannounced visit, but they were actually quite easy and open about it.

'She's in her bed, resting,' the lady said with a smile. 'It's just down the corridor. Turn right at the end and you'll find her.' And just like that I was moments away from facing my lifelong nemesis. Time seemed to slow down and part of me regressed into that frightened ten-year-old boy, rubbing the painful welt on his leg or holding a hand up to his bloodied face.

'Would you like me to come in with you, mate?' Richard's familiar voice in my ear and gentle hand on my shoulder steadied me and gave me resolve. I nodded that it was a good idea. We walked down the corridor together, around the corner and there she was. I don't know what I'd been expecting: a stout woman in her black nun's garb growling and barking orders; wicked Winifred waiting there with her hand raised to slap me for being such a horrible, sinful little boy.

When we stepped closer to her bed I was shocked to see a frail, shrivelled-up husk of a human being lying on sheets in the foetal position. Suddenly, I wasn't angry or nervous. Instead, I felt immensely sad for her. But we'd come all this way so I decided to speak.

'Sister Winifred,' I said, and her eyes shot open.

'Who is that?'

'My name's Gregory. I don't know if you remember me but I was one of the boys at St Patrick's Orphanage in Armidale in the 1960s. When you were there too.'

Her wrinkled face betrayed no signs of recognition; she just stared back at me. I continued, 'You were very cruel to me and the other children.' Winifred's eyes narrowed a little as I ran through all the ugly things she had done and how much it had hurt me back then and affected much of my life since. I explained to her how terrified I had been when she locked me under the stairs in the pitch black, how much it hurt when she belted me, how she'd made my life a misery when I'd done nothing wrong and how – as an enforcer of twisted dogma – she'd made me ashamed and confused about my place in the world.

When I finished, she held my gaze for a few moments and I saw something finally dawn on her. She did recognise me after all. Sister Winifred's wizened features curled into a wide, bitter smirk. 'Oh yeah!' she said, as if she'd just recognised a crook in a police line-up. 'You were one of *those* boys.'

Richard's body tensed and I could sense he was about to lose it. I just looked at Winifred in shock. I hadn't been expecting to be judged by her. It seemed nothing would make this woman see history differently.

We hurried back out into the car park. I was so shaken I sat slumped behind the wheel, unable to drive. When I recomposed myself Richard and I checked into a motel and talked over what had happened. It didn't take long for me to feel sorry for Winifred again. It was obvious she had lived a miserable life and she had paid her penance by carrying that misery around with her. I, on the other hand, was finally putting my life together and becoming a happier person. I had great things that I wanted to do and places I wanted to go. She, it seems, did not.

I put Winifred's words aside and instead reflected on the withered person in the middle of that bed, all alone in a place that smelled like impending death. I truly felt for her. I know she could have had a much better life if she hadn't been willing to be so mean. That was a good lesson for me – I didn't want to be like that. I'd been mean to myself for years and realised I'd just seen the result of continuing up close with my own eyes.

The encounter with Winifred got me thinking about Dr Freeman. I made some phone calls to try to track him down, too, but he had passed away. Richard suggested I try to talk to Dr Freeman's family instead, but they weren't the ones who tarred and feathered me with the sloppy diagnosis of being a teenage sociopath, so I let that idea slide.

During the final years in the forest, when my weight plummeted and I was constantly sick and full of pollutants, I could sometimes barely move through lack of energy. Sometimes, total exhaustion would king-hit me like a drunk in a pub and it would be lights out. I recall walking pissed into Byron Bay one New Year's Eve, standing outside a hotel and suddenly realising 'Shit! I'm going to be asleep in a few seconds', before collapsing onto the pavement where I slept for seven hours.

But since re-entering society and dramatically improving my health, I still found everything physical to be a huge effort. When I finally went to a doctor, blood tests showed there was a perfectly good reason for this: I had hepatitis C – a little memento from my days spent sharing needles with Meredith in Sydney. 'Shit!' was all

I could say when the doctor informed me. Frightening worst-case scenarios swirled through my head and I had unpleasant visions of my father's early demise through cirrhosis of the liver.

'It's all right,' said the GP. 'There's something we can do about it nowadays, though there are side effects and you're going to feel pretty crook while you're on it.' The drug is called Pegasys Interferon. 'You can expect severe depression and loss of hair,' he added.

Depression? Well I'd had some experience with that, so I was sure I could manage. As for the hair loss, no disease was going to have my mane. I went home that day and for the second time in my life I took all my hair off. 'I won't be losing it to a disease, a drug or anything else,' I said through a stiff upper lip. It turned out being bald for a while was the least of my worries. Having weekly injections of Pegasys Interferon was like being given a regular intravenous dose of pure misery. I lost a huge amount of weight, my skin grew so sensitive I wanted to rip it off, and I was left nauseous and severely depressed. There were, however, two upsides: the first was that I had hepatitis C subtype genome 1A, which meant I only had to do a six-month program. The second was that the treatment worked. In the ten years since, my scans have all been clear. I was cured of a disease that, once upon a time, would have put me in an early grave.

And I felt great. It was as if my life-force batteries had been thoroughly recharged. I completed my undergraduate studies and roughly eight years after my low ebb of playing with sticks and babbling to aliens and my ancestors in the forest, I graduated with a Bachelor's Degree in Social

Science from Southern Cross University. I received a pass in just one unit – from the late Trevor Lucas for Deviance in Society. In every other unit I received a high distinction, a distinction or a credit. I know Trevor would have been very pleased.

38

A DEGREE OF PEACE

My degree represented far more to me than just a piece of paper to hang on a wall. The four years I spent studying 'the origin, development, organisation and functioning of human society' helped me weave myself into the social fabric of the very country that had forgotten me. It had been a quid pro quo: by slowly letting people into my life, from Leanne and my classmates to Trevor, Richard and other mentors at university, I came to know myself better and only then did I begin to feel comfortable taking my place.

For a man who had always avoided mirrors, I was pleased to discover that the truest reflections of me were the ones that shone back from my relationships with fellow human beings. After all those years bristling at people's well-meant inquiries about who I was and where I was from, I realised that people never automatically hated me, judged me or were afraid of me.

I had badly misread a lot of people. I had badly misread myself, too. I wasn't the devil or Charles Manson after all, I was just a guy – someone in the line at the supermarket, a brother, a friend, a fellow traveller – who was doing his best. I used to think I was the ugliest person on earth but those reflections I saw in my friends proved otherwise. Being me has never been about how I look (which, it turns out, is pretty regular), it's about who I am as a person, who I choose to be, and whether I elect to care or not to care, to love or to hate.

For decades I chose hatred. I considered my parents the most wicked, loathsome people to ever stride upon the earth, but I've come to love them. Truly love them. The process of healing began while talking things over with my ancestors in the forest, it sharpened during my epiphany, and crystallised as I pursued my studies. A lot of the debris that was strewn across that park-bench battle-field was the ruins of my relationships with my parents. All the spite, resentment, judgement and the spitting on graves. I came to realise I have nothing to 'forgive' Mum and Dad for. It's not my place to judge anyone. All I can do is try to understand them, look at them through a different lens – something I learned on my first day at uni.

In Dad's case I realised I had empathy. I don't believe he ever had the opportunity to be the best person he could, and that's something I can relate to in my own way. He hit alcohol hard and his addiction really sprang out of his inability to cope after his mother died. I love Dad dearly today because I understand him and I can see that he never wanted to be the man he became – the one who hurt his family. I believe his shame about it is why he drowned himself in a room filled with sherry. I wish he hadn't. I know we'd have ended up great friends.

I've had a little more trouble reconciling with Mum. I believe that, unlike Dad, she did have choices in life and she made some pretty bad ones. I may not necessarily like my mother but I love her deeply and respect her as my ancestor. I hated my very name for decades but now I embrace it and hold it dear. It is the name my mother and father gave me and I am proud to tell the world that I am Gregory Peel Smith.

Gone, too, is my fear of religion and the superstitions that used to haunt me. The Catholicisation of me as a boy had a profound, long-lasting impact that made the supernatural a very real threat in my life. I remember one cursed homeless night being curled in the foetal position in a church yard and under physical attack from demons. The assault was as real to me as every other beating I'd copped throughout my life.

I don't believe in demons today. The ancestors helped show me that religion is man's construct to explain things we don't understand and it was Sociology that helped me put a name to some of the concepts and understand them better.

There came a point, too, where I realised I had betrayed the trust of everyone. For a long time no one could depend on me for anything. The painful part of that realisation was that it contradicted my belief in honesty and keeping my word. Blowing up the townhouse in Tamworth had been me keeping my word. But there were plenty of people I gave my word to along the way who I ended up letting down: Clary Davis and Danny Doyle, John Parkes, Wiremu and countless others who'd depended on me in one way or another, who I just walked away from.

After my epiphany, the ironclad guarantee of my word became sacred to me. The decision that day to change myself was imbued with immense meaning – and it began by keeping a vow to myself. Today that remains an integral part of who I am. If I say I will do something, to the best of my character and ability, I will do it. If I tell myself I will be there at the end, then that's where you'll find me.

Graduating with a Bachelor Degree turned out not to be the end, but rather the beginning of my time at Southern Cross University as I was invited to do my Honours thesis. The only question was what I should do it on. 'Mate, why don't you do it on yourself?' Richard suggested. 'If you're an expert on anything, you're an expert on your life and what happened to you and others like you.' So, in 2008 I commenced my Honours Degree on the experiences of children at a New South Wales orphanage I called The Chalet. In truth it was about St Patrick's Orphanage, Armidale. I called it *I'd Like to Tell You a Story But I'm Not Sure if I Can*. The thesis explored the stories of five adults who, as children, spent time at St Patrick's and had been too afraid and ashamed to tell anyone what happened to them.

One of the recommendations of the Senate's 2004 *Forgotten Australians* report was that oral history research of former care residents be undertaken as a matter of priority so the public could gain an understanding of what we went through while in 'care'. The overarching aim of my Honours thesis was to make a modest contribution towards that objective.

Around that time I was contacted by a lecturer named Dr Sandy Darab from the Social Sciences Faculty at Southern Cross University. She wanted to offer me some casual work tutoring and marking assignments. 'Do you think you'd be interested, Gregory?' she asked.

For a moment I couldn't quite believe what she was saying. Where once I couldn't get a job – not even a lousy interview for a gig as a cleaner – here I was, qualified with a degree after years of study, being offered paid work without even having to sit for an interview. 'Here, have a job.' Just. Like. That.

'Yes, Sandy,' I said. 'I'd be very grateful for some work.'

With my first pay cheque I bought a nice pair of black leather shoes. It was the very first new pair I had ever owned. I was fifty-three years old. I didn't even need to try the shoes on; I already knew what my foot size was from my days as an inmate at Yawarra. A guard had told me and handed me a pair on my arrival, and from then on whenever I scrounged used shoes from op shops I knew what size to look for.

For a long time after I emerged from the forest I suffered severe foot pain. I figured all the years traipsing up and down the eastern seaboard, living hard in the bush and breaking my toes on cold, uneven ground had left me with 'bad feet'. Two years after I bought my first new pair of shoes in Coffs Harbour, I was in a shoe shop on the New South Wales Central Coast when a salesman suggested measuring my feet before trying some shoes on.

'You look a bit bigger than a nine,' the man said as I sat down for a fitting.

'Nup. I've been size nine, tops, my whole life,' I assured him. 'I can't imagine I've suddenly grown.'

When I placed my foot on the black and silver measurer and the salesman moved the slide rulers around I was amazed to discover I'd been wearing shoes two sizes too small since 1974 (except when it came to my Maxwell Smart boots, of course). It was a classic symptom of being a Forgotten Australian. I was the product of a brain-washed, don't-ask-questions care-home upbringing that had carelessly pushed me into little pigeonholes. I'd been crammed underneath the stairs, dressed in ill-fitting clothes, packaged up as an idiot and stuffed into an arbitrary shoe size – all because no one in the system ever had the slightest concern for me.

Still, I was grateful for the knowledge and the comfier shoes, and thankful that I even had money to spend on such luxuries.

Like Richard, Sandy Darab and I got on really well and she took me under her wing. She mentored me as an academic and showed me how to tutor students and mark their work. After six months I was asked to give lectures and tutorials in Australian Politics at Southern Cross University. The first time I stood up in front of a classroom full of students I was terrified. But when I looked back at them and recalled how scared I had been when I was in their shoes, I realised they were looking to me for guidance, so I did the very best I could.

After a couple of staffing changes at the university, Sandy took over as the supervisor for my Honours thesis. It was a lot of work, particularly considering I could barely string a written sentence together just a few years earlier. The subject matter taxed me at an emotional level, too. Revisiting other people's trauma from their time in the orphanage brought up many unexpected and painful memories. I spent a lot of time consulting with my psychologist, Christina North, and she also found herself on the receiving end of a couple of emergency phone calls when I'd become dissociated and disoriented. Christina was invaluable to me, as was Sandy.

Leanne, too, was incredibly supportive throughout my studies – a kindness that extended to her mum, Bev. While writing my Honours thesis I was faced with a catastrophe when my computer suddenly crashed. Since I didn't have the funds to replace it I became incredibly stressed and anxious. Bev was visiting with Leanne and when she heard of my predicament said she'd lend me the money to buy a new one. Up until then I'd always had second-hand computers so I'm forever grateful to Bev for the opportunity to own my very first new laptop. She even helped me choose it.

One morning in 2010 I was driving to work when my phone rang. It was Sandy. 'Are you sitting down?' she asked in her best official-sounding voice.

'Yeah, why?'

'The results just came back for your thesis.'

In an instant I was overcome by emotion. I had to pull over.

'. . . And?' I pressed her.

'First Class Honours!' Sandy was still trying to sound secretarial, but I could tell she was jumping around in her office. I sat in the car and let the news sink in. For some reason my mind cart-wheeled back through time to the bleak days at school when I was poor old Pus Head. Now I was Gregory Peel Smith BSocSc (Hons 1st Class).

I stayed on as a casual tutor at Coffs Harbour where I continued to lecture in Politics and Sociology. They also gave me an office – another milestone in my long journey up from the bottom. When I lived in the gutters of Sydney I used to look up to the office workers who hurried past me and I considered them paragons of success. Now that I had an office all of my own, what did that make me? A success? I definitely didn't feel like one but I was finally cognisant of how far I had come.

I have to admit to a certain amount of satisfaction in putting my name on the door and hanging my degree on the wall, right alongside the 1973 psychiatric report that warned visitors to my office to beware of the sociopath. It was supposed to be a cheeky 'get stuffed' to the late Dr Freeman's misdiagnosis, but, deep down, I still put more weight in his words than I did in my own degree.

Sadly, I was still a fraud.

39

HERE . . . AT THE END

It was only after gaining a PhD that I stopped feeling like the world's biggest fake. My First Class Honours opened up a pathway to pursue my own doctorate, and this time I knew what I wanted my research to focus on.

The aim of this study [is] *to explore how individuals who lived in out-of-home child care in Australia before 1974 experienced, during adult years, a sense of belonging in relationships with significant others, and in relation to community and a sense of self.*

So began my thesis, *Nobody's Children: An Exploration Into Adults Who Experienced Institutional Care.* Two years prior, in 2009, the then Prime Minister Kevin Rudd had issued a national apology to the Forgotten Australians and recognised them as a vulnerable group with 'special needs' in their senior years. To better understand what some of those needs might be I wanted to research how a Forgotten Australian might experience feelings of belonging – or not belonging, as the case so often was.

Having spent much of my life adrift in the world in the wake of such 'care', I believed it was important for the wider community (the taxpayers who would help address the ongoing medical and mental health fallout) to understand the severe, long-term impacts that social disconnection had on many thousands of Forgotten Australians. Like me, a lot of the participants had never even heard about the 2004 Senate report that first described Forgotten Australians so I wanted to finally give them a voice, too.

Over four years, beginning in 2011, I interviewed twenty-one care leavers from right around the country and researched out-of-home care policies and practices in minutiae to provide an in-depth account of what it did to people's lives. My central finding was that the majority of care leavers had significant difficulties in developing relationships in their families, in their communities and in society more broadly.

At a research level the interviews lifted the lid on a deep, collective reservoir of anger and shame. Many tears were shed, including by me. I found that more than thirty per cent of my participants had serious drug and alcohol problems at some point in their lives, just as I had. This is significantly higher than among the general population. Although many questions remain, my PhD filled in a lot of gaps in society's knowledge of Forgotten Australians.

Researching and writing a PhD was a harrowing intellectual and emotional odyssey that required a great deal of time, focus, understanding, patience and support. The irony, for me, was that cataloguing human disconnection enriched my own life with strong, caring relationships. I had started visiting Dad's sister, my lovely Aunty Desley, on the New South Wales Central Coast. Our chats were illuminating and I drew wisdom and comfort from the insights she gave into my father's own troubled life.

Along with Dr Sandy Darab, Dr Yvonne Hartman (another academic attached to SCU's Social Sciences Faculty) became a co-supervisor of my thesis. On top of the guidance, mentorship and their help in editing, these two amazing women also became my friends.

In December 2015 I submitted my PhD to the Higher Degree Research Department for assessment and in 2016, after national and international peer review, it was conferred.

On graduation day at SCU's Lismore Campus, each student was allotted three tickets for family and friends, but I asked if I could have five. I invited Leanne – the amazing woman who had stood by me even at my very worst – Richard Hil, Aunty Desley, my sister Glenda and my daughter Katie, who I had finally started having a bit of contact with. There were others who I'd have loved to share the day with, not least my psychological lifeline, Christina North, but I was told five tickets was the absolute limit.

Before the official ceremonies began, there was a big parade of some 200 graduates through the main street of Lismore, led by the city's pipe band.

Crowds of townspeople lined the footpaths and applauded as we waltzed through the CBD. After a block or two a woman dressed in a flowing bright red gown caught my eye. She was waving, pacing along beside us and jumping up among the crowd. 'Gregory! Gregory!' she yelled over the clapping and cheering. 'I'm so proud of you, Gregory Smith!'

It was Christina North – she'd driven 230 kilometres from Bonville to see me graduate. 'I wasn't going to miss it,' she told me later with a big hug. 'The red dress was to make sure you didn't miss me.'

The graduation ceremony took place inside the beautiful Whitebrook Lecture Theatre at SCU's Lismore campus. Those receiving their PhD were the first on the stage. There was applause as the Chancellor handed me a blue leather folder containing my PhD and shook my hand while my principal supervisor, Professor Mark Hughes, read a summary of my research and presented me to the other academics. Throughout the ceremony my mind and my body remained tethered. I didn't zone out and I wasn't dissociated, but I did get quite overwhelmed, particularly when people started calling me Dr Smith.

Straight afterwards I was separated from my friends and family because the press wanted to interview me. Word had got around that a PhD candidate at the local university used to be a homeless man.

A few weeks after graduation I unlocked my office in Coffs Harbour one morning and sat down at my desk, feeling that something was oddly different. I glanced around the room but everything seemed in order. Still, I couldn't shake the feeling that something weird had happened when I'd walked through the door, so I got up and retraced my steps. That's when I noticed it. My colleagues had changed the nameplate on my door to 'Dr Gregory P. Smith'.

I was touched by the gesture but also a bit embarrassed by the honorific, and it was months before I could bring myself to change the auto-signature on my emails to include 'Dr'. Finally, Sandy Darab pulled me aside. 'I don't want to hear any of this nonsense about you being a fraud again,' she told me firmly. 'You're an expert in your field. In fact you are *the* leading academic in this field.'

I had no choice but to obey. Sandy and Yvonne – my loyal colleagues in the School of Arts and Social Sciences – were my forthright and steadfast academic sounding board. They were wise, kind and intuitive. When I graduated they gave me a beautiful book cataloguing the birds of planet earth. 'We know how much birds mean to you,' Yvonne said. I had to wipe away a tear. The very first written words of my academic life – the journal I had to keep during the tertiary preparation course at Southport TAFE – had been bookmarked with the feather I had picked off the ground near my beachside camp. Now a book of a billion feathers heralded the completion of my crowning academic work.

Sometimes I think back to those awful nights as a little boy when I'd tried to outrun the scary giant ball in my dreams. Today it feels as if the tables have turned and I'm chasing after the ball, just trying to keep up with the commitments, appointments, responsibilities and plans that vie for my time. My greatest ambition isn't so much to chase the ball, it's to simply enjoy my life and share what's left of it with the people I love.

In May 2016 my long-lost littlest sister, Roma, texted me to say she was going to be near the Coffs Coast in the middle of the month and would I like to catch up. We arranged for Leanne and me to drive up to Wooli where

Roma had rented a holiday house. I set out in the morning with Leanne and arrived at the address Roma had given me about lunchtime. When we pulled up I noticed three cars were already there, including a little Suzuki parked up the driveway that, strangely, had its numberplates covered with tissue paper. Worried that I might have the wrong house, I did a lap of the block, but when we pulled up again the address matched the one Roma had texted.

Leanne and I started walking towards the house when Roma burst through the front door and gave me a big hug. I was standing there marvelling at her when suddenly the front door flew open again and Wendy appeared. 'Oh my god! Two of you!' I exclaimed, and started to weep. I embraced Wendy, too, and all of us cried and said how good it was to see each other. The front door swung open again. It was Glenda, the eldest of the girls. That tipped me over the edge – I was a sobbing wreck and spent much of the afternoon wiping tears from my eyes. We cried, we laughed and we gave thanks that we were all still here. They told me they were proud of me.

The estrangement that had been forced upon my sisters and me has not been easy to overcome, though we're trying. While Lynette and Louise weren't there that day I'd been glad to catch up with Lynette in Tamworth during my trip to confront Winifred in 2009, and Louise had contacted me when I was in the final stages of completing my PhD. She told me her daughter, Victoria, had been accepted at SCU and was due to attend the Coffs Harbour campus.

On checking my enrolments I noted that I would be teaching Australian Politics to my niece – a delightful blooming flower on our weathered family tree. I asked Louise if she'd mind doing me a small favour. I was eager, I explained, to get my hands on an Oxley High School tie. She said she'd try.

A week or so later, a package arrived in the mail containing a length of sky blue polyester fabric with the ridiculous anchor of Tamworth embroidered in gold right in the middle. It was the tie I had always coveted for the inner validation it represented. 'Thank you, Louise!' I said beaming. 'Thank you!'

Long after the graduation parade through Lismore had dissipated, after the lights had been turned off at the White-brook Lecture Theatre and the celebration dinner with friends and family had ended, I went home as Dr Gregory P. Smith to quietly reflect on my own. I pulled the tie out of the drawer I'd been keeping it in, looped it around my neck and fashioned a knot as best I could. Then I turned to face the mirror to see how I looked.

EPILOGUE

It has been eighteen years since I walked out of the forest, but in many regards I'm still finding my way in the only fashion I know – by just putting one foot in front of the other. A few years ago, however, I finally succumbed to a long and strong urge to return to the wild. Well, sort of.

With money I earned as a casual lecturer at Southern Cross University, I purchased my own forest – twenty-five acres of humble regrowth bushland outside of Grafton in northern New South Wales. Leanne and I put down a slab and erected a decent two-room steel shed and a rainwater tank. We bolted solar panels to the roof and wired the juice to some batteries just inside the front sliding door. It's a hell of a lot more comfortable and sophisticated than the lava rock at Goonengerry, but it's 100 per cent off the grid. We spend time there with our two little dogs, a handful of fussy chooks, and monitors, snakes, lizards, marsupials and a glorious population of native birds. Bats, too. Still, life is not always rosy.

More than fifty years of disenfranchisement and estrangement has left its mark on me and I face extreme challenges in living with others. I know this is not easy for those I love and those who love me, but I continue to work hard on building, cementing and understanding these relationships. You're never too old to learn! Since that first surprise get-together with my long-lost sisters, we've decided to make being a family a bit of a family tradition. At the time of writing, we've headed to the Coffs Coast once every year to catch up, compare notes on life, swap stories and just enjoy one another. I love my little sisters. All of them, forever.

Over the years I have had periodic contact with my treasured daughter, Katie, now a beautiful mother of two herself. Sometimes it has been turbulent as she has endured a lot and done it all without a parent to lean on. Lately, though, that's started to change as Katie and I have begun to spend more time together. She is strong and smart – much more so than me. In mid-2017 she told me I was going to be the grandfather of a little boy, and meeting him was one of the greatest joys of my life. The reality, however, is that Katie and I still have a lot of healing ahead of us.

I think Leanne put it best after I started receiving accolades for my PhD. Suddenly I was being interviewed in the press, fielding requests to appear on panels and give speeches, and I was even invited to give testimony at the Royal Commission into Institutional Response to Child Sexual Abuse. Leanne is a gifted artist and amid all this hubbub she presented me with a beautiful card. Inside it she wrote: *I have watched you walk along your track and seen it turn into a trail, then a road and now a highway . . .*

Who knows where the road will lead but there are many things I want to achieve as it guides me forwards. For a bloke who for so long recoiled from any contact with society, I now find myself strongly community-minded. I serve on the board of Anglicare North Coast and I'm a consultative forum member of Wattle Place – an initiative of Relationships Australia (NSW) that advocates for the rights of the State's Forgotten Australians and advance social policies that affect them. I am also a founding member of VoiceUp Australia, a group that provides a social and advocacy platform for adult survivors of childhood violence. A lot of people need a lot of help.

At an academic level I have received a research grant to further explore issues that affect Forgotten Australians. I've pondered taking a close look at the impacts that have been handed down to the offspring of care leavers like me – people like my Katie.

In early 2017, after years working part-time on a casual basis, I finally secured permanent employment when Southern Cross University offered me a job as a fully-fledged lecturer and research fellow. It was the first full-time position I'd held since I was sacked from the Tamworth flour mill for 'lying about a fight'. There was, however, a catch: the job was based not at my beloved Coffs Harbour facility but at the university's campus at Lismore – a good 130 kilometres from the solar shack near Grafton and a solid 210 kilometre haul from the little nook I still rent behind Robert and Glenys's place at Coffs. Oddly enough, it's only a relatively short drive should I ever wish to pop up to the mountaintop at Goonengerry.

People have often asked me if I've been back to the forest and the answer is yes – four times since I staggered out onto Mill Road, close to death, circa 1999–2000. The initial pilgrimage was in 2005 with my loyal, adventurous and persistently interested friend, Professor Richard Hil. The second time, eleven years later, I was on my own. I had been offered the opportunity to share my life in a book and I felt compelled to ask the forest if that would be OK. Maybe, I thought, I'd get a word of advice from my ancestors at the long-dormant fireplace. It turned out that the rocks around it were still there but the elders weren't. The third visit was with Craig Henderson, the fellow who helped me tell my story. And the last time was with Leanne. She deserved to see it. I don't think I'll go back there again.

Nowadays I also rent a little room at the top of a hill in Lismore to be closer to work during the week. Where once I was homeless I now have three beds where I can lay my head! Swings and roundabouts. I sometimes also lecture on the Gold Coast, and while I will always hold a special fondness for the campus at Coffs Harbour where my academic career truly blossomed, I love teaching at Lismore, too. I have good friends there – and the place is set amid an ancient rainforest.

Dr Gregory P. Smith
February 2018

ACKNOWLEDGEMENTS

When I left the forest and began my journey towards socialisation some very special people were strategically placed along the way. Too many to mention here.

The late Trevor Lucas was the first person to take me aside and show a genuine interest in what I was trying to do. Never to be forgotten.

Richard Hil was the first human being with whom I felt I could unashamedly share my previously unmentionable life without fear of being judged. I thank you for your kindness and friendship over the years.

Two very special ladies I am privileged to call my friends are Yvonne Hartman and Sandy Darab. Wow – thank you so much for the things you have both taught me and continue to teach me. You are my inspirations.

A very special acknowledgment for Leanne Maynard and her mum Bev Edsall, both of whom I have the highest regard for.

For their ongoing support I must thank Barbara Rugendyke and Mark Wittleton from Southern Cross University. Your kindness and generosity haven't gone un-noticed, nor have your behind-the-scenes decisions and actions for many years before this book came to fruition.

There are two people without whom producing this memoir would have been impossible:

Sophie Ambrose at Penguin Random House. A very savvy individual, Sophie was able to address all of the reasons I could conjure *not* to put these memories into a book. She has been kind and energetic all the way to the end. One day I would like to explore the pathways and trails of *her* special forest in Britain.

The other is Craig Henderson. Craig and I hit it off from the moment we first met. A man with an ability to develop a deep understanding of a fellow human's lived experi-ence. After I told him I'd been diagnosed as a sociopath he promptly invited me into his home to meet his beautiful wife Lizzie and their daughters Katie and Abigail. Without Craig, this book wouldn't exist.

To my daughter, Katie, and my sisters Glenda, Louise, Lynette, Wendy and Roma, you mean the world to me.

Discover a
new favourite